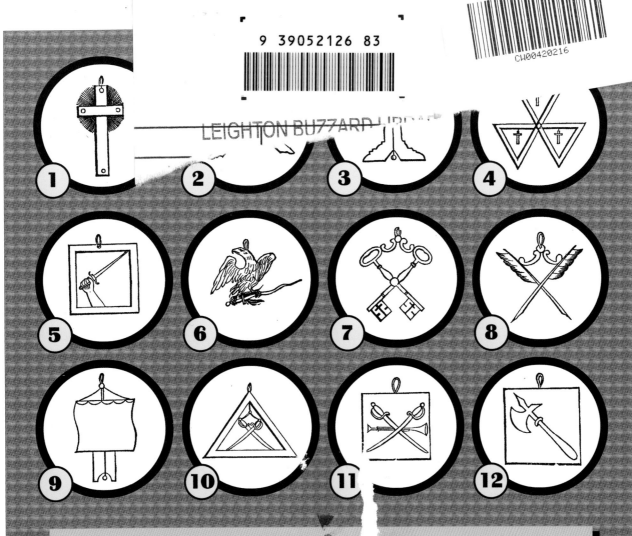

American Masonic Templar Jewels of Office

The jewels of office used by American Masonic Templars is considerably different than those used in the United Kingdom and Canada, as are the names of the various offices. 1: Commander 2: Gerneralissimo 3: Captain General 4: Prelate 5: Sr. Warden 6: Jr. Warden 7: Treasurer 8: Secretary 9: Standard bearer 10: Sword Bearer 11: Warder 12: Guards

The
Compasses
and the
Cross

The
Compasses
and the
Cross

A History of the Masonic Knights Templar

Stephen Dafoe

Author of **Nobly Born**

Lewis Masonic

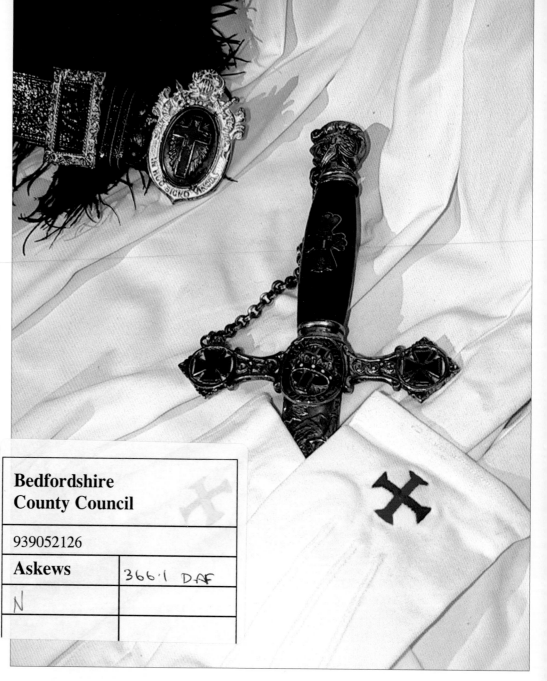

Page 2: **A nineteenth-century Masonic Templar ceremonial sword takes the foreground to one of the emblems of mortality used in Masonic Templarism.** *Sarah Burns*

Right: **A collection of Masonic Templar regalia.** *Stephen Dafoe*

First published 2008

ISBN 978 0 85318 298 6

Published by Lewis Masonic

an imprint of Ian Allan Publishing Ltd, Hersham, Surrey KT12 4RG.

Printed in England by Ian Allan Printing Ltd, Hersham, Surrey KT12 4RG

Code: 0809/B2

Visit the Lewis Masonic website at www.lewismasonic.com

Contents

Acknowledgements

> **Dedicated to the memory of my parents James and Ruth Dafoe, who always bought me books.**

The medieval Templars were unique in that each member of the Order worked together for a common cause, with each man applying his talents where they were most needed and beneficial to the greater good of the Order. The same can be said with the production of this book, which would not exist without the tireless efforts of many people.

Acknowledgements must be made to Frank Gibbs who signed my petition to become a Freemason and to Clare Faulkner who sponsored me in my desire to become a Royal Arch Mason and latterly a Knight Templar.

With respect to this particular book I am indebted to my agent Fiona Spencer Thomas, the good people at Lewis Masonic and my editor Jay Slater who worked with me on my previous book, *Nobly Born: An Illustrated History of the Knights Templar*. Additional thanks must be made to a number of friends and colleagues who contributed to the completion of this work: Sarah Burns who provided the cover photography, Gordon Napier who meticulously crafted two original sketches of Templar regalia from the slimmest of historical records, Sir Knight Stephen McKim, who lent his hand with his uniquely creative digital art and Sir Knight Carson Smith who provided a number of photographs from his extensive collection of Masonic Templar memorabilia. I would be remiss if I did not acknowledge S. Brent Morris for his assistance in providing additional images from the archives of the Ancient and Accepted Scottish Rite (Southern Jurisdiction) and to the brethren of Loyal Lodge No 251, Barnstaple, for their kind permission to include their portrait of Thomas Dunkerley. Additionally, I am grateful to my friend, brother and fellow author Chris Hodapp for being kind enough to write the Foreword to the book. Lastly, no illustrated book would be possible without the efforts of the designer, Alan Gooch, who meticulously and artistically blended the text and images into the present volume you now hold.

Foreword

W HEN Stephen Dafoe asked if I would be interested in writing the Foreword to *The Compasses and the Cross*, his kind invitation came at an important moment in my own Masonic life. On the one hand, I was just getting involved as an officer in my own hometown Knights Templar Commandery, outfitted with its traditional black, Civil War-era long coat, a ceremonial sabre, ostrich plume-festooned 'fore and aft' hat, and learning my first sword drills. On the other hand, I was also a part of a new medieval period recreation Knights Templar unit, that would confer the Masonic Templar orders in chainmail hauberks and gauntlets, steel helmets, and white mantles, while brandishing sharp-edged broadswords.

As Templar kit goes, I have it in spades.

The romance of chivalry is a curious human preoccupation that has waxed and waned throughout history. The real Middle Ages were a particularly brutal, impoverished, ignorant, and altogether filthy collection of years to have the misfortune of finding oneself inhabiting by the accident of birth. And yet, it was from this turbulent moment in time that so much mythological idealism sprouted and took root in the collective consciousness of the West. The fraternity of Freemasonry has not been immune to chivalry's alluring influences and heroic principles.
At the centre of the chivalric universe stands the Knight Templar, and without him, there would be no King Arthur, no *Ivanhoe*, no Narnia, no *Lord of the Rings*, and no Jedi Knights of the *Star Wars* universe. From the Order's humble beginnings in the Holy Land at the end of the First Crusade, the Knights Templar became legends in their own time, the superheroes of Outremer, alternately lionised and distrusted by all of Europe. Their meteoric rise over such a short lifetime – from obscurity, to stardom, to destruction, across just 200 years – seems like a storybook tale, too fantastic to be true.

In the early 1800s, the Romantic period of art and literature arrived like a ton of bricks, dressed up in armour, and delivered on a white steed. And at the centre of it all was Sir Walter Scott's *Ivanhoe*. *Ivanhoe* was *The Da Vinci Code* of its day, and its influence was felt everywhere, especially in Britain, Canada, and the United States. Apart from creating the modern legend of the character of Robin Hood, and introducing the love-struck Templar, Sir Brian de Bois-Guilbert, the book fanned an international craze for all things medieval. People actually changed their manner of speaking and letter writing to take on the more florid style of Scott's characters, and every man, deep down inside, wanted desperately to brandish a sword and to be a knight. *Ivanhoe* was unquestionably

Banner of the American Knights Templar displaying the cross and crown. This banner holds a prominent place in the Knights Templar Room at the George Washington Masonic National Memorial in Alexandria, Virginia.
Stephen Dafoe

A stained glass window depicting the crucifixion of Jesus Christ towers over the Knights Templar room at the George Washington Masonic National Memorial in Alexandria, Virginia. The century old facility has one level dedicated to each of the various Masonic bodies.
Stephen Dafoe

that made these gentlemen value these bogus decorations. For it was he that created… reverence for rank and caste, and pride and pleasure in them… Sir Walter had so large a hand in making Southern character, as it existed before the war, that he is in great measure responsible for the war.'

Romantic notions of the Knights Templar have not been confined to the 1800s, and the Templars have touched Freemasonry in different ways at different periods. The Order of DeMolay was started as a Masonic-affiliated group for boys in 1919, and based its initiatory rituals on the story of the arrest, conviction and death of the last Grand Master of the Knights Templar, Jacques de Molay. And for many years after the publication of 1989's *Born In Blood* by John Robinson (who was not a Mason at the time of its writing), it was anecdotally said that its modern telling of the supposed Templar origins of Freemasonry was responsible for more men joining lodges than any other book.

Today, thanks partially to the success of *The Da Vinci Code*, the Knights Templar are popular again. They appear in novels (like Raymond Khoury's *The Last Templar*), movies (like 2005's *Kingdom of Heaven*), and even computer games (like *Hellgate London*). And it is likely the Masonic order of Knights Templar will be a beneficiary of this newfound interest as young men rediscover Freemasonry, and become excited at the prospect of themselves becoming a Templar knight. Such a prospect is as alluring today for many as it was in Sir Walter Scott's time.

I have had the great fortune to have known Stephen Dafoe since 2005, when he made the arduous trek from his Canadian home to Indianapolis, where he spoke at Lodge Vitruvian No. 767. For several years before, I was a great admirer of his works about the Knights Templar, as well as his magazine, *Templar History*. But in the last year, Stephen has produced two very different, but equally important, volumes about the Templars that are unlike any other works about the Order. His *Nobly Born* (2007, Lewis) is a lavishly illustrated and straightforward telling of the history of the Knights Templar that casts aside sensationalist speculation and brings his talents as a reporter to bear on what has been for others an illusive subject. I can honestly say that, for anyone looking for a one-volume history of the Knights, *Nobly Born* should be at the top of the list.

The Compasses and the Cross is something very different. In this meticulously detailed work, Stephen has taken on 250 years of cherished Masonic Templar mythmaking and slain a whole barnyard full of sacred cattle. Even during Freemasonry's operative period,

responsible, at least in part, for the explosion of new fraternal orders that sprung up all around the world in the 1800s, patterning themselves after medieval knights.

Not everyone thought such influences were a good idea. In his 1883 memoir, *Life On The Mississippi*, American humorist Mark Twain placed the blame for the American Civil War firmly at the doorstep of Sir Walter Scott and *Ivanhoe*. According to Twain, Scott 'set the world in love with dreams and phantoms; with decayed and swinish forms of religion; with decayed and degraded systems of government; with the sillinesses and emptinesses, sham grandeurs, sham gauds, and sham chivalries of a brainless and worthless long-vanished society. He did measureless harm; more real and lasting harm, perhaps, than any other individual that ever wrote.'

Twain railed that Scott's influence 'made every gentleman in the South a Major or a Colonel, or a General or a Judge, before the war; and it was he, also, when masons were a guild of stonecutters building cathedrals and castles, there was an irrepressible desire to claim descent from something ancient and legendary. The earliest mason guilds asserted their kindred members had built the Tower of Babel and King Solomon's Temple. Likewise, when speculative Freemasonry appeared in Scotland and England after the Restoration, ushered in by the Enlightenment, modern Freemasonry made claims to more ancient beginnings. Even when the so-called higher degrees developed, seemingly overnight, they were declared to be of great antiquity, dragged to Europe out of the mists of ancient Egypt or the sacred dust of the Holy Land, 'rediscovered' in a long forgotten scroll, or 'accidentally' unearthed in a musty bookstall. No one wanted to join an organisation whose rituals were written last week.

The trouble with mythmaking within the windowless temples and tyled meetings of a fraternal organisation that cherishes its reputation of secrecy is that, occasionally, outsiders believe the myths, too. Thus it has been with the tall Templar tales of Freemasonry. The result has been a literary avalanche of speculative stuff and nonsense that can be traced back to a few very specific episodes of wishful thinking or deliberate fable weaving of our Masonic forefathers. What Stephen has done is to trace the legends of Masonic Templarism back to their sources and shine the light of truth on them, once and for all.

For a fraternal organisation like Freemasonry, which prides itself on its inclusion of men from all economic and religious walks of life, having an appendant organisation that requires a belief in Trinitarian Christianity and makes 'Christian soldiers' seems like an anachronism to many. *The Compasses and the Cross* explores and explains where those notions came from.

But it is important to understand that this book is not some blunt instrument of debunkery. It is a thoroughly researched history of the development of the Knights Templar within Freemasonry, and the very different paths it took in continental Europe, England, Scotland, Canada and the United States – and make no mistake, Masonic Templarism is very different in all of those places. Hence, my own ersatz Civil War uniform and anachronistic chapeau that is common across the US, but unknown elsewhere.

Stephen graciously acted as the technical reader for my own book, *The Templar Code For Dummies* (Wiley, 2007), co-written with Alice Von Kannon, and I am honoured to have been able to return the favour. The book you hold is destined to be a unique resource for those studying the history of Freemasonry and its labyrinthine degrees and orders. There is no other volume I know of that investigates this important phase of Masonic history in such careful detail. Stephen has not set out to burst bubbles, but to understand where they came from, and how they became what we see in commanderies and preceptories around the world today.

So much in Freemasonry is explained to its members as 'the way we've always done it'. That clearly is not so, and that's no way to answer inquisitive students of the fraternity. If you want to know why, how and when the Knights Templar rode on their steeds into Masonic history, I urge you to read on.

Christopher L. Hodapp
Indianapolis, Indiana
May 11, 2008

A bronze statue of a valiant knight on his horse rests on a table below the stained-glass crucifixion scene in the Templar room of the George Washington Masonic National Memorial. Although the armour is of the wrong period for the Templars, it is not at all uncommon with the way the Templars have been portrayed in Masonic iconography over the years.
Stephen Dafoe

Introduction

Knighthood in Black & White

Batman: *'Haven't you noticed how we always escape the vicious ensnarements of our enemies?'*

Robin: *'Yeah, because we're smarter than they are!'*

Batman: *'I like to think it's because our hearts are pure.'*

Batman, episode: *The Cat and the Fiddle* (1966)

THERE were no videogames or computers to keep me entertained when I was a child. In fact, having been born in the early 1960s, I was four years old when Canadian television stations began to broadcast in colour. It would be another decade before my family purchased a colour television set, largely because they subscribed to the myth that the new technology emitted radiation that would damage one's eyes. In retrospect, it is possible that my parents' adherence to the myth was an attempt to cover the reality that colour television sets were quite simply outside our family budget.

However, as was the case with many middle-class Canadian children, viewing the world in black and white did not prevent me from enjoying the live-action escapades of Batman and Robin. It didn't matter to me that The Green Hornet lacked a particular shade of green and the Red Skeleton wasn't… red (granted, the latter was a bit of a stretch). What was important for me was that I enjoyed television, not for the richness of Technicolor, but for the richness of the stories the medium presented. Television provided me with a portal into the lives and events of real people. I couldn't wait to race home from school each day and watch my favourite heroes on TV, believing that their adventures were happening for real.

Eventually I came to realise that Batman wasn't a superhero fighting crime and the villains of Gotham City, but an actor named Adam West. Suffice to say, The Joker, The Riddler and The Penguin were also played by actors. With this realisation came the understanding that the stories being presented to me were not true; rather they were written to entertain children and to sell breakfast cereals. Although I had become less concerned about the fate of Batman and Robin at the end of a cliffhanger, knowing that they would escape from Mr Freeze's clutches by the next episode, I still enjoyed watching the programmes because the characters stood for honesty and integrity. The fact that they were not real people didn't detract from my desire to create my own adventures with the never-ending supply of toys made in their likeness.

As such, I couldn't wait for Christmas in 1967 in the hope that Santa Claus would bring me the new Corgi Batmobile I had asked him for. While my belief in my favourite television characters waned in time, there were some that I wanted to hang on to for a while longer. St Nick didn't let me down, for under the tree was not only the Batmobile I'd been hoping for, but also a Batboat and trailer as well. Now I didn't have to wait for the next episode to air as I could invent my own adventures any time I wanted to. And unlike the television series at the time, my adventures were in colour! But there was more under the Christmas tree than my shiny new Batmobile. My parents always bought books for me during the festive season, and this year's crop included a hardcover edition of Sir Walter Scott's *Ivanhoe*, albeit a child's version of the story.

Suddenly, the black and white television images had been replaced by the black and white text of a historical novel. More importantly, my interests

The author's interest in chivalry was developed as a child through the 1960s *Batman* television series and through the pages of Sir Walter Scott's *Ivanhoe*.
Author's Collection

Although my makeshift sword succumbed to the rigours of bloody battle, my interest in knights in shining armour continued to grow throughout my life. Looking back, perhaps it was a subconscious attempt to stay connected with the deeply planted notions of heroism and integrity that I developed as a child in front of an old black and white television set. Regardless of the reasons, I have always viewed the knight as the embodiment of self-sacrifice in the name of a higher purpose.

It would be some three decades after my childhood role-playing, on 8 June 1999, that I knelt before the Presiding Preceptor of King Baldwin Preceptory No. 6 in Belleville, Ontario, and had the mantle of a Masonic Knight Templar placed over my shoulders. By this time I had been a member of the Masonic fraternity for seven years, having been attracted to the fraternity by the integrity and honesty of my sponsor Frank Gibbs.

Sir Walter Scott, the author of *Ivanhoe* and *The Talisman*, two novels that dealt with the Knights Templar.
Jupiter Images

began to drift from the adventures of the caped crusaders to the adventures of medieval crusaders. Although I understood that the story presented in Scott's classic novel took place a long time ago, I did not grasp that the book was a work of fiction that had been written a century and a half before I received my copy. Neither did I realise that the book was written at a time when men dressed like characters in the novel, believing that they were a direct continuation of the Templars of old. But it would be many years before I became aware of the Masons, let alone the Masonic Templars. As a child, I only knew of the Templars as portrayed in Scott's novel – a group of bad guys like The Riddler or Joker, but without the amusing costumes and penchant for theatrics.

After hungrily devouring *Ivanhoe*, I was dashing around the living room with a bath towel around my neck as a cloak and rubber boots and gloves serving as armour. With a cardboard tube as a sword and a toilet roll as my dagger, I slashed and hacked my way through the house defeating the bad guys that I had learned of in *Ivanhoe*. I never realised that Scott's depiction of the Templars was as fictional as Adam West's portrayal of Batman.

Fifteen years have now passed since I became a Freemason, and nine since I became a Templar. In that time, I have always striven to understand the philosophy and history of the Orders to which I belong. That said, there have been periods of time where I have accepted information presented to me on the history of the Templars and their connection to Freemasonry as willingly as I once accepted the stories presented on my family's black and white television set.

But I have not been alone in that acceptance. I have had the company of my Masonic brethren, both past and present, who have subscribed to the long-held belief that like the phoenix rising from the ashes Freemasonry also rose from the ruins of the destroyed Templar Order.

It is my hope that this book will help my fellow Masonic Brethren and Templar Fratres to let go of the myth once and for all.

Stephen Dafoe,
18 March 2008,
Morinville, Alberta, Canada

The Templar-Freemason Myth

'If a man is offered a fact which goes against his instincts, he will scrutinise it closely, and unless the evidence is overwhelming, he will refuse to believe it. If, on the other hand, he is offered something which affords a reason for acting in accordance to his instincts, he will accept it even on the slightest evidence. The origin of myths is explained in this way.'

Bertrand Russell (1872-1970)

Many early Masonic historians traced the origins of the Masonic craft back to the biblical stone masons who built the Tower of Babel or the builders of the pyramids.
Jupiter Images

WE FREEMASONS can be a funny lot. Never content with simply being part of an organisation that has survived and thrived for three centuries, we are constantly searching for evidence that the Masonic Craft must stem from some ancient source. Whether it is making connections between the philosophy and workings of Freemasonry and that of the stone masons who erected the Tower of Babel or ancient Egyptians who built the pyramids, we Freemasons will do our best to create as old a lineage for the Masonic institution as possible. This pedigree, usually concocted from the slimmest pieces of circumstantial evidence or the greatest leaps in logic, has allowed some Masonic speculators to create a history of Freemasonry that extends back to the time of creation and makes provision for the Craft to stop at every important stage in human history. What these theories lack in credibility have been more than made up for in the credulity of many Masons, who are eager to hang on to their beliefs, long after they have been proven to be false or inaccurate.

But can the average Freemason of today be blamed for subscribing to such notions, for the wildest of Masonic speculations are often constructed from information found within the rituals and traditional histories of Freemasonry, or books written about the history of Freemasonry? At the earliest stage of our Masonic careers we are 'called on to make a daily advancement in Masonic knowledge' [1] and yet, few Freemasons are instructed in just how to go about the task by their senior brethren, many of whom are as uninformed about the history and teachings of Freemasonry as they were when they first entered the Craft. As I lamented in my paper *Reading, Writing and Apathy: The Rise and Fall of Masonic Education* [2], we Freemasons have allowed the ritual to serve as the means and ends of Masonic education, which has had devastating results. If we are no longer willing to provide extra-ritual education, we must, therefore, be solely responsible for those members who walk away from our ceremonies with a literal interpretation of our rituals.

But where does the new Mason turn for guidance, if not to the members of his Lodge, Chapter or Preceptory? Certainly not to official Masonic publications. As I argued in the aforementioned paper, the quality of North American Masonic literature has been in a state of steady decline for many years, having reached its peak in the 1920s with the publication of *The Builder*, the monthly publication of the National Masonic Research Society. It has long been my opinion that there has yet to be a North American Masonic publication to successfully take its place. Sadly, many of today's Masonic magazines offer little for the thinking Freemason to think about; the publications' editors preferring to fill their pages with self-congratulatory photographs of Masons presenting cheques, receiving awards or frying battered fish. [3] On the rare occasions that these publications do offer some enlightenment, rather than seeking out articles that will help

Unfortunately, many Masons seem incapable of discerning between traditional and actual history. As such, a number of modern Freemasons believe that Hiram Abif met his end at the hands of three impatient 'operative' masons. [6] It is ironic that such falsehoods are perpetuated by impatient 'speculative' masons who never took the time to investigate the traditional histories presented in Masonic rituals. They muddy the waters by accepting the speculations presented in popular books on the Craft, books that are written to titillate the preconceived notions of the people who buy them.

Freemasons understand the history, symbolism and teachings of the Craft, they regurgitate the same tired articles on dead presidents and baseball players who once wore a Masonic apron.

Fortunately, companies like Lewis Masonic continue to publish quality works on Masonic subjects that provide the knowledge so greatly needed by Freemasons today. However, it is more often than not the popular works of speculative research that the new Mason reads first. In many lodges a brother will rush forward to be the first to help the newly raised Master Mason understand the history and mystery of Freemasonry by thrusting a well-worn copy of *The Hiram Key* or *Born in Blood* [4] into his hands along with the exhortation, 'Read this and you'll begin to understand.'

While these books have a place in the annals of Masonic literature and should be read, albeit with a critical eye, they are often accepted as gospel by Masons and non-Masons alike. As such, the speculative theories presented in these books have come to be accepted as the missing link between post-1717 Freemasonry [5] and earlier groups such as the Egyptians, megalithic builders and the Knights Templar. What many Masonic authors and Freemasons fail to consider is that the traditional history of our various Masonic organisations was not intended to be taken literally. Rather they were mythological stories, based upon historical or biblical events, intended to teach a certain philosophy or ideology by allegory and metaphor.

Nowhere is this trend more prevalent than in the story of the Knights Templar, which has developed into a chicken and egg scenario over the years with respect to the medieval Order's connection to Freemasonry. Did the rise and development of Freemasonry give birth to the Masonic Knights Templar, or did the demise of the original Knights Templar give birth to Freemasonry itself?

While it would be easy to lay the blame for both theories at the foot of modern speculative writers, the fact remains that the Masonic chicken and Templar egg arguments were created by Freemasons themselves. This traditional history or mythology was picked up by non-Masonic writers and treated as actual history, which, in turn, gave Freemasons further evidence to support the theories that they themselves had created. As we will see through the course of this book, the Templar-Freemason myth has taken different forms over the years, evolving and developing as Masonic Templarism grew and flourished.

Eighteenth Century Masonic References to the Templars

As POPULAR as the notion is today, it is important to understand that in the early days of Freemasonry in its post-1717 form, there is no mention of the theory that Freemasonry was created by the medieval Knights Templar as a means of continuing their teachings after they were suppressed by the Catholic Church in 1312. Rather, the earliest Masonic documents, if they mention the Templars at all, point to the notion that Freemasonry pre-dated the Templars and the crusades that saw their birth.

The first printed histories of Freemasonry were contained in Dr James Anderson's *The Constitutions of the Free-Masons*, first published in 1723, to be revised and expanded in 1738 as the *New Constitutions*. [7] Although both editions contain more historical fiction than historical fact, they were products of the age [8] and we cannot be too critical of its author. What remains relevant to our present discussion is that the 1723 edition of Anderson's *Constitutions* contains what can be considered to be the first published reference to a connection between Freemasonry and the crusading Orders, although none are specifically identified by name and Dr Anderson's reference to them is almost in passing. Speaking of the vast influence Freemasonry has had on the history of the world since the time of creation, Anderson tells his reader:

'In short, it would require many large Volumes to contain the many splendid instances of the mighty influence of Masonry from the creation, in every Age, and in every Nation, as could be collected from Historians and Travellers: but especially in those Parts of the World where the Europeans correspond and trade, such Remains of ancient, large, curious, and magnificent Colonading, have been discovered by the Inquisitive, that they can't enough lament the general Deviations of the Goths and Mahometans; and must conclude, that no Art was ever so much encourag'd as this; as indeed none other is so extensively useful to Mankind. 'Nay, if it were expedient, it could be made appear, that from this ancient Fraternity, the Societies or Orders of the Warlike Knights, and of the Religious too, [9] in process of time, did borrow many solemn Usages; for none of them were better instituted, more decently install'd, or did more sacredly observe their Laws and Charges than the Accepted Masons have done, who in all Ages, and in every Nation, have maintain'd and propagated their Concernments in a way peculiar to themselves, which the most Cunning and the most Learned cannot penetrate into, though it has often been attempted; while They know and love one another, even without the Help of Speech, or when of different Languages.' [10]

Although Anderson's New *Constitutions* expanded on his mythical history of Freemasonry, especially with respect to Scottish Freemasonry, he did not have much to add regarding Freemasonry during the time of the crusades, other than to maintain his position of 15 years earlier that the Craft pre-dated the crusaders. [11]

Andrew Michael Ramsay was another well-known eighteenth century Freemason, who held views similar to those of Dr Anderson. Although Ramsay does not appear to have been as active a Freemason as Anderson, he is none the less equally well known today for his singular contribution to the Craft: an address he is alleged to have given to the Grand Lodge of France in 1737, a year before Anderson published his *New Constitutions*. This address, known as 'Ramsay's Oration', exists in two forms: 'The Epernay' version and 'The Grand Lodge' version. [12] Although the two versions are slightly different in tone, they contain the same commentary with respect to the Freemasons during the time of the crusades:

'At the time of the Crusades in Palestine many princes, lords, and citizens associated themselves, and vowed to restore the Temple of the Christians in the Holy Land, and to employ themselves in bringing back their architecture to its first institution. They agreed upon several ancient signs and symbolic words drawn from the well of religion in order to recognise themselves amongst the heathen and Saracens. These signs and words were only communicated

The Rev James Anderson DD was the author of The Constitutions of the Free-Masons, published in 1723 and later revised in 1738.
Author's collection

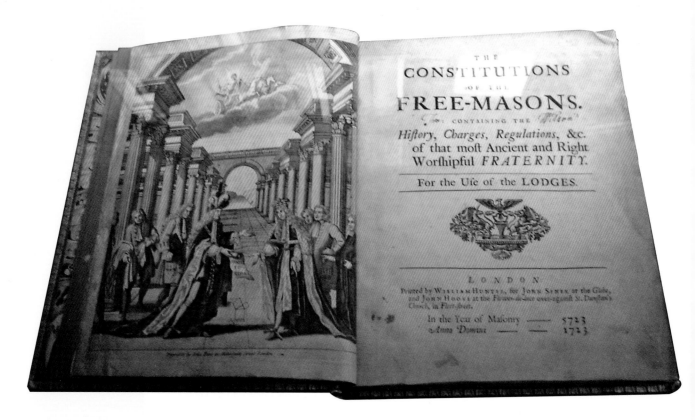

to those who promised solemnly, and even sometimes at the foot of the altar, never to reveal them. This sacred promise was therefore not an execrable oath, as it has been called, but a respectable bond to unite Christians of all nationalities in one confraternity. Some time afterwards our Order [Freemasonry] formed an intimate union with the Knights of St John of Jerusalem [The Hospitallers]. From that time, our Lodges took the name of Lodges of St John. The union was made after the example set by the Israelites when they erected the second Temple, who, whilst they handled the trowel and the mortar with one hand, in the other held the sword and the buckler.' [13]

As we will look at the story of Chevalier Ramsay and his famed Oration in greater detail in Chapter 6, let it suffice to say that this address provided the foundation stone upon which Freemasons would erect the so-called high degrees of Freemasonry, [14] a system in which the degree of Knight Templar held and continues to hold a prominent place.

There were other eighteenth century Freemasons who made reference to the crusading Orders and their connection to Freemasonry, which are worth noting. Among them was William Preston, a Scottish Freemason, who is best remembered as the author of *Illustrations of Freemasonry*, published in 1772. It was a book that Thomas Smith Webb, the founding father of the American Rite (erroneously referred to as the York Rite), borrowed heavily from in creating his *Freemason's Monitor* or *Illustrations of Masonry* in 1797 – a quarter century after Preston's work.

Like Anderson, Preston created an ancient pedigree for the Craft in his history of the Order, but his journey began with the druids, rather than the time of creation, as Anderson had maintained. [15] Although both writers observed that Freemasonry pre-dated the formation of the Knights Templar, Preston went a step further by mentioning them specifically by name:

'During the reign of Henry II (1154-1189) the Grand Master of the Knights Templar superintended the Masons, and employed them in building their Temple in Fleet-street, A.D. 1155. [16] Masonry continued under the patronage of this order till the year 1199, when John (1199-1216) succeeded his brother Richard [Richard the Lionheart] on the throne of England. Peter de Colechurch was then appointed Grand Master. He began to rebuild London-bridge with stone, which was afterwards finished by William Alcmain in 1209. Peter de Rupibus succeeded Peter de Colechurch in the office of Grand Master, and Geoffrey Fitz-Peter, chief surveyor of the king's works, acted as deputy. Under the auspices of these two artists, Masonry flourished in England during the remainder of this and the following reign.' [17]

What is interesting about Preston's account is that, although he points to Freemasonry pre-existing the crusades, he makes no mention of the Templars themselves being Freemasons. Rather, Preston describes the relationship between the two groups as being strictly a matter of business – an arrangement that is not at all removed from historical reality. Certainly the Templars would have employed many 'operative' masons over their nearly two hundred year history, but Preston, like many Masonic writers of his day, confuses the operative masonry practised by rough-handed medieval stone workers with the speculative masonry practised by the well-manicured men of leisure who were their namesakes.

Another Masonic writer contemporary with Preston was William Hutchinson, who published his book *The Spirit of Masonry in Moral and Elucidatory Lectures* in 1775, three years after Preston's *Illustrations of Masonry* hit the press. Like Preston and Anderson before him, Hutchinson's book was sanctioned by the Grand Lodge of England [18] and the author continues the opinion that Freemasonry predated the time of the crusades. But Hutchinson did more than simply preserve the status quo of Masonic history; he provided his reader with a far more detailed fictional account of the connection between the crusaders and craftsman. It was Hutchinson's belief that the Roman Catholic priests were Masons who initiated the crusaders into the mysteries of Masonry so that they might protect themselves from spies and identify themselves to one another as comrades. The story is told in Hutchinson's chapter entitled 'The Secrecy of Masons' and is worth repeating in its full form:
'Soon after the progress of Christianity in England, all Europe was inflamed with the cry and madness of an enthusiastic monk, who

prompted the zealots in religion to the holy war; in which, for the purpose of recovering the holy city of Judea out of the hands of infidels, armed legions of saints, devotees and enthusiasts, in tens of thousands, poured forth from every state of Europe, to waste their blood and treasure, in a purpose as barren and unprofitable as impolitic.

'It was deemed necessary that those who took up the ensign of the cross in this enterprise, should form themselves into such societies as might secure them from spies and treacheries; and that each might know his companion and brother labourer, as well in the dark as by day. As it was with Jeptha's army at the passes of Jordan, so also was it requisite in these expeditions that certain signs, signals, watch-words, or pass-words, should be known amongst them; for the armies consisted of various nations and various languages. We are told in the book of Judges, 'that the Gileadites took the passes of Jordan before the Ephramites; and it was so, that when those Ephramites which were escaped said, let go over, that the men of Gilead said unto him, Art thou an Ephramite? If he said nay, then said they unto him, say now Shibboleth, and he said Sibboleth, for he could not frame to pronounce it right. Then they took them and slew them at the passage of Jordan.'
'No project or device could answer the purpose of the crusaders better than those of masonry: the maxims and ceremonials attending the master's order had been previously established, and were materially necessary on that expedition; for as the Mahomedans were also worshippers of the Deity, and as the enterprisers were seeking a country where the masons were in the time of Solomon called into an association, and where some remains would certainly be found

Preston's reference to the Templars in his *Illustrations of Freemasonry* makes the claim that the Templars employed operative masons during the reign of King Henry II of England.
Author's Collection

William Preston was one of the early Freemasons to reference the Knights Templar; however, his connection was that the Templars employed operative masons as builders.
Author's collection

THE
SPIRIT
of
MASONRY

in
MORAL and ELUCIDATORY
LECTURES.

by Wᵐ Hᴜᴛᴄʜɪɴꜱᴏɴ

The Second Edition

CARLISLE

Printed by *F. Jollie*

MDCCXCV.

Title page from William Hutchinson's *The Spirit of Masonry in Moral and Elucidatory Lecturers* published in 1775. Hutchinson provides his reader with a rather fanciful connection between the crusaders and the Freemasons.
Author's Collection

of the mysteries and wisdom of the ancients and of our predecessors. Such degrees of masonry as extended only to the acknowledgement of their being servants of the God of nature, would not have distinguished them from those they had to encounter, had they not assumed the symbols of the Christian faith.

'All the learning of Europe in those times, as in the ages of antiquity, was possessed by the religious; they had acquired the wisdom of the ancients, and the original knowledge which was in the beginning, and now is, the truth; many of them had been initiated into the mysteries of masonry; they were the projectors of the

enterprise, and as Solomon in the building of the temple, introduced orders and regulations for the conduct of the work, which his wisdom had been enriched with from the learning of the sages of antiquity, so that no confusion should happen during its process, and so that the rank and office of each fellow-labourer might be distinguished and ascertained beyond the possibility of deceit; in like manner the priests projecting the crusades, being possessed of the mysteries of masonry, the knowledge of the ancients, and of the universal language which survived the confusion of Shinar [19] and initiated the legions therein who followed them to the Holy Land; hence that secrecy which attended the crusaders.

'Among other evidence which authorises us in the conjecture that masons went to the holy wars, is the doctrine of that order of masons, called the higher order, we are induced to believe that order was of Scottish extraction; separate nations might be distinguished by some separate order, as they were by singular ensigns: but be that as it may, it fully proves to us that masons were crusaders.' [20]

Thus far we have seen that throughout the whole of the eighteenth century, from the time of the formation of the Grand Lodge of England in 1717 until the closing decades of the century, Masonic writers subscribed to the belief that Freemasonry was in existence long before the time of the crusades and the military Orders who were formed during them. If there was a connection between the two, it lay in the Masonic belief that the crusading Orders, like the Templars or Hospitallers, embraced the ceremonies of Freemasonry. It was a belief that would be carried into the nineteenth century by a number of Masonic writers who remained eager to add their own embellishments to the mythical history of their Order and its association with the Knights Templar of old.

An Anti-Masonic Interlude

Aʟᴛʜᴏᴜɢʜ there were many Masonic writers who wished to draw a connection between the Craft and the crusaders, there were others who wished to put forth a different argument and twist concerning the connection between the Templars and the Freemasons. Chief among them was Augustin Barruel, author of *Mémoires pour servir à l'histoire du Jacobinisme* published in 1797 and 1798. [21] Barruel's book, which was first translated into English by

Robert Clifton in 1798, argued that the French Revolution was the result of the anti-Christian and anti-social principles of secret societies such as the Freemasons. [22] But there was more to Barruel's claims than pinning the French Revolution on the Freemasons; the author was of the belief that Freemasonry was a direct lineal descendant of the suppressed medieval Templars. On this subject, Barruel said:

'Yet, following nothing but the archives of the Free-masons themselves, and the apparent affinities which subsist between them and the Knights Templars, we are entitled to say to them, "Yes, the whole of your school and all your Lodges descend from the Templars." After the extinction of their order a certain number of criminal Knights, who had escaped the general proscription, formed a body to perpetuate their frightful mysteries. To their pre-existing code of Impiety they added the vow of vengeance against Kings and Pontiffs who had destroyed their order, and against all Religion, which proscribed their tenets. They formed adepts who were to perpetuate and transmit from generation to generation the same mysteries of iniquity, the same oaths, and the same hatred against the God of the Christians, Kings and Priests. These mysteries have descended to you, and you perpetuate their impiety, their oaths, and hatred. Such is your origin. Length of time, the manners of each age may have varied some of your signs and of your shocking systems; but the essence is the same, the wishes, oaths, hatred and plots are similar. You would not think it, but everything betrayed your forefathers, and everything betrays their progeny.' [23]

As Robert Cooper pointed out in his book *The Rosslyn Hoax*, this appears to be the first suggestion, at least from a non-Masonic writer that Freemasonry began after the original Templars. [24] Given that Barruel was a member of the same church that had suppressed the Templars in 1312, his claim certainly gained some legitimacy, at least amongst his coreligionists. Barruel was born at Villeneuve de Berg, France, in 1741 and entered the Society of Jesus (Jesuits) at the age of 15. However, the storm of controversy surrounding the Order drove him from France and he remained on foreign shores until the suppression of the Jesuit Order in 1773. Although he returned to France for a number of years, Barruel later sought refuge in England during the French Revolution. It was here that Barruel wrote *Mémoires pour servir à l'histoire du Jacobinisme*, a book that was greatly contested by English, French and German Freemasons. Among those to refute Barruel's claims, both anti-Masonic and historical, was a Scottish Freemason named Alexander Laurie.

Nineteenth Century Masonic References to the Templars

IN 1804, Laurie, who was a bookseller and stationer to the Grand Lodge of Scotland, but would go on to serve variously as Grand Secretary and Joint Grand Secretary of that body, published a book on the history of Freemasonry and the Grand Lodge of Scotland. While Laurie is often credited as the author of the book, it was probably the work of Sir David Brewster. [25] In 1859, his son, William Alexander Laurie – himself then Grand Secretary – reproduced his father's book in an expanded format under the long-winded title of *The History of Free Masonry and the Grand Lodge of Scotland with Chapters on The Knights Templar, Knights of St John, Mark Masonry and R. A. Degree to which is added an Appendix of Valuable Papers*. Although William did not incorporate major changes to the original, he managed to alter the existing chapters with more factual information than that used by Brewster and published by Laurie's father. [26] But while the revised version may have contained information that was more historically accurate than the earlier work, the commentary on the Knights Templar and their connection with Freemasonry is no more credible than that published in the eighteenth century. In chapter two of the 1859 version (see Appendix II for the complete chapter), Laurie offers his reader the following romantic and erroneous information:

'To prove that the Order of the Knight Templars was a branch of Free Masonry would be a useless labour, as the fact has been invariably acknowledged by Free Masons themselves, and none have been more zealous to establish it than the enemies of the Order [Barruel]; the former have admitted the fact, not because it was creditable to them but because it was true; and the latter have supported it, because, by the aid of a little sophistry, it might be employed to disgrace their opponents.

'The Order of Knight Templars was instituted during the Crusades, in the year 1119, by Hugo de Payens and Godfrey de St Omer, and received the appellation because its members originally resided near the church in Jerusalem which was dedicated to our Saviour. Though their professed object was to protect those Christian pilgrims whose mistaken piety had led them to the Holy City, yet it's almost beyond a doubt that their chief and primary intention was to practise and preserve the rites and mysteries of Free Masonry. We know at least that they not only possessed the mysteries, but performed the ceremonies and inculcated the duties of Free Masons; and it is equally certain that the practising of these rites could contribute nothing to the protection and comfort of the Catholic pilgrims. Had they publicly avowed the real object of the institution, instead of that favour which they so long enjoyed, they would have experienced the animosity of the Church in Rome. But as they were animated with a sincere regard for the Catholic faith, and with a decided abhorrence for the infidel possessors of Judea, it was never once suspected that they transacted any other business at their sacred meetings but that which concerned the regulation of their Order, the advancement of religion and the extirpation of its enemies.' [27]

As a point of interest, Chapter 5 of William Alexander Laurie's book perpetuated the reverse myth that the disbanded Templars created Freemasonry. However, as this myth and its evolution are covered in detail later in the book, we will return to the present discussion. Laurie was not the only nineteenth century Masonic author to add his own embellishments to the fictional story of a Templar-Freemason connection, nor was the myth confined to England and Scotland. The story of Freemasonry practised by the crusaders was also embraced across the pond where American Masonic writers were only too eager to graft their own accompaniments onto the story.

Although Thomas Smith Webb's history of the Templars found in the 1818 version of his monitor (see Appendix III) contains many historical errors, to his credit, he does not make mention of the Templars having practised the rites of Freemasonry. However, one of his protégés, Jeremy Ladd Cross, reprinted much of Laurie's 1804 history of Freemasonry in the 1851 version of his *The True Masonic Chart or Hieroglyphical Monitor*. The addition of Laurie's work, referred to as *A History of Freemasonry by a Brother*, certainly did its part to help perpetuate to American readers the long-standing erroneous claims that the Templars embraced Masonic rites and ceremonies.

But other American ritualists and writers would take the claims even further.

The anonymous author of *The Templar's Text Book*, published in 1859 (see Appendix IV) with Cornelius Moore's *The Craftsman*, offers the following Masonic fiction in the course of the dramatic rise and fall of the medieval Knights Templar:

'This Order (The Templars) had no connexion with ancient Freemasonry, save that the rites and mysteries of Masonry were practised and preserved by them; and from an early date, none could be admitted to the honours of the Order until they had first received the several degrees of Masonry up to the Royal Arch.' [28]

The author of *The Templar's Text Book* was not the only Masonic writer to perpetuate this twist on the myth. Writing in his 1867 two-volume book, *History of the Knights Templar of the State of Pennsylvania*, Alfred Creigh, who was the then historiographer of Knights Templar of Pennsylvania and the United States, presents a fanciful account in his introduction. Speaking of Henry II of England and Gilbert de Clare, the First Earl of Pembroke (1100-1147), Creigh tells his Masonic Templar readers:

'It is recorded that in this reign Knights Templar were first initiated into the mysteries of Freemasonry, from which period they gave it patronage, and the Grand Master of the Temple was appointed to superintend the Lodges, by which appointment pre-eminence was confined to the Orders of Knighthood, over the Society of Freemasons. By this junction of the two Orders, Freemasonry assumed a more important character and higher position in the eyes of the world and continued to increase in general estimation down to the reign of Richard I. It is generally believed that it was at this period that the first connection was formally established with a Masonic Lodge and the Knights Templar. Before that event, individual Knights were initiated into Masonic mysteries and patronised the Society of Freemasons, but subsequently and after the suppression of the Order and their dispersion throughout Christendom, and after they regained stability and freedom from

SIT LUX ET LUX FUIT

Title page of William Alexander Laurie's *The History of Free Masonry and the Grand Lodge of Scotland* with *Chapters on The Knights Templar, Knights of St John, Mark Masonry and R. A. Degree to which is added an Appendix of Valuable Papers. Author's Collection*

persecution, this Order of Knighthood was conferred exclusively on those who had previously passed through the higher degrees of Freemasonry.' [29]

Creigh seems to share the opinion of the author of *The Templar's Text Book* that no man could be admitted to the Templar Order until he had passed through the so-called higher degrees of Freemasonry. Like a number of Masonic writers of the eighteenth and nineteenth centuries, neither author offers valid proof to support their claims, which are, of course, historically absurd. As we will see in Chapter Five, the initiation ritual of the medieval Knights Templar makes no mention of a masonic prerequisite, either operative or speculative, nor does it offer anything beyond a passing similarity to the Craft rituals as they developed from the seventeenth century onwards.

But just as we have to be careful in casting criticism on eighteenth century writers like Anderson and Preston, who were writing for a particular age and audience, we must also be cautious in levelling our disapproval towards the nineteenth century North American writers. It is important to understand that the books quoted above were penned for a general readership; rather they were written for American Templars, who were required to pass through the Craft and Royal Arch degrees before taking the Templar Orders. [30] As such, Creigh and his contemporary may have been welding modern Masonic requirements onto the medieval Order as part of their traditional histories.

While we may never truly know the motives of the men who created a mythology about the Knights Templar that has formed the basis for historical fact in the minds of many modern-day Masons, what remains certain is that these men, no matter how well intentioned, have done more damage than good in their treatment of the subject. Although these writers can perhaps be forgiven for creating the myth of a direct connection between the Templars of old and their modern namesakes to help attract men to the relatively new chivalric grades, the time has long since passed for Freemasons to put aside this notion.

Nearly three centuries have passed since Freemasonry came into a formal existence, more than two hundred since the emergence of Templar organisations attached to Freemasonry. Given that the original Templars were destroyed before reaching either milestone, it is time for Masonic Templars to be satisfied with their longevity. Also, the fanciful versions of how the Order came into existence should be replaced with what actually happened, for the real story of how the Templar orders evolved is as interesting as the mythological accounts.

We are fortunate that the Great Priory of England and Wales has included an introduction in its ritual book, which provides members of the order with information that makes the distinction between the Templars of old and their Masonic counterparts. Speaking of the evolution of the Christian degrees in the mid-eighteenth century, the Great Priory tells us:

'The most important of these were a masonic Templar Rite and a Rose Cross Degree, neither of which has any historical or ritual connection with the old Military Orders of the mediaeval Rosicrucians.' [31]

Unfortunately, not all grand bodies are as thorough in outlining the distinction. In the early part of the twentieth century, The Sovereign Great Priory of Canada, which is the autonomous governing body for Masonic Templars in that country, took great pains to ensure that every man who was consecrated a Knight Templar understood the story of how Masonic Templarism came into being. However, it excluded The Third Historical Sketch from the ritual, a situation that has allowed Canadian Masonic Templars to subscribe to the myths of an earlier age. From the discarded address we read the following:

'The great mistake which has caused so much confusion about the character of the Modern Templar degrees, as allied to Free Masonry, arises mainly from not knowing or not distinguishing, the great difference between the Masonry of to-day and that from which it is derived. The Templar degrees refer to and represent the connection which it is supposed formerly existed between the old Templar Order and the Ecclesiastical Christian builders, who, on separating from the Cloisters, associated themselves with the building Guilds, of which modern Speculative Masonry is supposed to be the outcome – but this revival forms no part of the present Templar system of the British Empire, excepting by alliance.

'The introduction of the Templar degrees into Free Masonry originated on the Continent of Europe soon after Speculative Free Masonry was imported there from England, and was at first chiefly confined to those in the higher ranks of social life, who were ambitious that Masonry should be considered the descendent of the old Religious and Military Order of the Templars. This desire was based upon a fiction that, at the dissolution of the Order (1312 AD), certain Knights joined the Guilds of Stone Masons in Scotland, and thus gave rise to Free and Accepted Masonry.' [32]

Before we can examine and deconstruct the myth that the Templars fled to Scotland where they created Freemasonry, we should first understand the rise and fall of the original Knights Templar.

References for Chapter 1

1. Taken from the Charge to the Entered Apprentice Mason, as presented in the ritual of the Canadian Rite, this instruction is one of several contained in the piece, which points out to the newly made Entered Apprentice his duties to his God, his neighbours and himself.

2. This paper was originally presented to Lodge Vitruvian No. 767 in Indianapolis, Indiana, in July 2005. It was published in its entirety in *Heredom: The Transactions of the Scottish Rite Research Society Volume 14*, and is available online at www.scottishrite.org/what/edu c/heredom/articles/vol14-dafoe.pdf

3. The fish fry is a popular fundraising activity common to North American Lodges, but more especially among the lodges of the United States. It is a common point of ridicule by Masons who are unhappy that Freemasonry is shifting from philosophy and intellectualism to what they perceive as Freemasonry's attempt to remodel itself after the service clubs.

4. *The Hiram Key* by Christopher Knight and Robert Lomas offers, among a myriad of theories, the idea that Jesus and his brother James were striving to establish a Kingdom of Heaven on earth using Masonic style rituals. The authors offer the theory that the Templars uncovered these lost writings of Jesus and buried them beneath the Rosslyn Chapel. *Born in Blood*, by John J. Robinson, offers an interesting theory connecting the Templars to the Freemasons via the Peasants' Revolt of 1381. Both books, although speculative in nature, have been extremely popular among Freemasons.

5. Freemasonry came to a formal and public existence on 24 June 1717 when four London-based lodges united to form a Grand Lodge. This does not imply that Freemasonry magically appeared out of the ether on this date, as it is clear that Masonic lodges must have existed prior to this time for four lodges to bond under one governing umbrella.

6. The rituals of Craft or Speculative Masonry are built around the story of the building of King Solomon's Temple. In the allegorical retelling, Hiram Abif is murdered by three craftsmen who are intent on learning the secrets of a Master Mason, before completing the temple. The biblical depiction, while mentioning a superior craftsman named Hiram or Huram, makes no mention of his demise.

7. *The Rosslyn Hoax*, Robert L. D. Cooper, Hersham, Surrey, Lewis Masonic, 2006, p.40.

8. 'James Anderson: Man and Mason', David Stevenson, published in *Volume 10 of Heredom*, the *Transactions of the Scottish Rite Research Society*, pp.93-94. As Stevenson pointed out in his paper, Anderson has been derided over the years by Masonic scholars who followed him, without giving consideration to the era in which he wrote his work or what the publication was designed to do. Perhaps these historians wished to show just how scientific the subject of Masonic history had become.

9. Anderson's reference to 'the Societies or Orders of Warlike Knights, and of the Religious too' is probably an allusion to the secular knights who fought in the crusades and the military Orders like the Templars, Hospitallers and Teutonic Knights, who took on a religious as well as militant role.

10. *The Constitutions of the Free-Masons*: James Anderson (London 1723) pp.44-47. Facsimile reprint by the Masonic Service Association of the United States, 1924.

11. Cooper. Op. cit. p.41.

12. 'Andrew Michael Ramsay and his Masonic Oration', Lisa Kahler, published in

Heredom: The Transactions of the Scottish Rite Research Society Volume 1, 1991.

13. An excerpt from the Grand Lodge version of Ramsay's Oration as reproduced in *Ramsay's Oration: The Epernay and Grand Lodge Versions* by Cyril N. Batham found in *Heredom: The Transactions of the Scottish Rite Research Society Volume 1, 1991*. See Chapter 6 for a detailed explanation of the two versions and Ramsay's motivations in penning the address.

14. Kahler. Op. cit.

15. Cooper Op. cit. pp.43-44.

16. This temple was actually the Order's second location in London and is still in existence today. It is most commonly referred to as the Round Church in London.

17. *Illustrations of Masonry*: William Preston, p.135.

18. Cooper. Op. cit. p.44.

19. The author is making reference to the biblical story of the Tower of Babel.

20. *The Spirit of Masonry in Moral and Elucidatory Lectures* (second edition): William Hutchinson. Carlisle. F. Jollie, 1775, pp.112-115.

21. Barruel's work comprised four volumes, the first two of which were published in 1797 and the final two in 1798.

22. *The Catholic Encyclopaedia*: Augustin Barruel, www.newadvent.org/cathen/02 310a.htm (accessed 30 Dec 2007.) Also: *An Encyclopaedia of Freemasonry and its Kindred Sciences* (Vol. 1): Albert G. Mackey, Chicago, The Masonic History Company, 1927, p.99.

23. *Barruel – Memoirs Illustrating the History of Jacobinism Part II: The Antimonarchical Conspiracy* (Vol. 2). Hartford, Hudson & Goodwin, 1799, pp.212-213.

24. Cooper. Op. cit. p. 58.

25. Cooper. Op. cit. pp. 56. Also *The History of Freemasonry*, Chap. XXV, *Legend of the Dionysiac Artificers*: Albert G. Mackey, New York, Gramercy, 1996, p.166. Cooper suggests that although Laurie allowed his name to stand as author of the work, Sir David Brewster was the ghost-writer. Mackey also makes the claim that it was Brewster and not Laurie who wrote the book.

26. Ibid. p.56.

27. *The History of Free Masonry and the Grand Lodge of Scotland with Chapters on The Knights Templar, Knights of St John, Mark Masonry and R. A. Degree to which is added an Appendix of Valuable Papers*: William Alexander Laurie, Edinburgh, Seton & Mackenzie, 1859, pp.29-30.

28. *The Craftsman, and Templar's Text Book and, also Melodies for the Craft*: Jacob Ernst, 1859, pp.249-250.

29. *History of the Knights Templar of the State of Pennsylvania* (Vol. 1): Alfred Creigh, Philadelphia, J. B. Lippincott & Co, 1867, p.12.

30. In some American jurisdictions Freemasons are also required to take the degrees of the Cryptic Rite in addition to those of the Craft and Capitular degrees. These degrees are being offered with increasing frequency over the course of a Saturday afternoon or weekend to help bolster sagging membership numbers.

31. *Ritual No. 1 – The Order of the Temple and Drill, The Great Priory of the United Religious, Military and Masonic Orders of the Temple and of St John of Jerusalem, Palestine, Rhodes and Malta of England and Wales and its Provinces Overseas*. London, Chancery of the Orders, 2007, p.3.

32. This address is taken from the Third Historical Sketch, which once formed an important part of the ritual of the Sovereign Great Priory of Canada. Although it was present at the turn of the twentieth century, all attempts to discover its origin and discontinuance have remained unanswered by the Grand Body in Canada. The entire lecture has been reprinted in its original form in Appendix V: A Tale of Two Templar Origin Stories.

Premiers Templiers
En Habit De Guerre A Cheval

The Origin of the Knights Templar

'We have found a strange footprint on the shores of the unknown. We have devised profound theories, one after another, to account for its origins. At last, we have succeeded in reconstructing the creature that made the footprint. And lo! It is our own.'

Sir Arthur Eddington (1882-1944)

This eighteenth century French illustration entitled *Premiers Templiers* (The First Templars) is a romantic depiction of the humble origins of the Order, when it was alleged that the Templars were so poor they had to share one horse.
Author's collection

It WOULD be difficult to understand the history of Masonic Templarism without first having a reasonable understanding of the history of the religious and military Order which it serves to emulate. Given that the Order's well of historical knowledge has been poisoned with misinformation over the years, often by well-meaning members of the Masonic fraternity, it is in our best interest to study the Templars' history without the speculative embellishments and fanciful notions that have been welded onto their armour. In this way, we can examine Templarism as it evolved and exists within our Masonic environment. Also, it can be compared against Templarism as it existed in the arid and dry battlefields of the east or the fertile fields or the west, which financed the brethren at war.

While the chapters within this book are not intended to be a comprehensive analysis of the Templars and their near two-century reign as Christendom's most feared and revered warriors, it is hoped that they will provide sufficient information to give the reader a good overview of their story in a historical context, while putting a few long-standing myths and misconceptions to rest. [1]

If one were to chronicle the history of a group of Masonic Knights Templar, one would start by acquiring the minute books of the Preceptory or Commandery and studying what the group recorded in its formative years, for even the most inefficient of archivists would have made notes on their meetings. Unfortunately, we have no such minute books for the men who gathered together in the early years of the twelfth century AD to protect the interests of Christendom. Rather, we are left with a series of chronicles written half a century after the Order was believed to have been conceived.

The reason for this is that the men who wrote about the Templars did so from the perspective of the Order's later notoriety. Although these same men wrote of other events contemporary with the Templars' beginnings, the Order does not appear to have been of interest to them. Even when the Templars had acquired the reputation to warrant the attention of the chroniclers, the stories they told are hardly synoptic in nature. Like the Masonic writers who would tell their story many centuries later, every author who wrote about the Templars during their existence did so by adding their own spin, bias and flavour; facts were not always the most important ingredient in the mix.

There are three men credited with chronicling the story of the Templars: William of Tyre (1130-1190), Michael the Syrian (1126-1199) and Walter Map (1140-1210). Much of what has come to be the accepted story of the formative years of the Knights Templar is derived from the chronicle of William of Tyre, despite the fact that William had no particular love of the Order and what he perceived they had evolved into. Writing during the second half of the twelfth century, William paints a portrait of the early days of the Knights Templar that will no doubt appear familiar to members of the Masonic Templar Orders

(see Appendix V: A Tale of Two Templar Origin Stories for a comparison between the two):

'In this same year, (1118) certain noble men of knightly rank, religious men, devoted to God and fearing him, bound themselves to Christ's service in the hands of the Lord Patriarch. They promised to live in perpetuity as regular canons, without possessions, under vows of chastity and obedience. Their foremost leaders were the venerable Hugh of Payens and Geoffrey of St Omer. Since they had no church or any fixed abode, the king gave them for a time a dwelling place in the south wing of the palace, near the Lord's Temple. The canons of the Lord's Temple gave them, under certain conditions, a square near the palace which the canons possessed. This the knights used as a drill field. The Lord King and his noblemen and also the Lord Patriarch and the prelates of the church gave them benefices from their domains, some for a limited time and some in perpetuity. These were to provide the knights with food and clothing. Their primary duty, one which was enjoined upon them by the Lord Patriarch and the other bishops for the remission of sins, was that of protecting the roads and routes against the attacks of robbers and brigands. This they did especially in order to safeguard pilgrims.' [2]

And so William provides us with the traditional rendering of the Templars' story. A number of nobly born knights led by Hugues de Payens and Geoffrey St Omer took an oath of poverty, chastity and obedience and obligated their swords to defend Christian pilgrims, who were attacked while visiting the shrines sacred to their faith. Being poor and homeless knights, Baldwin II granted them a portion of his royal palace to serve as a home base.

William goes on to state that for nine years after their foundation, the knights had no uniform of their own; rather they wore the humble garments offered to them by their beneficiaries. Additionally, William reveals that in that period of time, the Templars remained nine in number. [3] This piece of information has opened the door for a number of authors to suggest that nine men were simply not enough to protect the pilgrims against the vast number of Turks and Saracens hanging around outside the city walls; therefore the Templars must have been digging for treasure under the Temple Mount, which is how they got so fabulously rich. Of course, as we will see in the next chapter, the Templars' wealth had nothing to do with excavating the Temple Mount; rather it came from excavating the deep pockets of European monarchs.

But while William tells us that the Templars remained nine in number in their first decade of existence, another of the early chroniclers tells us a different story altogether. In the account of Michael the Syrian, Jacobite Patriarch of Antioch, the founding members of the Templar Order number 31 and not nine as we saw in William's account:

'At the beginning of the reign of King Baldwin II, a Frank came from Rome to pray at Jerusalem. He had made a vow never to return to his own country, but to take holy orders, after having assisted the king in war for three years, he and the thirty knights who accompanied him, and to terminate their lives in Jerusalem. When the king and his nobles saw that they were renowned in battle, and had been of great use to the city during their three years of service, he advised this man to serve in the militia, together with those attached to him, instead of taking holy orders, to work towards saving his soul, and to protect those places against thieves.

'Now this man, whose name was Hough de Payen, accepted this advice; the thirty knights who accompanied him joined him. The king gave them the house of Solomon for their residence, and some villages for their maintenance. The Patriarch also gave them some villages of the Church.' [4]

Although Michael's version of the story has received less mileage than William's over the centuries, it does provide some answers to questions raised by the more popular version. For example, if the Templars were but nine in number how was it possible for them to defend the pilgrims against the attacks of 'robbers and brigands' as both accounts indicate. But perhaps more importantly, why would the King of Jerusalem offer a group of men, who couldn't gather together a quorum

over a decade span of time, a portion of his Royal Palace?

It is unlikely that we will ever know which, if either account was the most accurate, but it seems that the mission and privileges given to the founding members is more plausible given Michael's number of knights. But where Michael's account lends plausibility to the Templars' story, the account of Walter Map, seems to remove it entirely. Walter, who was the Archdeacon of Oxford and a clerk in the kingdom of King Henry II of England, was the farthest removed in terms of time and geography, but also the farthest removed in terms of reality. In Walter's account, the task of defending Christian pilgrims did not fall on the shoulders of nine or even thirty-nine men, but on the head of one man, a Burgundian knight named Paganus.

In Walter's romantic story, Paganus was troubled after seeing pilgrims regularly attacked at a horse pool near to the City of Jerusalem and took it upon himself to come to their rescue. [5] Initially, Paganus took on the attackers single-handily, and it wasn't until they became too much for him to handle that he went to the canons of the Temple of the Lord looking for assistance. The canons were only too happy to offer a

King Louis VII kneels at the feet of the Cistercian abbot Bernard of Clairvaux who preached the second crusade called by Pope Eugenius III.
Jupiter Images

Facing Page:
This collection of eighteenth century French illustrations shows a romantic depiction of the various classes within the Temple Order. Clockwise from top left: serving brother in black mantle; Templar in the dress of the house; treasurer or paymaster of the house of the Temple; Grand Master of the Order in red ceremonial robes; Knight Templar in the original habit of the Order before the cross was added; Templar in the regular garments of a knight.
Author's collection

hand and granted Paganus a hall to serve as a base of operations in order for him to gather more knights to the cause.

Although Walter's account is undoubtedly a work of fiction, it is certain that the hero of his piece, Paganus, was Hugues de Payens, as no two chronicles seem to render the name of the founding father of the Templars the same way: Payens, Payen, Pedanis, Pedano and Paganus all appearing over the years as variations.

If we were left with just these three divergent chronicles to compose a snapshot of the early years of the Templars, we would be hard pressed to gain any real insight and would be left to speculations. Fortunately there are other primary sources of information, written much closer to the actual events, which help to clarify the beginnings of the Order.

The first of these comes from a charter written by Simon, the Bishop of Noyons, sometime between 1130 and 1131, documenting a donation granted to

Hugh, Master of the Knights of the Temple. In the preamble, Simon wishes the order the strength to persevere in 'the life of the religious order you have entered'. The Bishop of Noyons goes on to say:

'We give thanks to God, because through his mercy he has recovered the order which had perished. For we know that three orders have been instituted by God in the Church, the order of prayers, of defenders and of workers. The other orders were in decline while the order of defenders had almost completely perished. But God the Father and our Lord Jesus Christ, God's Son, had mercy on His Church. Through the infusion of the Holy Spirit in our hearts, in these most recent times He deigned to repair the lost order.'[6]

At first glance, this statement would seem to indicate that the Templars had existed in some form prior to their official formation and had recently been restored. However, it is important to note that what Simon was referring to by the three orders was a natural division in society that existed at that time. At the top of the societal food chain was the order of prayers: the churchmen who looked after ecclesiastical matters. Next to the order of prayers was the order of defenders: the aristocracy of medieval Europe, who were charged with defending the interests of their liege lord and protecting the weak and poor under their care. Lastly, was the order of workers: the peasant class who made up the bulk of society and owed their fealty to the nobility. However, the context in which all of this is placed is within the context of religion. The Church was the hub around which the medieval world turned and the central rallying point for the medieval community; however, the nobility were often the least likely to keep up their end of the faith. As such, Simon was commending the Templars for restoring this decline and for setting an example for other secular knights to follow.

The next primary source we have which sheds some light on the early

Templar Knight – Templar Sergeant. The nobly born Templar knight was dressed and armed differently than his ignobly born counterpart the sergeant. Sergeants, because they were infantrymen, did not receive full chain-mail armour, as did their mounted counterparts.
Gordon Napier

years of the Templars was written between 1135 and 1137 by another Simon – Simon de St Bertin, a monk from the St Omer area. In his *Gesta abbatum Sancti Bertini Sithensium*, Simon suggests that the founding members of the Templars were soldiers from the First Crusade who had stayed behind when the majority had returned to Europe with the spoils of war. In writing about the events following the crowning of Godfrey de Bouillon, who was the first King of Jerusalem in all but name, [7] the St Bertin monk tells us:

> 'While he [Godfrey] was reigning magnificently, some had decided not to return to the shadows of the world after suffering such dangers for God's sake. On the advice of the princes of God's army they vowed themselves to God's Temple under this rule: they would renounce the world, give up personal goods, free themselves to pursue purity, and lead a communal life wearing a poor habit, only using arms to defend the land against the attacks of the insurgent pagans when necessity demanded.' [8]

Simon was not alone in making the suggestion that the original Templars were crusaders. Otto, the Bishop of Freising, writing some time between 1143 and 1147 in his work, *Chronicon*, claimed that during the time of the Investiture controversy [9] a number of knights who realised that their swords were intended for a more noble purpose headed for Jerusalem on crusade, where they formed a new type of knighthood dedicated to bearing arms against Christ's enemies:

> 'Around this time, while the kingdom of the Romans was divided in civil and parricidal war caused by a desire for domination, others, despising what they had for Christ's sake, and realising that they did not bear the belt of knighthood without good reason, headed for Jerusalem. And there they began a new type of knighthood. Thus they bear arms against the enemies of Christ's cross, so that continually carrying the mortification of the cross on their bodies; they might appear to be in life and lifestyle not knights but monks.' [10]

Although the Templars may have appeared as monks rather than knights, they actually accommodated both aspects of society, which is what made them so unique. It was this unusual dichotomy that caught the eye of Bernard of Clairvaux, a man who was largely responsible for the success of the fledgling Templar Order. Bernard was born into a noble family in 1090 at Fontaines, which is just outside the old Burgundian capitol of Dijon. Bernard's father was a knight by the name of Tescelin and his mother was a woman named Aleth, who was from the Montbard family. [11] Aleth's younger brother Andrew, who would have been Bernard's uncle – despite being considerably younger – is believed to have been one of the founding members of the Order, but was certainly a member at some point, having been elected to the position of Grand Master in 1154.

The story of Bernard's early years is often coloured with a similar mythos to that of the Templars themselves. What is known is that Bernard did not become a knight like his father, but rather entered the religious life at a young age; first attending school at St Vorles at Châtillon-sur-Seine, where Tescelin owned property. Although Bernard's family accepted his being educated at St Vorles, they opposed his decision to enter a monastic life. But the young man prevailed and in 1112 Bernard, along with thirty-two other young men who also sought the ascetic life, entered the newly formed Citeaux Abbey, birthplace of the Cistercian Order. [12] Within three years of joining the Cistercians, Bernard was sent by Stephen Harding, the abbot of Citeaux, to form a new abbey at Ville-sous-la-Ferté.

There is an interesting parallel between the story of Bernard's early monastic career and Michael the Syrian's account of the early career of the Templars. For in both stories we have a single man, accompanied by thirty-some others entering a new vocation and, after a three year period of service, proceeding to bigger and better things. While the connection is probably one of pure coincidence, it must be remembered that Michael's account was written well after Bernard and Templars had risen to fame in Christendom. Given Bernard's influence upon the success of the Order, there may have been an underlying allegory.

Speculations aside, the request to form this new abbey had come from Count Hugh of Champagne, [13] a man who was once Hugues de Payens' liege lord and a man who eventually renounced his worldly possessions to join the Templars himself in 1125. Although the land provided by the count was a virtual swamp, Bernard chose to call the new abbey Clairvaux or clear valley and remained its abbot until his death in 1153.

With the sole exception of the Templar's Rule of Order, Bernard's *De laude novae militae* or 'In Praise of the New Knighthood', written between 1128 and 1138, is one of the most valuable primary source materials in terms of providing us with a picture of the early days of the Order and how they differed from all that had existed before them. The document served the dual purpose of praising and encouraging the Templars and acting as a recruitment flyer, but regardless of the personal motivations behind Bernard's praise of the fledgling Order, the letter served to inform Christendom of this new knighthood.

Bernard referred to the Templars as a new kind of knighthood because their method of fighting was twofold; like secular knights, they waged war against flesh and blood, but of far greater importance to the Cistercian abbot, the Templars waged war against 'a spiritual army of evil in the heavens'.

While Bernard regarded neither type of warfare as being worthy of his highest praise, it was the combination of the two that set Bernard's hand to quill in writing his letter praising the fledgling Templars:

> 'But when one sees a man powerfully girding himself with both swords and nobly marking his belt, who would not consider it worthy of all wonder, the more so since it has been hitherto unknown? He is truly a fearless knight and secure on every side, for his soul is protected by the armour of faith just as his body is protected by armour of steel. He is thus doubly armed and need fear neither demons nor men.' [14]

Bernard's letter continued the theme introduced several decades earlier in Pope Urban's speech at Clermont, which launched the First Crusade: that the knight who fought and killed in the name of Christ was not committing murder, nor was he engaging in evil. Indeed, as the Cistercian abbot wrote, 'The knights of Christ may safely fight the battles of their Lord, fearing neither sin if they sdmite the enemy, nor danger at their own death; since to inflict death or to die for Christ is no sin, but rather, an abundant claim to glory.' [15] Bernard saw a win-win situation in this twofold nature. The Templars won a victory for Christ whenever they killed one of his enemies in battle, and won a victory for themselves should they be slain in the process.

Combining the best attributes of the monastic and warrior lifestyle, Bernard wrote of the dichotomy that existed in the Templars, marvelling that this new knighthood appeared gentler than lambs and yet were fiercer than lions. In fact the abbot was unsure as to whether they should be referred to as monks or soldiers, but decided that it would be best to recognise them as both. This new form of knighthood was, to the Cistercian abbot, a stark contrast from the secular knighthood of the day and he spared no feelings in condemning the latter for their ways. It was customary for secular knights to adorn their horses and armour with gold, silver and precious jewels. To Bernard these were not the trappings of a warrior, but rather the accessories of a woman and he spared no feelings in calling matters as he saw them. Indeed, Bernard saw the secular knight of his day as anything but masculine, their long flowing hair and longer flowing tunics being feminine accoutrements. By contrast, the Templars were to keep their hair well tonsured, as proscribed in their own Rule of Order.

In pointing out the lifestyle of the knights of Christ, Bernard does so to shame those knights who, according to the abbot, were 'fighting for the devil rather than for God'. [16] Indeed, the manner in which the Templars lived was a stark contrast with the lifestyle that the nobly born secular knight was accustomed to. Although secular knights, especially those who had come on crusade, usually owed their fealty to a lord or baron, the Templars were far more restricted in what they could and could not do. They came and went at the call of their superior, ate what he provided them, wore what he gave them to wear and, above all, lived together without the company of women. Unlike the secular knight, whose noble birth may elevate his station in life, the Templar knights had no such distinction among them, although they were, for the most part, nobly born also. This lifestyle was not to everyone's taste and morale was said to be low at times.

This state of low morale is addressed in another letter of encouragement to the Templars, written sometime between 1119 and 1135. Unlike, Bernard's *De laude novae militae*, the authorship of the *Letter to the Knights of Christ in the Temple at Jerusalem* remains somewhat of a mystery as it was signed simply Hugh Peccator or Hugh the Sinner. What is clear about the document is that it was intended to reassure the Templars of their mission and to boost troop morale, which had been sagging due to the number of people who had told the Templars that their mission did not please God. In the opinion of their critics, the Templars ought to love Christ's enemies, rather than fight them; and furthermore, if the Templars wished to enjoy eternal life, they ought to lay down their arms and embrace the life of monks.

The writer of the letter defends the active life of the Order and informs the reader that each man has a calling from God and that it is their duty to heed that calling, drawing a metaphor that each part of the body has a separate function and if all served the same purpose, the body would die:

'See, brothers, if all the parts of the body had the same duties, the body could not survive. Listen to what the Apostle says: 'If the foot should say, "I am not an eye, therefore I am not part of the body," isn't it still part of the body?" [17]

While the importance of the letter lies in the insight it provides into the early Templars rather than who actually wrote it, there are two candidates for the person of Hugh Peccator. The first and most widely accepted candidate is Hugues de Payens himself. Certainly if morale was low among his brethren, it would be expected that he would take action upon it. However, the style and content of the letter makes de Payens seem a less credible candidate. [18] The second possibility is Hugh de St Victor, of the Augustinian Abbey of St Victor at Paris. Although not the most favoured candidate, the fact that the manuscript is headed with the words Prologus, magistri hugonis de sancto victore strongly indicates that he was the author of the letter. [19]

What is particular noteworthy is that it was the Abbey of St Victor that provided the canons of the Order of the Holy Sepulchre with their rule, and it is within the Order of the Holy Sepulchre itself that a final account of the early days of the Knights Templar can be found. Written sometime after the Battle of Hattin in 1187 (4 July 1187), *The Chronicle of Ernoul and Bernard the Treasurer* [20] presents us with another

interesting piece of the Templar puzzle. The writer tells us that after the victory of the First Crusade, when most had returned home with the spoils of war, a number of knights stayed behind, attaching themselves to the Church of the Holy Sepulchre. [21] Among those who had taken on the ascetic life, were a number of former knights who realised that the Kingdom of Jerusalem was still in need of men-at-arms. Seeing no conflict between fulfilling both vocations, they decided to elect one of their number to serve as Master and to lead them into battle should the need arise:

'At that time Baldwin was king. So they came to him and said: "Lord, advise us for God's sake. We have decided to make one of us a master who may lead us in battle to help the country." The king was delighted with this, and said that he would willingly advise them and aid them.' [22]

The account goes on to say that Baldwin summoned the Patriarch of Jerusalem, bishops, archbishops and barons of the country to discuss the proposal. All agreed that the former knight's idea was a good one and the prior of the Holy Sepulchre released the knights from their allegiance to him. Afterward, the new knighthood was granted quarters in the Temple of Solomon (al-Aqsa Mosque) from which the order derived their name. What is particularly interesting about this account is that the Templars and

The Temple Mount at Jerusalem viewed from the east. The al-Aqsa Mosque on the left is where the Templars were granted quarters by King Baldwin II after their formation in 1119-1120. The building was believed to be the Temple of Solomon and it was from this connection that the Order became known as Templars.
IStockPhoto.com
Luis Alvarez

Hospitallers both followed the liturgy of the Church of the Holy Sepulchre and, although erroneously thought to be the Dome of the Rock, it is the dome of the Holy Sepulchre that was depicted on the obverse of the Grand Master's seal. [23]

So far we have looked at nine sources, which can be considered contemporary sources; for although some were written many years after the Templars had started, all were written by people alive when the order still existed. As divergent as the sources seem at first glance, there are areas in which the authors agree. The principal area where the nine accounts are synoptic is in their description of the purpose and need of the Templars as a force to protect the sacred shrines of Christendom and the pilgrims who ventured to worship at them. Although the crusaders had succeeded in removing the Muslims from the City of Jerusalem, they had, despite capturing considerable territory, not managed to defeat them entirely.

While the Crusader States of Edessa, Antioch and Tripoli were relatively safe places for the Christian faithful to congregate, the roads between them were paved with danger. Pilgrims were often attacked in areas where they would gather to take water. Malcolm Barber recounts the story of a Russian Abbot named Daniel and his feelings in passing the town of Bashan in 1106:

> 'And this place is very dreadful and dangerous. Seven rivers flow from this town of Bashan and great reeds grow along these rivers and many tall palm trees stand about the town like a dense forest. This place is terrible and difficult of access for here live fierce pagan Saracens who attack travellers at the fords on these rivers.' [24]

The abbot's story was not an exaggeration; a decade and a half later an event occurred which may have been the catalyst for the formation of the Templars. At Easter in the year 1119, a group of seven hundred Christian pilgrims, who were travelling to the River Jordan after visiting the Church of the Holy Sepulchre, were attacked by a group of Muslims from Tyre and Ascalon. Three hundred of the pilgrims were slain and another sixty were carried off as slaves. [25] Although King Baldwin dispatched a group of knights to the scene, they arrived too late to be of assistance [26] and one can only imagine the reaction of the residents of Jerusalem when the knights returned to the city with the news of the murdered and captured pilgrims. But as great a loss as the slaughter of three hundred pilgrims was, another massacre a few months later would add to the already unstable landscape that was present in the Crusader States.

On 28 June 1119, some 700 knights and 4,000 foot-soldiers were killed at the Battle of Ager Sanguinis (Field of Blood) when the army of Roger of Salerno, the regent of Antioch, was surprised and outnumbered by the army of Ilghazi. Among the dead was Roger himself, who was beheaded at the foot of a large golden crucifix, which the army had brought with them from the basilica of Antioch. For whatever reason, Ilghazi failed to press on to Antioch, which was now depleted of its defences. Having learned of Roger's death and the slaughter of the Antiochan army, and anticipating that Ilghazi would attempt to besiege the city, King Baldwin and Pons of Tripoli, who had come to assist Roger in his mission, moved on to Antioch preparing for a battle which never came. With Roger dead and Antioch's legitimate heir Bohemund II too young to rule his principality, Baldwin II took on the role of its regent, further taxing the resources of his own kingdom.

Those who lived in Jerusalem were already afraid to venture outside the city walls without an armed escort, and certainly the tragedy at Easter and the massacre in June would have done little to change their mind on the matter. What made matters worse was the fact that Jerusalem was inland and as such not as popular a place for settlement as the coastal cities of Acre and Tyre. Writing of the time of King Baldwin I, the successor of Godfrey de Bouillon as King of Jerusalem, William of Tyre gives the following account:

> 'At this time the king realised with great concern that the Holy City, beloved of God, was almost destitute of inhabitants. There were not enough people to carry on the necessary undertakings of the realm. Indeed there were scarcely enough to protect the entrances to the city and to defend the walls and towers against sudden hostile attacks.' [27]

William's claims are certainly supported by the small numbers that Baldwin and Pons were able to spare in 1119 to support Roger of Salerno. In reviewing the situation in the Latin States, especially in the City of Jerusalem we see that the need for an organised military force was indeed a logical and necessary objective, if for no other reason to give the perception that Jerusalem was a secure place for Western Christians to settle and visit. As such, King Baldwin II would surely have welcomed an offer of assistance from a group of knights. The question that remains is who were these knights and just how many of them were there?

The Founding Fathers

MANY modern books dealing with the Knights Templar, in keeping with William of Tyre's assertion that there were nine members of the order at the time of the Council of Troyes, [28] list the names of nine men believed to be the founders of the order. This list of names seems to have originated with Charles du Fresne du Cange (1610-1688) who was a French historian specialising in Byzantine and medieval history. Du Cange wrote a book entitled *Les familles d'outre-mer*, (published in 1869 long after his death) in which he lists the founders as: Hugues de Payens, Godefroid de Saint-Omer, Andre de Montbard, Geoffrey Bisol, Payen de Montdesir, Archambaud de Saint-Aignan, Gundomar, Godefroy and Roral. [29] However, none of the contemporary accounts we have dealt with thus far provide us with any names other than Hugues de Payens and Geoffrey de St Omer. [30] As such, we can have little doubt that they were indeed the founders of the Order. Additionally Andrew de Montbard served as Master in 1153 and Payen de Montdidier served as Master of the Order in France, so it is possible that both were involved in the early days of the Order, but with respect to the others, nothing can be said with any real degree of certainty.

What also remains uncertain is whether or not the original members were veterans of the First Crusade. Modern historians seem split down the middle with respect to this idea, although many of the contemporary accounts indicate the Templars were involved in the victory of the First Crusade, having either taken up residence in the area or joined with the Order of the Holy Sepulchre as *The Chronicle of Ernoul and Bernard the Treasurer* suggests.

In studying the primary accounts it seems more and more likely that the first Templars were either veterans of the First Crusade, knights who had come east in the years that followed, or perhaps a combination of both. Certainly it seems possible if not probable that their number were greater than the nine knights in nine years, which Barber suggests carries a suspicious symmetry. [31]

Nailing Down the Date

THE NEXT area in which historians disagree is the actual date that the Templars started. William of Tyre's date of 1118 has long been accepted and modern day Masonic Knights Templar derive their calendar year, which they refer to as Anno Ordinis, upon it. [32] But other than William's account, the majority of the primary sources do not specify a date,

instead simply referring to the Templars' official sanctioning as having occurred during the reign of King Baldwin II. As Baldwin II was crowned King of Jerusalem at Easter, 1118, following the death of Baldwin I, it is possible that William was correct.

But in recent years, Templar historians have begun to discredit this date and have put forth a notion that the Templars actually began in 1119 or 1120. Malcolm Barber, arguably one of the world's foremost authorities on the Templars, identifies the formation of the Order as occurring between 14 January and 13 September 1120. [33]

What we do know is that the Templars first received ecclesiastical recognition at the Council of Nablus, held in January of 1120. [34] Although not a church council per se, it was none the less called by Baldwin II and Warmund, Patriarch of Jerusalem, to deal with a number of secular and religious matters confronting the kingdom at that time. As we have seen, the Kingdom of Jerusalem was not the Utopia that some chronicles wished people to believe; times were hard, threats from enemies were great, the citizens lived in constant fear and the ability to deal with any of it was limited by a lack of manpower.

Of the twenty-five canons [35] that came out of the council, one is particularly interesting in light of the Templars' dual role as warriors and monks. The Truce of God – which was upheld at the Council of Claremont in 1095, when Urban launched the First Crusade – prohibited clerics from fighting at any time; however, canon twenty penned at the Council of Nablus stated that a monk should not be held guilty if he takes up the sword and shield in defence. Quite simply put, the kingdom needed all the muscle they could muster, but what is interesting in this canon is that it seems to be in keeping with the account of the crusaders who had attached themselves to the Order

Charles du Fresne du Cange (1610-1688) is the man responsible for the widely publicised list of founding members of the Knights Templar. *Author's collection* of the Holy Sepulchre found in *The Chronicle of Ernoul and Bernard the Treasurer*:

> 'We have left our lands and our loved ones, and have come here to raise up and exalt the law of God. So we rest here eating and drinking and spending, without doing any work. We do not perform any deed of arms either, although this country has need of that. We obey a priest, and so we do no labour of arms. Let us take advice, and with our prior's permission we shall make one of us our master, who may lead us in battle when necessary.' [36]

A Probable Origin of the Knights Templar

ALMOST nine centuries after the Templars began there is simply no way of knowing with absolute certainty the precise details of their early origins. Only those who were there when the Order began could tell us for sure, but as they are now long dead, the best we can do is to piece together the bits and pieces they have left for us to assemble. From those pieces, we can assemble the following account, which is only as accurate as the information used to put it together.

After the conquest of Jerusalem the crusading armies, for the most part, left the Holy City, taking with them the spoils of war. Other knights, remembering that the purpose of the crusade was as much a matter of pilgrimage and dedication to God as it was a war of liberation, vowed to stay in the Holy Land, perhaps taking their lead from Godfrey de Bouillon who refused to be called king in a city where Christ was crucified, instead choosing the title Advocatus Sancti Sepulchri or Defender of the Holy Sepulchre. The knights attached themselves to this Church of the Holy Sepulchre, which worked in tandem with the Knights Hospitaller, who began as an Amalfitan hospital for poor pilgrims and had been in operation near to the Sepulchre since 1080. Perhaps having seen enough blood over several years of hacking their way east, these knights had given up their knightly vocation and taken up the contemplative life.

Although their Muslim enemies had been driven out of the city and out of the Crusader States that had been founded along the path to Jerusalem, they had not been driven out of the Holy Land altogether and many of their number were as dedicated to taking the area back as the crusaders were to keep it. Over the years the security of the region began to face a serious decline and after the massacre of 700 pilgrims at Easter, 1119, and the Battle of Ager Sanguinis in June of the same year, the former knights, now living the ascetic life, began to question their choice. Perhaps some of them had been already been serving with both the cross and the sword as it was certainly not unknown for priests to take up arms when the need arose as they had at the Field of Blood.

At some point Hugues de Payens who may have first come to the Holy Land with the crusaders or later with his lord Hugh, Count of Champagne, got the idea that a man could serve two masters and lead an active as well as a contemplative life. He spoke to his fellow knights, chief among them Geoffrey de St Omer, who also may have been a veteran of the crusade, and together they arranged for a number of knights, although we don't know for sure how many, to support the idea.

They approached Baldwin II, who was in desperate need of assistance. Not only was Baldwin responsible for his Kingdom of Jerusalem, but also the Principality of Antioch, which he became regent of following the death of Roger of Salerno at the Field of Blood. In addition Baldwin would have felt some responsibility in protecting the other Crusader States that were under threat from the Muslims who came closer and closer to their walls each day. Baldwin was thrilled with the idea offered by the knights and after consulting with the Patriarch of Jerusalem, other ecclesiastics and the barons of the country, approached the Prior of the Church of the Holy Sepulchre, asking that he free the former knights from their allegiance. The prior accepted the request and granted his charges their freedom and his blessings.

At the Council of Nablus, held in January of 1120, the new knighthood was first given its ecclesiastic recognition. As they were no longer attached to the Holy Sepulchre, Baldwin II granted them part of the al-Aqsa Mosque, which at that time served as the royal palace and was believed to be the Temple of Solomon itself. From this base of operations the knights began to take up their dual role as a monastic and military order that would patrol the roads surrounding the kingdom, protecting the pilgrims in the process and acting as a deterrent against further incursions into Baldwin's land.

Although the Order had been recognised and was supported by the king and patriarch, they largely relied on donations and wore simple clothing provided to them for their use, having taken monastic vows of poverty, chastity and obedience. There were some within the city, however, who did not approve of this new style of knight, believing that it was wrong for a Christian to take up arms. Rumours and accusations travelled the kingdom, which sapped the fledgling order of its esprit de corps. Eventually letters praising the Order were written and the Order slowly began to grow and prosper.

While it is admitted that the previous history of the origin of the Knights Templar is a speculation on the part of the author, it is a more realistic and plausible account than Walter Map's notion of a one-man army or William of Tyre's notion of an order that couldn't muster a quorum of men over a decade of existence. It is likewise a more realistic treatment of the origins of an Order which rose in prominence throughout Christendom over the next century, ultimately becoming powerful enough to finance and influence kings. It is towards this rise in power, an area that has been glossed over in Masonic Templar rituals, that we will now turn our attentions.

References for Chapter 2

1. For a detailed history of the Templars see *Nobly Born: An Illustrated History of the Knights Templar*, Stephen Dafoe, 2007, Lewis Masonic.

2. William of Tyre: *The Foundation of the Order of Knights Templar* – Medieval Sourcebook www.fordham.edu/halsall/source/tyre-templars.html. Professor James Brundage translation. Accessed 13 December 2007.

3. Ibid.

4. Burman, Edward: *The Templars: Knights of God*, pp.19-20.

5. Barber, Malcolm: *The New Knighthood*, p.7.

6. Nicholson, Helen: *Contemporary reactions to the foundation of the Templars*. www.deremilitari.org/resources/sources/templars1.htm

7. Godfrey de Bouillon refused to wear a crown of gold where Christ had worn a crown of thorns. As such he accepted the title of Defender of the Holy Sepulchre. Nomenclature notwithstanding, de Bouillon was the first of the Christian kings.

8. Nicholson. Op. cit.

9. The Investiture Controversy occurred during the 11th century between Henry IV, the Holy Roman Emperor, and Pope Gregory VII. The controversy involved who had the power to control church appointments (investitures).

10. Nicholson. Op. cit.

11. Meadows, Dennis: *A Saint and A Half*, p.92.

12. Op. cit. p.100.

13. Tobin, Stephen: *The Cistercians*, p.53.

14. Bernard of Clairvaux, *In Praise of the New Knighthood*. www.the-orb.net/encyclop/religion/monastic/bernard.html

15. Ibid.

16. Ibid.

17. *Letter to the Knights of Christ in the Temple at Jerusalem*: Nicholson, Helen, www.the-orb.net/encyclop/religion/monastic/hughssin.html. In this section the author, possibly Hugues de Payens or Hugh de St Victor, is quoting from I Corinthians 12:15. This is one of many scriptural references used in the document to support and defend the Templars' lifestyle and mission.

18. Barber. Op. cit p.42.

19. Ibid. It is interesting to note that Barber mentions the prologue tying Hugh de St Victor to the letter; however, Nicholson makes no mention of it in her book, *The Knights Templar: A New History*. In Nicholson's book she states that the Latin used in the letter is of too poor a quality for a theologian and yet of too good a quality for a knight.

20. *The Chronicle of Ernoul and Bernard the Treasurer* was edited by L. de Mas Latrie in 1871 and is likely to have been based on a French version of William of Tyre's book. The Ernoul mentioned in the title is generally believed to be a squire named Ernoul who was part of the company who travelled with Balian of Ibelin, a major figure in the history of Jerusalem. Balian of Ibelin was the central character in Ridley Scott's film *Kingdom of Heaven* about the loss of Jerusalem to Saladin in 1187. Bernard was the treasurer of Corbie Abbey in France.

21. The Temple of the Holy Sepulchre or Church of the Holy Sepulchre is one of the most sacred sites in Christendom and is believed to be the very spot where Christ's body was placed after the crucifixion. The shrine was built by Constantine the Great sometime around AD325, but damaged by the Persians in 614 when they captured Jerusalem. It was restored in 630 by Emperor Heraclius and remained a Christian church when the Muslims took control of Jerusalem until it was destroyed in 1009 by al-Hakin bin-Amir Allah. The church was rebuilt in 1048 and completely reconstructed sometime in the mid-twelfth century.

22. Nicholson : *Contemporary reactions to the foundation of the Templars*, op. cit.

23. Nicholson: *The Knights Templar*, p.29.

24. Barber. Op. cit. p.6.

25. Burman. Op. cit. p.19. Burman attributes the story to the work of Albert of Aix. And other credible historians such as Malcolm Barber recount the story, with Barber attributing it to Albert of Aachen's (Aix) *Historia Hierosolymitana*.

26. Barber. Op. cit. pp.9-10.

27. Burman. Op. cit. p.17.

28. The Council of Troyes was where the Templars' Rule of Order was drafted and approved. It was also at this council that the Templars were granted the right to wear white garments.

29. Burman. Op. cit. p.21. This listing is likely taken from *Les familles d'outre-mer* published by Emanuel Guillaume Rey in his work *Inédits de l'histoire de France*

(1869). The spellings used are those of Burman's book.

30. A letter from Baldwin II does make mention of an Andreum and Gundemarum and the roster from the Council of Troyes lists several Templars in attendance. It is likely that du Cange cobbled together his list of nine knights from a combination of the primary sources and the Council of Troyes documents.

31. Barber. Op. cit. p.10.

32. Anno Ordinis (AO) is Latin for Year of the Order and is used in Masonic Templar circles as a calendar. AO is arrived at by deducting 1118 from the calendar year – thus 2008 becomes 890 AO. Similar calendar calculations are used in the various branches of Freemasonry.

33. Barber. Op. cit. p.9. Barber indicates that a charitable grant issued to Hugues de Payens from Thierry, Count of Flanders, and date 13 September 1128 mentions the grant was given in the order's ninth year, which would make the year of foundation 1120.

34. Ibid. p.9.

35. The 25 canons of the Council of Nablus largely dealt with such matters as church tithes, adultery and bigamy, homosexuality, sexual relationships between Muslims and Latins, the prohibition of Muslims dressing like Christians, and theft. It was believed by the organisers of the council that the problems confronting the kingdom were due to the sins of its population.

36. Nicholson – *Contemporary reactions*, op. cit.

Templars on the Mount 1120-1187

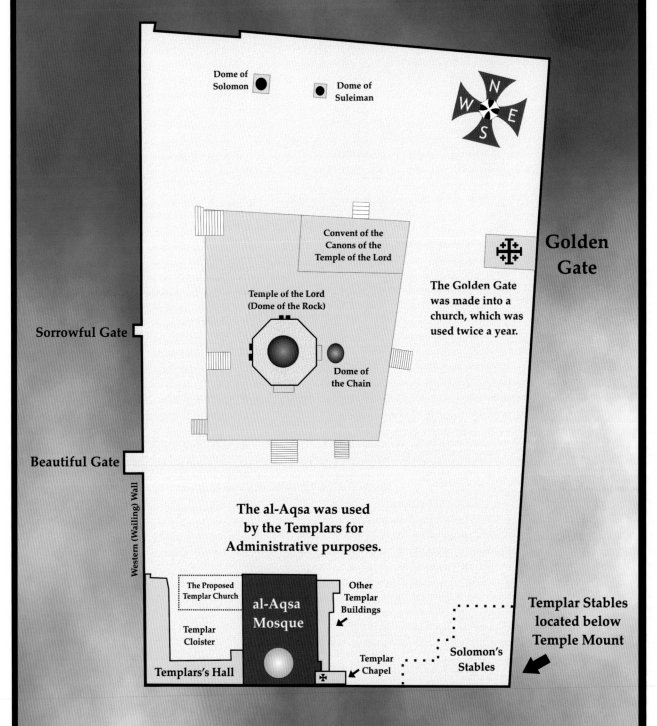

Dome of Solomon

Dome of Suleiman

Convent of the Canons of the Temple of the Lord

Temple of the Lord (Dome of the Rock)

Dome of the Chain

Sorrowful Gate

Golden Gate

The Golden Gate was made into a church, which was used twice a year.

Beautiful Gate

Western (Wailing) Wall

The al-Aqsa was used by the Templars for Administrative purposes.

The Proposed Templar Church

al-Aqsa Mosque

Other Templar Buildings

Templar Cloister

Templars's Hall

Templar Chapel

Solomon's Stables

Templar Stables located below Temple Mount

The Rise of the Knights Templar

'Nearly all men can stand adversity, but if you want to test a man's character, give him power.'

Abraham Lincoln (1809-1865)

Diagram depicting the Templars' headquarters on the Templar Mount from their formation in 1120 until the loss of the City of Jerusalem in 1187. From 1191 until 1291, the Templars based their headquarters at the port city of Acre.
Stephen Dafoe

THE RITUAL and ceremonies used by Masonic Knights Templar offer the new member but the briefest snapshot of the history of the original medieval Order and even then limit its focus primarily to the origin of the Order and its ultimate demise less than two centuries later. Sadly, the new Masonic Templar is given little information on the Order's rise to wealth and power, which is an important component in understanding the history of the Knights Templar. For example, the Canadian ritual, in the course of telling the origin of the Templars, offers the following passage as its only commentary on how the Order acquired its wealth:

'Many generous pilgrims and Crusaders supplied them [the Templars] with money and other aid, and Hugo, Count de Provence, admiring their disinterested deeds, desired to have his name enrolled as the ninth original member of the Order.'[1]

Other rituals, if they make mention of the matter at all, seem to gloss over it as quickly as the Canadian ritual does. With so little information for the Masonic Knight Templar to draw from, the brevity of the ritual opens the door for the Order's members to fill the gap with misinformation, which, as we saw in Chapter 1, is largely drawn from the many popular speculative books that are offered to the members by well-meaning brethren. The purpose of this chapter is to disassemble the main myth regarding the Templars' rise to wealth and power, while providing the reader with an accurate version of what happened.

In Chapter 1 we learnt that Sir David Brewster, the probable author of Laurie's 1804 history of Freemasonry, was of the belief that the chief and primary intention of the medieval Templars for assembling at Jerusalem in the early decades of the twelfth century was to practise and preserve the rites and mysteries of Free Masonry.[2] Although Brewster offered his reader no evidence to support the claim, many of the authors who followed him subscribed to the idea, with each subsequent writer adding his own twist or turn to the story.

While many of the Masonic writers of the eighteenth and nineteenth centuries may have been of the belief that the Templars went to the Holy Land to preserve Masonic secrets, authors writing closer to the present time have given the Templars a different reason for gathering on the Temple Mount. For these authors, it was not the secrets of Freemasonry that needed to be uncovered; rather, it was the secrets that lay buried in the ruins of Solomon's Temple. This theory, which we will see in due course came out of the mouth of the Chevalier Ramsay, seems to have been accepted by many of today's Freemasons with the same enthusiasm as the equally absurd theories presented to earlier generations of Craftsmen.

A large part of the theory revolves around the inability of these authors to accept that the Templars were formed to deal with the treacherous conditions that confronted pilgrims travelling to the Levant in the decades that followed the First Crusade. Basing their theories on William of Tyre's assertion that there were but nine Templars in their first nine years of existence, these authors argue that the Order surely couldn't have had a chance of protecting pilgrims from thousands of marauding infidels and therefore must have been up to something else. Since they weren't able to protect pilgrims, they must, therefore, have been digging up the Temple Mount looking for buried treasure; for what else could explain the meteoric rise of the Templars from relative obscurity to international fame and fortune in a few short years?

Like the speculative theories presented by the writers of the eighteenth and nineteenth centuries, the modern myth of secret Templar excavations requires an incredible amount of credulity combined with an utter lack of understanding about the history of the Order and the world in which they operated. It is this combination that has allowed publishers to churn out book after book chronicling just what the Templars found whilst digging in the rubble. Whether it was the Ark of the Covenant, the Holy Grail, or even the severed and mummified head of Jesus Christ, [3] these authors contend that it was the shovel and not the sword that kept the Templars occupied in the first decade of their existence. Regardless of the trinket the Templars are alleged to have discovered, the books all seem to follow a similar pattern and logic:

- There weren't enough Templars at the start to protect pilgrims; therefore the idea was merely a cover for their secret activities.

- The Templars had learnt that something was buried under the Temple Mount from secret traditions, secret documents or secret knowledge – any and all of which the Templars kept secret from everyone but the modern authors.

- The Templars discovered said artefact(s) after covertly digging under the Temple Mount in the ruins of Solomon's Temple.

Charles Warren, shown examining a shaft in this nineteenth century engraving, made extensive explorations of Jerusalem and its environs during the 1867 Palestine Exploration Fund's project. Many modern-day authors have claimed that Warren or his contemporaries discovered Templar artefacts under the Temple Mount.
Author's collection

- The discovery made them rich and the knowledge of the same so frightened the Catholic Church that it granted them special privileges to keep their mouths shut about the discovery.

- All of this is proven by the fact that Sir Charles Warren, Charles Wilson or Montague Parker – or sometimes all of the above – discovered Templar artefacts during their excavations of Jerusalem in the late nineteenth century.

- These artefacts are currently in the possession of a Scotsman named Robert Brydon, who received them from his grandfather, who in turn received them from Warren, Wilson or Parker. The artefacts' existence proves all the previous parts of the theory.

There is, of course, not a shred of credible evidence to support the claims made in such books, and as the theory was deconstructed in detail in my last book [4] I'll give but a brief synopsis of that deconstruction here.

Templars Leaning on a Shovel

As we saw in the previous chapter, the idea that there were but nine Templars in the first nine years of their existence was put forth by William, Archbishop of Tyre in his version of the Templar's origin story. Other accounts paint a different picture and a composite study of the primary source materials available to us reveals that it is more than probable that there were more than nine Templars at the onset. Even Malcolm Barber doubted William's claim, charging that the notion of nine knights in nine years carries a suspicious symmetry. [5]

But even if there were just nine Templars between their formation in 1120 and the Council of Troyes in 1129, to accept the idea that the Templars could laze about the Temple Mount during the day, whilst digging beneath it all night is to disregard the history of what was going on around them. As we have seen, the Templars' early privileges were granted by Baldwin II, a man who took on the additional responsibility for the administration of the Principality of Antioch following the death of its regent during the Battle of Ager Sanguinis in 1119. This monarch's resources were stretched even further in 1122 when Joscelin, the Count of Edessa was captured. In fact, Baldwin was also captured while returning from Edessa the following year, and remained imprisoned until 1124, which certainly

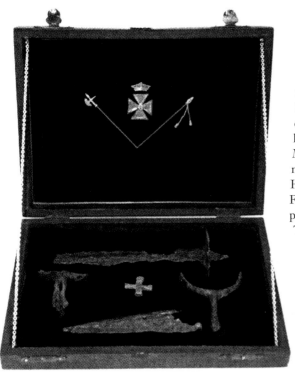

didn't help the Christian cause in the east. Given that the Christians were involved in a number of battles such as the Siege of Tyre in 1124 and the Battle of Azaz in 1125, it is a large leap in credulity to accept that the Templars could have continued to receive the support of eastern Christians had they not been willing and active participants in some of the conflicts going on around them. The idea that they could stand about the Temple Mount leaning on shovels, whilst their coreligionists were defending Christian interests, simply doesn't hold water.

Templars on and under the Mount

BUT supposing that the fledgling Templars had some spare time on their hands to do a bit of archaeological digging, where is the proof that they did so? Certainly the primary source materials have offered no evidence to support the claim. But why would they, for as the modern authors contend, the Templars' mission was secret and they did a fantastic job of keeping it hidden from everyone except the modern authors themselves, who uncovered the secret many centuries later. With no primary sources from which to support their theories, these authors rely on mythical legends and Masonic traditional histories, such as those found in the Royal Arch Degree, [6] to support their subterranean claims. To add weight to these claims and to bridge the gap between fiction and fact, these

authors will use legitimate archaeological digs to support their assertions.

The central launching point from which most of the Templar excavation theorists begin is the nineteenth century explorations conducted by a Freemason named Sir Charles Warren and his contemporary Charles Wilson. Warren is best known as having served as the head of the Metropolitan Police during the Jack the Ripper murders; however, in 1867 Warren travelled to the Holy Land on behalf of the Palestine Exploration Fund to conduct that organisation's first major project: an investigation of the site of the Jewish Temple as well as the fortification lines of the ancient City of David. Several years prior to this well-documented exploration, Captain Charles Wilson, a member of the Royal Engineers, took part in an Ordnance Survey of Jerusalem.

The purpose of the survey was to provide topographical maps that could assist in the improvement of the sanitary conditions of the city.

Depending on the book in which the theory is presented, Wilson, either during the Ordnance Survey conducted in 1864 or later 'Excavations at Jerusalem', between 1867 and 1870, discovered, according to the modern myth, a number of artefacts which consisted of the tip of a spear and the hilt of a sword as well as some spurs and a cross made of lead. These items, were, of course, Templar in origin and their discovery is used by the speculative authors to prove that the Templars must have been excavating under the Temple Mount. To add a degree of credibility to their claims, these authors point to the fact that the artefacts are currently in the possession of Robert Brydon, who inherited them from his grandfather, who had received them from the men who found them.

There are several problems with the chain of events, the least of which is the fact that the items were not discovered by either Warren or Wilson. [7] Rather, the artefacts were discovered by a man named Montague Parker, who conducted explorations between 1909 and 1911.

But unlike Wilson and Warren who conducted legitimate archaeological work on behalf of legitimate organisations, Parker's expedition was of a decidedly different purpose. Parker was motivated by a Swedish philosopher and eccentric named Valter Henrik Juvelius, who believed he had deciphered a coded passage in the Book of Ezekiel, which disclosed the location of Solomon's Treasure. [8] Juvelius was unable to find backers for his expedition, but found in Parker

A collection of crusader-era artefacts in the possession of Robert Brydon, whose grandfather received them from Montague Parker prior to World War 1. Although several authors have claimed the items to be Templar in origin, and therefore proof that the Order excavated below the Temple Mount, the owner of the collection makes no such claims himself.
Robert Brydon

not only a willing believer in the potential value of buried treasure, but a man who was capable of finding the funding necessary for the journey. Parker was the son of the Earl of Morley and, as such, travelled in circles the Swedish mystic could only have dreamed of. While Parker's expedition is a matter of historical fact, Masonic authors such as Knight and Lomas have confused the legitimate expeditions of Wilson and Warren with the illegitimate treasure-hunting mission of Parker by having the latter taking part in the work conducted by the former. [9] Given that Parker was born in 1878, a decade after Warren and Wilson conducted their researches in Jerusalem, the Templars would have needed to have discovered a time machine under the Temple Mount for him to have been a participant in the earlier expeditions.

But research error aside, what remains important to the present discussion is that Parker did eventually visit Jerusalem and did some digging in the same areas that Wilson had explored four decades earlier. Parker's expedition was a spurious undertaking from the beginning; [10] he bribed officials, had his party dress as Arabs and eventually shut operations down when the winter rains came and prevented the work from continuing. Even after returning to his operation the following summer, he was unable to unearth the treasure he had hoped for. It was only after he and his party were caught, once again dressed as Arabs, trying to dig beneath the Dome of the Rock that Parker finally gave up, having narrowly escaped with his life. [11] However, it does seem that he found a few trinkets, which he sent to Robert Brydon's grandfather.

The fact that these items exist and are in Brydon's possession has allowed speculative authors to stretch the information to great ends in supporting their own theories. A typical example of letting one fact support an entirely different conclusion taken from Keith Laidler's book, *The Head of God*, follows:

> 'I spoke with Mr. Bryden [sic] at length about the finds, and he confirmed that the remains do exist. They have been dated to the twelfth century and comprise a spearhead, spurs, a sword hilt, and most telling of all, a leaden cross pattee, the symbol of the Templars.' [12]

The problem with Laidler's commentary is that he seems to have grafted an unrelated fact onto a set of related facts in order to make a connection that simply doesn't exist. It is a fact that Brydon has confirmed that the items exist. It is also true that Brydon has confirmed that they are dated to the twelfth century. Likewise, Mr Brydon has confirmed that the items

comprise a spearhead, spurs, sword hilt and a cross. All of this is correct, but Laidler adds the fact that the cross pattée was a symbol of the Templars, which, whilst being true, seems to have been added on to imply that Brydon himself claimed the cross and therefore all of the artefacts are Templar in origin; and therein lies the problem.

In the course of researching my last book *Nobly Born*, I spoke to Mr Brydon about the artefacts in his possession. [13] During our conversation, Brydon confirmed that the pieces had belonged to his grandfather, who had received them from a man named Parker sometime before the First World War. However, he was quick to point out that, although the pieces were medieval in origin and of the type likely to have been used by the Templars, there was simply no way to positively identify them as being Templar in origin. [14] In fact, Brydon said that Parker's letter, which makes absolutely no mention of Warren or Wilson, merely implied that they were Templar in origin, quoting the words of his grandfather's letter from memory, 'These are relics of our Brethren of former days.' Brydon went on to say that the items were really just archaeological detritus, and had no real historical value, which is why they were never turned over to a museum, although Brydon stated that they were put on display in Rosslyn Chapel for about five years. Rather, Brydon's grandfather accepted the gift of his friend with the same admirable respect in which it was delivered and placed them in a tasteful presentation case, which has been part of the family's archives since that time.

Like the myth that the Templars were formed to preserve the secrets and mysteries of Freemasonry, the notion that the Order was started as a cover for a secret treasure hunting expedition is without foundation. But if the Templars didn't find some hidden treasure, how did they get so fabulously rich all of a sudden? The simple fact is that the Templars didn't become wealthy overnight. Like any good business plan, the Templars' rise to power was slow and steady and greatly assisted by the support of a few influential and powerful friends.

Friends in High Places

During the first decade of their existence, we see an interconnection between some of the key players in the Templars' story, which must seem suspicious to some. For example, Bernard, the first abbot of Clairvaux Abbey, was the nephew of Andrew de Montbard, an early, if not founding member of the Order. Bernard, in turn, would not have founded his new abbey if Hugh the Count of Champagne had not granted land to the Cistercian Order and requested that they build on it. Hugh, in turn, was a powerful count who had as one of his vassals a certain Hugues de Payens, the founder of the Templar Order. Of course the roles were to reverse in 1125 when Hugh divorced his wife, disowned his son, granted his lands and interests to his nephew Theobald and joined the Templars, thereafter to take orders from his former vassal Hugues de Payens. It was Theobald who hosted the Council of Troyes, at which the Templars received their Rule of Order, drafted in large part by Bernard of Clairvaux. While all of this may seem to some as a sort of conspiracy involving the early movers and shakers of the Templar Order, the fact of the matter is that back scratching is not a modern invention; a favour granted today, may result in a reciprocal favour a few years down the road. It wasn't as much a matter of what the Templars knew as who they knew, that got them moving on the road to wealth and power.

A prime example of this is in the situation of Fulk V, the Count of Anjou. Fulk joined the Templars in 1120 as an associate member. While it is well known that Templar knights were not permitted to marry, the Rule of Order made provisions for married men to join the Order. [15] Although Fulk did not stay a member for long, he continued to grant the Templars an annual allowance of thirty 'pounds Anjou' (as the local currency was known) long after returning to his homeland. But this would not be Fulk's only connection with the order. After the death of his wife, Fulk was persuaded to marry Melisende, the daughter of King Baldwin II. Upon Baldwin's death in 1131, Fulk became King of Jerusalem, and it is hardly surprising that he continued to patronise his former comrades, the Templars.

In fact, it is likely that Fulk had a firm hand in selecting Robert de Craon as Master of the Order after the death of Hugues de Payens in 1136.

De Craon had acted on Fulk's behalf as early as 1113 [16] and a charter from Fulk dated 22 September 1127 lists de Craon as a witness. [17] Given the fact that Fulk was King of Jerusalem when Hugues de Payens died, often filled important positions with men he knew he could trust [18] and had a previous relationship with both the Templars and de Craon, it is not too far a stretch to suppose that Fulk may have had a hand in a fellow Angevin being elected to the post of Master of the Temple. He certainly would not have been alone, as later Masters of the Order would be elected as a result of the outside influences of European kings. [19]

But western monarchs were not the only members of high society to bestow favours and privileges on the Templars. For most of their history, the Templars had the listening ear and ready hand of the popes to guide them on the path to fame and fortune. Among them was Pope Honorius II, who granted the Templars the right to wear white robes after the Council of Troyes and Pope Eugenius, who, around the time of the Second Crusade (1145-1149), granted the Order the right to affix a red cross to their garments. However, neither of these papal favours did much to assist the Order financially. It was Pope Innocent II who was the Holy Father who provided the Templars with the best gift.

On 29 March 1139, Innocent penned the bull Omne datum optimum, which granted the Templars privileges that would propel them on their path. Henceforth, the Templars answered only to the Master of the Order and he only to the Pope. Templar loyalty was to the Order and the Church alone, and members were prohibited from making any oath to anyone outside the Order and were forbidden from joining another Order or returning to secular life. [20] Of course, these aspects of the bull were not much different than what had been outlined in the Rule of Order adopted by the Templars at the Council of Troyes a decade earlier; however, Innocent's bull

Pope Innocent II (left) was the author of the papal bull Omne datum optimum, penned in 1139, which granted the Templars special privileges. Pope Eugenius III (right) authorised the Templars to affix the red cross on their white robes around the time of the second crusade (1145-1149). *Author's Collection*

legitimised the practices by giving them the papal seal of approval.

But Omne datum optimum did expand the Templars' privileges by allowing for the admission of priests into the Order. For the first time in their history, the Templars were allowed to have their own chaplains who, after a period of one year's service, could be made members of the Order by taking Templar vows and swearing loyalty to the Master. [21] In addition to making allowances for the Templars to have their own clergy, the bull granted the Order the right to construct their own oratories or private chapels where they could conduct their religious services unhindered.

But certainly the greatest gift of Omne datum optimum was the provision that excluded the Order from having to pay tithes to the Church. Prior to the bull the Order had been obligated to give the Church one tenth of all produce harvested from its lands. While the exclusion of paying tithes would prove to be of great economic benefit to the Order, it was but one half of the benefit, for the Templars were now permitted to collect tithes from the laity or the clergy provided the bishops of the area approved. [22]

Fields and Fortunes

It is in the fertile fields of the Templars' western holdings that we see the true growth of the Order in terms of its wealth. For once the Templars were given a piece of property they would begin to work the land as quickly as possible to maximise the economic benefit of the gift. Of course there was often no rhyme or reason as to where these land grants would be given, but the Templars were adept at linking their properties together in a support network and often smaller Templar holdings would be grouped around the largest preceptory in the area. The arrangement was an effective one because the larger house could provide communal support to the smaller houses and the Order's resources such as men, horses and supplies could be shared between the houses in the network.

In these networks, it made sense for the Order to cultivate the land themselves; however, where the Order had few land holdings and houses to support them, it made greater sense to let the land to a tenant and take a share of the crop. This type of arrangement, while beneficial to the sharecroppers, also benefited the Templars; for it allowed them to amass large quantities of grain from their outlying properties without expending valuable resources. However, even in areas where the Order had large quantities of land, small plots were often rented to tenants.

Temple Cressing in Essex, which had 85 tenants working small plots of land by 1185, [23] provides us with perhaps the finest surviving example of the sheer magnitude of Templar farming. Cressing is home to two surviving grain barns believed to have been built by the Order around 1206 and 1256 respectively. [24] Records from the property dating to just after the Templars' suppression in 1312 show the scale to which the property was being farmed at the time. In addition to a livestock population consisting of more than 700 animals, the property was reported to have 601 arable acres, of which 121 were growing beans, peas and drage (a course type of barley), another 73 sown with oats and 252 growing wheat. [25]

Wherever the Order was involved in the growing of grain crops it needed mills to process the harvest and Cressing was no exception; an inventory taken in 1308 shows that the Order had a windmill and a watermill on the estate. [26] While this may seem like no big deal in modern times, it is important to understand that in the twelfth century mills were few in number, due to the costs of constructing and maintaining them. As such, many mills were constructed by the Templars and Hospitallers who had the financial resources necessary to build them as well as the manpower to keep them operating. By constructing mills the military Orders were able to derive additional revenues by processing crops harvested by their tenants as well as other farmers in the area.

Of course not all land donated to the Templars was as ready to grow crops as Cressing. Often land that was too difficult for the owner to cultivate, due to a lack of manpower, was handed over to the Order, who increasingly had the means and men necessary to work the land properly. Like the Cistercian monks, the Templars became adept at cultivating marginal land and even where the land was not particularly suitable for crops they would make the best use of it that they could. One such property was Temple Bruer in Lincolnshire, which was given to the Order in the mid-twelfth century by William of Ashby. [27] Located on a barren heath, the property was best suited for grazing and by the mid-thirteenth century the Order had a flock of approximately 400 sheep grazing the property at Bruer. [28] Although the Templars were never as active in sheep rearing as their Cistercian cousins, the Order did maintain substantial flocks in Yorkshire as well as in the Iberian Peninsula. In England the Order established two water-powered fulling mills, which were used for manufacturing cloth and, like the grain mills operated by the Order near their agricultural operations, the fulling mills were certainly used to full revenue-earning potential.

In fact, as the Templars expanded they became particularly adept at involving themselves in every aspect of the process from field to fair. They grew the crops on their land, processed the crops at their mills, and transported the grain with their own wagons or those of their tenants to the trade fairs and markets where they could be converted to cash.

As we saw earlier in this chapter, many authors have put forth the idea that the Templars' wealth and power came from some relic buried beneath the Temple Mount. If the Templars uncovered anything, it was the formula for creating a well-disciplined organisation capable of managing its many branches and business interest in the East and West. In this sense the Templars were in many ways the medieval equivalent to a modern international corporation. Like any modern corporation, the Templars quickly learnt that the key to financial success wasn't just working for their money, but getting their money to work for them.

The wheat barn at Temple Cressing in Essex is one of two surviving barns originally constructed by the Templars. This barn was constructed in the mid-thirteenth century.
Mira Vogel

The Borrowers and the Bankers

ONE OF THE common myths about the Knights Templar is the notion that they invented the modern banking system as we know it. While it is certainly true that the Templars took part in a wide variety of financial activities, the simple fact is that the Templars did not operate as a bank – at least not in the modern sense of the word. For example, while the Templars

Left: **Temple Bruer in Lincolnshire from a nineteenth century engraving. Bruer was one of the properties where the Templars raised sheep.**
Author's collection

accepted deposits from their clientele, the Order did not pool those deposits and lend them out to other clients like banks do today. [29] Rather, the Templars had an absolute hands-off policy with respect to money given to their trust. As such, Templar banking, if it can be called such, was largely limited to offering safety deposit boxes to their clients. This was certainly nothing new as other monastic Orders had been engaged in similar activities for many years prior to the Templars. [30]

However, the Templars did not lock their own strong boxes as tightly as those of their clientele and, as their assets grew, the Templars began to lend money at interest, something that was forbidden by the Church. But they were not the first money lenders in Europe as many suppose; the Jews had been engaged in money lending for many years before the Templars became involved in the practice, largely due to the fact that it was one of the only occupations open to them.

While many authors have credited the Templars with great ingenuity in international finance, an objective view of history shows that they were not so much innovators as they were opportunists. Quite

The Round Church of the London Temple as it appears today. In 1185, the London Temple became home to the royal treasure and in 1204, King John placed the crown jewels in the Templars' care for safekeeping.
Stephen Dafoe

simply, they were in the right place at the right time. After the victory of the First Crusade, the establishment of the Latin States and the evolution of the Military Orders, pilgrimage to the Holy Land multiplied. And along with the increase in the number of travelling pilgrims came the increase in opportunity to make a profit from them.

One of the earliest documented loans made by the Templars took place during the early years of the Order. In 1135, a man named Petre Desde obtained a sum of 50 morabitins from the Templars to finance a journey from his home in Saragoza, Spain, to Jerusalem. According to the document drafted for the sum, Desde was not being given a loan; rather the money was being provided to him by the Templars 'out of charity'. [31] In exchange for this act of Templar kindness, Desde agreed to give the Order his home, lands and vineyards in Saragoza upon his death. While the Order could hardly be accused of taking interest on their loan, the benefit of their charitable considerations far outweighed any interest they might have charged Desde while the man was alive.

Of course not all methods of lending money involved the need for the borrower to turn over his earthly possessions to the Templars on his death. Often the loan document would carry a clause that said if the money depreciated in value between the time it was borrowed and the time it was repaid, the Order was to be compensated for the loss of assets. In 1170 a man named Raimon of Cornus and his nephew Ricart pledged a farm to Elias, Master of the Temple of St Eulalia, in exchange for a loan of 200 sous Melgueil, 100 being given to each man. If the money depreciated before it was repaid, the men were to pay the Templars a silver mark for every 48 sous 'in love' until the loan was repaid in full. [32] In addition, the document stated that while the Templars held the farm as security on the loan, the produce yielded from the property was to be kept by the Order and did not count towards the repayment of the loan.

Although the Templars did not limit themselves to lending money to pilgrims and farmers who found themselves a little short between crops, their involvement in money lending was largely an ancillary activity to their original mandate of assisting pilgrims, as the loan given to Petre Desde would seem to indicate. However, within a decade of that initial loan, the Order had begun to finance the crowned heads of Europe and their journeys to the East. But by this time they were not so much financing a pilgrimage to the Holy Land as they were financing a holy war.

In 1147, during the Second Crusade, King Louis VII left France for the Holy Land accompanied by an army that included 130 Templar knights, one of whom was Everard des Barres, the Master of the Order in France. By the time Louis and his army arrived in Antioch in the spring of 1148, the king had exhausted his financial resources getting there and needed to borrow money to continue. Although both the Templars and the Hospitallers lent the French king money, [33] the Templars' contributions to the campaign nearly brought the Order to a point of bankruptcy. [34]

The massive debt was incurred on 10 May, when des Barres travelled from Antioch to Acre to procure the funds from his brethren to allow Louis's crusade to continue. Later that year the king wrote to his regents back home instructing Abbot Sugar to provide 2,000 marks of silver and requesting Raoul of Vermandois to scrounge up 30,000 livres Parisis to repay the king's debt to the Order. This was not merely pocket change, for 30,000 livres equalled about half of the annual revenue of the French kingdom at that time. [35] When the regents had raised the funds to repay the loan, it was the Templars themselves who transported it from France to the Holy Land.

Templar Traveller's Cheques

THE ABILITY to transmit money, men and materials between locations had been well established by the time of the Second Crusade, due to the Templars' vast network of properties in the East and West, which we looked at earlier. Because the Templars had such an extensive network, a pilgrim could deposit his valuables in a Templar preceptory in France or England and withdraw the funds in the appropriate currency when he reached his destination in the Holy Land or wherever he might be travelling. If there was one area of financial activity in which the Templars were pioneers, it is in providing the lettre de change. There is, however, a great deal of misconception about just how the process worked. Many authors have suggested that the traveller was given an encoded document that could only be translated by another Templar; however, there appears to be little evidence to support the claim outside of one author quoting another until the idea becomes an accepted fact. Surviving examples of these documents disprove the claim, for they are not written in code, but rather in Latin. One example of this type of document was reprinted in 1884 in a book entitled *Documents Inédits sur le Commerce de Marseille au Moyen Age* by Louis Blancard. The lettre de change, dated 9 August 1229, indicated that Etienne de Manduel, who had travelled from the port of Marseille to Acre aboard a Templar vessel, had deposited a sum of 30 pounds of royal crowns (equal to 90 Saracen bezants) with a Templar named Bertrand de Cavaillon. The document indicated that de Manduel was to be paid the sum upon his arrival in the Holy Land. [36] The Templars would receive their profit on the transaction by either charging a fee for the service or in the rate of exchange between the two currencies.

Templar Safety Deposits

OF COURSE not all money deposited with the Templars was intended to be retrieved on foreign shores, and people often deposited coins, jewels, documents and other valuable with the Templars to be safeguarded while they were away. The owner's valuables would either be retrieved when he returned from his journey or as the owner might have need for his property from time to time. As we saw earlier, the Order had a strict rule that money deposited with the Templars belonged to the depositor and could not be touched or used except by its rightful owner. To do so would constitute theft and the Templars' Rule of Order dealt with thieves in its ranks by expulsion. No member of the Order was to have money on his person that he was not entitled to carry [37] and should any be found amongst his belongings upon his death he was to be denied a Christian burial. [38] In fact, if he had already been buried, his body was to be exhumed. It is doubtless that the Templars' strict adherence to their Rule of Order increased their reputation as men who could be trusted with money.

Sometimes this reputation for trustworthiness put them in a position to act as middle men for parties who did not trust one another. One such situation occurred in 1214 when King John of England offered to pay some French barons a pension in order to gain their support. However, the barons had little trust in the English king so John placed the money in the Templar preceptory at La Rochelle with the directive to pay the pensions out as the barons required them. [39] But regal deposits were not limited to pension funds, and larger centres of Templar activity, such as Paris and London, became home to the wealth of kingdoms. As early as 1185, the London Temple housed the royal treasure and in 1204 King John of England deposited the crown jewels there for safekeeping. [40] In France, kings from Philip II (1180-1223) to Philip IV (1285-1314) used the Paris Temple to storehouse their treasures. Even when Philip IV created his own treasury at the Louvre in 1295, he still made use of the services of the Paris Temple. [41] In fact,

Taxes and Tithes

As such, the Order was often called upon to collect taxes, tithes and debts on behalf of secular rulers, and William Marshal, the Earl of Pembroke, and King Henry II both used a Templar as their almoner. These almoners didn't just dispense regal charity to the poor. During the time of King John of England, his almoner, Roger the Templar, was in charge of collecting freight duties from the king's shipping interests. [43]

When crusader taxes were introduced in England in 1166 and again in 1188, both the Templars and the Hospitallers were utilised to collect the taxes. The best known of these, the Saladin Tithe, was levied to help finance the Third Crusade, which was launched in 1188 as a response to the fall of Jerusalem the previous year. The taxation required that every person was to give one tenth of his rents and movable goods for the purpose of retaking Jerusalem; however, knights and members of the clergy, who had taken the cross, were exempted from the taxation as they were already supporting the cause. [44] Under Pope Innocent III, the Templars derived an additional benefit from collected taxes. In 1202, he ordered that two per cent of the revenues from certain abbeys and religious orders should be sent to the Paris Temple for use in the Holy Land. Six years later he decreed that the alms of the Cistercians plus 2.5 per cent of the revenues deposited by the Bishop of Paris should be applied to the purpose and be used by the Patriarch of Jerusalem and the Masters of both the Temple and the Hospital.

just less than a decade before Philip IV organised his own treasury, the Templars were providing the French king with a package of financial services that were chronicled in a massive document that ran to 290 articles. [42] Whatever was deposited with the Order, the client had the assurance that the Templars would keep their hands off it until it was time to turn it over to the owner.

As we have seen throughout this chapter, the Templars' wealth and power did not come from uncovering some Holy relic buried beneath the Temple Mount, but from the fruits of their labours, which allowed them to convert donations and privileges into incredible wealth. As their economic activities increased, bringing them great wealth, trust and power, accusations of greed were launched against the Order. An English satirist, writing in the middle of the thirteenth century, while acknowledging the Templars for their resolute courage, none the less charged the Order with being too fond of pennies and looking after their own self-serving interests. [45] But the satirist's scathing remarks about the Order were minor charges compared to the horrendous accusations that would lead to the Templars' demise in the years that followed the loss of the Holy Land in 1291.

References for Chapter 3

1. First Historical Sketch, found in the Novice portion of the Order of the Temple as authorised by the Sovereign Great Priory of Canada. 1996.

2. *The History of Free Masonry and the Grand Lodge of Scotland with Chapters on The Knights Templar, Knights of St John, Mark Masonry and R. A. Degree to which is added an Appendix of Valuable Papers*, William Alexander Laurie. Edinburgh. Seton & Mackenzie. 1859. pp.29.

3. This ridiculous theory was presented in Keith Laidler's 1998 book *The Head of God*.

4. See *Nobly Born: An Illustrated History of the Knights Templar*, Chapter 5, Templars on the Mount, for a comprehensive look at the myth of Templar excavations on the Temple Mount.

5. *The New Knighthood*, Malcolm Barber. Cambridge. Cambridge University Press. 1996. p.9.

6. The traditional history of the Royal Arch Degree tells the biblical story of the building of the second Temple under Zerubbabel. In the process of clearing the ruins of Solomon's Temple, three workmen discover an opening to a subterranean area, where they make an important discovery.

7. In an e-mail correspondence of 17 January 2007, Felicity Cobbing, an executive of the Palestine Exploration Fund (PEF) stated: 'I do not recall any of the objects you describe being connected to either Charles Wilson's survey for the Ordnance Survey in 1864 (not the PEF – we were founded in 1865), or with Charles Warren's PEF explorations beneath the Temple mount 1867-1870.'

8. *In Search of Solomon's Treasure*, Silberman, Neil Asher. Biblical Archaeology Society, Vol. VI No. 4 (July/August 1980), pp.30-41.

9. In their book *The Second Messiah* authors Christopher Knight and Robert Lomas make the claim that: 'In 1894, almost eight hundred years after the Templars had begun digging under the ruined Temple of Jerusalem, its secret depths were probed again, this time by a British army contingent led by Lieutenant Charles Wilson of the Royal Engineers. They found nothing of the treasures concealed by the Jerusalem Church, but in the tunnels cut centuries earlier they found part of a Templar sword, a spur, the remains of a lance and a small Templar cross. All of these artefacts are now in the keeping of Robert Brydon, the Templar archivist for Scotland, whose grandfather was a friend of a certain Captain Parker who took part in this and other later expeditions to excavate beneath the site of Herod's Temple. In a letter to Robert Brydon's grandfather, written in 1912, Parker tells of finding a secret chamber beneath Temple Mount with a passage that emerged out in the Mosque of Omer [Dome of the Rock]. On breaking through into the mosque, the British army officer had to run for his life from irate priests and worshippers.' This statement contains numerous factual errors and is heavily romanticised, even where accurate. For a full rebuttal of such claims, see *Nobly Born: An Illustrated History of the Knights Templar*, Chapter 5.

10. *1909 Quarterly Statement of the Palestine Exploration Fund* p.3. The spurious nature of Parker's expedition was chronicled in the report as follows: 'Sensational reports have, from time to time, during the last few months, appeared in the London and provincial press relating to works of excavation which have been conducted by an English party of amateurs on Ophel. The operations have been carried on, with much secrecy, in and about the aqueduct discovered by Sir Charles Warren; and their object is locally supposed to be to find the Royal Treasures of David. It is believed that no result of value has been attained; but the work is in no way connected with the Palestine Exploration Fund, nor, so far as we can ascertain, does there appear to be with the party any trained archaeologist. By the last reports the work is suspended.' Parker had been forced to stop his dig due to the fact that the winter rain made it difficult to continue, but returned to his excavations in the summer of 1910.

11. Silberman. Op. cit.

12. *The Head of God*: Keith Laidler. p.178.

13. I telephoned Robert Brydon on 2 February 2007 after having made contact with him via Dr Karen Ralls, author of *The Templars and the Grail*. Mr Brydon, upon learning that I was writing a book about the Templars and interested in his artefacts, was reluctant to speak to me on the basis that he had dealt with several authors in the past, whom he asserted didn't listen to what he had told them.

14. Brydon's exact words were 'You couldn't say they were Templar at all.'

15. Fratres conjugate, or married brothers, were provided for in the original Latin Rule of the Order, which outlined the conditions on which they could be admitted. They were not permitted to wear the white habit of the knights and if the Fratre conjugati should die before his wife, a portion of his estate should be given to the Templars with the rest going to the widow for her future support.

16. Barber. Op. cit. p.36.

17. Op. cit. p.8.

18. Ibid. p.36.

19. Among them was Robert de Sablé, who was not even a member of the Templars when he travelled to the Holy Land with King Richard I during the Third Crusade in 1191. Yet de Sablé was elected Master of the Order in the same year. Additionally Reginald de Vichiers probably received the position in 1250 after assisting in providing ransom money for the release of King Louis IX.

20. *The Knights Templar: A New History*, Helen Nicholson, p.154.

21. Ibid. p.154.

22. Ibid. p.154.

23. *The Knights Templar in Britain*, Evelyn Lord, p.62. These tenants paid the Templars between 10 and 15s per virgate, which was approximately 12 hectares of land. Additionally the tenant would render other services to the Templars when required, such as ploughing, mowing and harvesting.

24. *Cressing Temple – The Documented History of Cressing Temple*. www.cressingtemple.org.uk/History/CThist.htm (accessed 16 February 2007).

25. Lord. Op. cit. pp.65-66.

26. Lord. Op. cit. p.65.

27. Lord. Op. cit. p.94.

28. Ibid. p.96.

29. Nicholson. Op. cit. p.162.

30. Barber. Op. cit. p.266.

31. Ibid. pp.78-79.

32. The Military Orders and economic growth, Cardiff University, School of History and Archaeology, http://www.cf.ac.uk/hisar/people/hn/MilitaryOrders/MILORDOCS9.htm

Translated by Helen Nicholson. The phrase 'in love' seems to have been placed to point out that the silver mark was being paid to cover the Templars' losses and not as a financial gain on the loan.

33. Nicholson. Op. cit. p.163.

34. Barber. Op. cit. p.67.

35. Ibid. p.68.

36. *Documents Inédits sur le Commerce de Marseille au Moyen-Age*, Louis Blancard,

Translation from the Latin by Dr Christian Tourenne.

37. *The Templar Rule*, Upton-Ward, pp.92 § 329.

38. Ibid. p.147 § 566.

39. *The Templars: Knights of God*, Edward Burman, p.82.

40. Ibid. p.81.

41. Nicholson. Op. cit. p.164.

42. Burman. Op. cit. pp.88-89.

43. Nicholson. Op. cit. p.161.

44. *Select Chartres of English Constitutional History*: William Stubbs (ed), p.189.

www.fordham.edu/halsall/source/1188Saldtith.html

45. Ibid. p.181. Nicholson quotes from a mid-thirteenth century work entitled *Sur les états du monde* (On the classes of society). The work criticises the different aspects of medieval society from the clergy to the Military Orders.

4 The Destruction of the Knights Templar

'A bitter thing, a lamentable thing, a thing, which is horrible to contemplate, terrible to hear of, a detestable crime, an execrable evil, an abominable work, a detestable disgrace, a thing almost inhuman, indeed set apart from all humanity…' [1]

Opening of Philip IV's order to arrest the Templars

Right: **Philip IV of France, known as le Bel, was the man who ordered the arrest of the Knights Templar in 1307.**
Author's collection

Left: **The Templars, who had for two centuries protected pilgrims in and around Jerusalem, would fall victim to the destructive power of the French Crown.**
Illustration by Bob Prodor

THE STORY of the destruction of the Knights Templar told in Masonic Templar rituals and Masonic histories, while on one hand sticking to a script common in the eighteenth and nineteenth centuries, on the other provides the reader with a couple of erroneous facts, which have come to be accepted as the official story. But before we can separate romantic fiction from historical fact, we should first be familiar with a few examples of the Masonic version of the story. In the Second Historical Sketch used by the Sovereign Great Priory of Canada during the Installation portion of the Order of the Temple, [2] the Masonic Templar is told:

'For two centuries after its formation in Palestine, the Templar Order flourished greatly, and was of essential service in the defence of the Christian Faith. Yet, strange to say, its overthrow was to be effected by men professing the same faith, but actuated by the base desire of possessing themselves of the treasures of the Order.

'To this end Philip the Fair, King of France, and Pope Clement V, in the year 1307, entered into an unholy league, binding themselves to destroy the illustrious Order.' [3]

Likewise, the history of the Templars presented in Thomas Smith Webb's monitor lays the blame for the demise of the Order in the united hands of the King of France and Clement V. Drawing from the works of the French historian the Abbé de Vertot (1655-1735) Webb tells his reader:

'This was the darling object the monarch had in view: this being accomplished, he immediately sent for the Archbishop of Bordeaux, whose ambition he knew had no bounds, and who would hesitate at nothing to gratify it; and communicated to him the power he had

Pope Clement V became pope in 1305 and ruled from France, finally settling in Avignon in 1309. Clement has been much maligned over the years for having plotted alongside Philip in the Templars' destruction. However, his participation came well after Philip had the Templars arrested.

Jupiter Images

received of nominating a person to the papal chair, and promising he should be the person, on his engaging to perform six conditions. The Archbishop greedily snatched at the bait, and immediately took an oath on the sacrament to the faithful performance of the conditions. Philip then laid upon him five of the conditions, but reserved the sixth until after the Archbishop's coronation as Pope; which soon took place in consequence of the recommendation of the king to the conclave.' [4]

The sixth condition, according to Vertot, Webb and myriad others who have told the story, was the destruction of the Templars. Although this information has gained wide acceptance over the years, the story of the demise of the Templars paints a different picture. While it is true that it was the pope's hand that ultimately sealed the Templars' fate, the notion that he was involved from the start is inaccurate. To understand the story, we should know a bit about the key players in the play.

The King of France

PHILIP IV took the throne in 1285, the eleventh in a continuous line of male heirs who proudly traced their lineage back to Hugh Capet, the founder of the Capetian Dynasty who took the throne in AD987. More than any of his ancestors, Philip regarded his throne as having been given to him in trust by God and, as such, felt it his duty to govern by the strictest of Christian principles. [5] Of course a considerable amount of his opinion must have been formed by the fact that his crusading grandfather, Louis IX, was proclaimed a saint during Philip's reign.

Philip was known as le Bel, or the fair, but the appellation was not due to his accommodating personality, but rather his handsome appearance. In fact a summary of his actions as king indicate that he

was often anything but fair. In a quest for money, to support the growing costs of military operations, and to relieve the massive debts accumulated by his father's war with Aragon, Philip fiddled with the currency, persecuted the Jews and Lombards and even levied a tax on the clergy in his lands. This last action prompted Pope Boniface VIII to issue the bull Clericis laicos in 1296, which prohibited secular rulers from taxing the Church without the pope's approval. Philip responded by forbidding the clergy on his lands from sending any money to Rome. The pope was not amused and began the process of excommunicating the French king in 1303. However, William de Nogaret, one of Philip's ministers, and Sciarra Colonna, one of the pope's Italian enemies, descended on the pontiff and had him arrested. Although he was freed from prison, he died soon after the humiliating ordeal. Oddly enough, Philip had turned on the very man who had canonised his grandfather. As such, it should come as no surprise that he would turn on the men who had helped free his grandfather when he was in an Egyptian prison. [6]

The Pope

BERTRAND DE GOT, who would take the papal name Clement V, was born in 1264 at Villandraut in Gascony and served as the Bishop of Bordeaux prior to his coronation a position that made him a subject of the King of England rather than the King of France. [7] Although Bertrand and Philip had been childhood friends, [8] Bertrand remained a strong supporter of Philip's enemy Boniface VIII. While many Masonic histories make the claim that Clement V succeeded Boniface VIII on the throne of St Peter, the fact remains that Benedict XI was elected to replace Boniface. On the death of Benedict, who had reigned for just eight months, Bertrand was elected by the College of Cardinals with a two-thirds majority vote. His election was a long drawn out affair, which took eleven months to resolve due to politics and controversies which still hung over from Boniface's reign. But Bertrand was not related to the Colonna or Orsini families who had caused Boniface problems, his status as Bishop of Bordeaux made him acceptable to the anti-French factions and the fact that he was a Frenchman by birth made him acceptable to the King of France. [9]

Although Bertrand was invited to Rome for his coronation, he ordered that the ceremony be held in Lyon instead. In fact Clement served his entire reign in France, ultimately choosing Avignon as his base of operation in 1309, a base that would be used by his successors until 1378. While this resistance to reigning in Rome has been used as evidence of Clement's subservience to the King of France, it was rather the case that the political situation in Rome was such that the new pope, like Pope Urban II, who had launched the First Crusade, did not feel safe in Italy.

The United Military Orders

JACQUES DE MOLAY, the last Grand Master of the Templars, left Cyprus for France in the autumn of 1306, the year after Clement became pope, and never returned to the island again. He, along with the Master of the Hospital, Fulk de Villaret, had been summoned to France by Clement in order to offer the pontiff their views on the prospects of a new crusade and the unification of the two Orders. Many accounts of the Templars' demise, including those written by Freemasons, have claimed that de Molay was summoned to France in order to lead him into Philip's trap. However, the facts show that this was not the case.

The idea to unite the Military Orders was certainly nothing new; the idea had been presented at the Council of Lyon in 1274. However, there were other Westerners such as Ramon Lull who wrote several treatises on recapturing the Holy Land. In 1292, a year after the fall of Acre, Lull suggested that the Orders should be united under a Bellator Rex or War King, who would serve as the leader of the united organisation. Thirteen years later, Philip IV offered to renounce his kingdom in exchange for being given the leadership role in a new Order to be called the Order of the Knighthood of Jerusalem. Successive leaders of this Order would be the sons of kings or royal appointees, should the king die without a male heir. [10] However, these plans by men who had never travelled east must have seemed impractical if not outright foolish to de Molay.

De Molay made a report to Pope Clement in May of 1307 and although the Grand Master presented the pros and cons of the concept, he was largely opposed to the idea. De Molay cited the fact that the two Orders had existed separately for many years and men who joined the Templars or Hospitallers conscientiously chose to join one over the other. Additionally, there had been a long rivalry between the Orders, which de Molay argued had been beneficial since one Order tried to outdo the other in its defence of Christendom. But perhaps most importantly, the unification of the Hospitallers and

Jacques de Molay
Master of the Temple
1293 - 1314

the Templars would see the creation of a new Rule for the new organisation. The Templars' Rule was stricter than that of the Hospitallers and de Molay did not want to see his Order softened by the introduction of Hospitaller ideas. By contrast, Villaret offered no ideas on the unification of the two Orders, largely due to the fact that his Order was just beginning its conquest of Rhodes. As such, he hoped that with the pope's assistance he could resist the French king's rising ambitions.

Jacques de Molay, the last Master of the Knights Templar, was born in AD1244 and joined the Order in France in 1265. He was elected to his post in 1293.
Author's collection

Domme in France was one of the locations in which the French Templars were imprisoned after 1307.
IStockPhoto.com Rafael Laguillo

Rumours of Heresy

BUT THE talk of a united Order was not the only rumour about the Templars being circulated; others of a far more sinister nature were being spoken behind closed doors. These rumours were circulated by a man who had been a member of the Order – a renegade Templar named Esquin de Floryan, who was spending a little time in prison. His accusations against the Order, which he eventually brought to Philip's attention in the hopes of lessening his sentence, contained four items. Esquin told the French king that when the Templars were received, they were instructed to deny Christ and spit on His Holy Cross. During their reception they were made to kiss the receptor on the buttocks, navel and mouth and because the Templar Rule prohibited them from having sex with women, the new brethren were told that it was permissible to engage in sexual activity with each other. But perhaps most horrifying of all, the Templars did not worship God, but rather an idol. [11] After hearing the renegade Templar's account, Philip informed the pope of what he had learnt and turned

the matter over to his right hand man, William de Nogaret, who began an investigation of the Templars by interviewing a number of brethren who had been expelled from the Order. Additionally, a survey was conducted to learn just what properties the Templars owned. However, to keep under the Templars' radar, the assessment was broadened to include all religious Orders who held land in the kingdom.

On 24 August 1307, Clement wrote to Philip informing him that he was planning to launch an investigation into the recent accusations levelled against the Templars, but that the investigation would not begin until October. [12] However, Philip had no intention of waiting that long; his mind was already made up on the matter and there was a possibility that de Molay could set sail for Cyprus, where the Order had sought refuge after the fall of Acre, at any time. On September 14 the king issued a letter to his bailiffs throughout the kingdom outlining the Templars' crimes and ordering their arrest at a later date, which was to be kept secret until the time had arrived.

The Arrest of the Templars

PHILIP's men acted upon the orders on 13 October 1307, and in a series of simultaneous raids on Templar properties throughout France, virtually every Templar in the country was taken into custody. The king's men would certainly have been well acquainted with the technique for they had previously acted upon similar orders when Philip had earlier had the Jews and Lombards rounded up. [13] Although the dawn raids were a huge success in capturing the Templars, there were those who managed to escape. The official sources record twelve Templars evading the bailiffs' irons, although there may have been as many as four dozen. Among those who fled was Gérard de Villiers, the former Master of France, who along with a number of brethren and Imbert Blanke, the Master of Auvergne, crossed over into England. [14] There were other brethren of lower rank who managed to escape, but ultimately most found themselves imprisoned with their brethren; even Blanke was later captured and went on to play a role in defending the English Templars during the trials held in that country.

Modern authors have claimed that the Templars learnt of Philip's arrest orders soon after they were issued and escaped in large numbers to re-establish the Order elsewhere (see Chapter 8). However, scholars such as Barber, Nicholson and Demurger are of the belief that the Order had little or no advance notice of the planned arrests, although Demurger provides evidence that de Molay was at least aware of the allegations and rumours circulating about the Order. [15]

The Interrogation of the Templars

WITH the Templars in prison, Philip wrote to the other Western rulers explaining the reasons why he had imprisoned the Order, urging that they take similar action against the Templars in their lands, a request that was denied. While Philip was undoubtedly surprised by their reaction, Clement was appalled – not by the failure of other Christian rulers to comply, but rather by Philip's failure to seek his permission before arresting the Templars. But there was little the pontiff could do: the Templars were already being interrogated and Philip was not about to let them loose.

Within a week of their arrests, Philip put the Templars through a series of interrogations to extract confessions that confirmed the accusations levelled against the Order. On 19 October, the 138 Templars arrested in Paris began to make their depositions.

To ensure that only the right information was received from the Templars, the jailers were instructed to keep the brethren in isolation, to inform them that both the king and pope were aware of the scandalous nature of their reception ritual and that they would be pardoned if they confessed to the accusations against them. By contrast, a refusal to do so would result in death. To help persuade the Templars in complying, the jailers were instructed to use threats and torture before the brethren were sent to meet with the inquisitors. The tactic worked and the king got the confessions he desired. Of the 138 extant depositions from the Paris inquisitions of October and November 1307, only four Templars were able to resist the tortures inflicted upon them. Even Jacques de Molay, the Master of the Order, confessed in the fear of the tortures that awaited him if he refused.

On the strength of the confessions Pope Clement issued the bull Pastoralis praeminentiae on 27 November 1307, which ordered the arrest of the Templars throughout Christendom. However, compliance with the pope's directive had different results in different places.

Torture was used on members of the Order in Naples. However, given the fact that Charles II was a relative of Philip IV, his methods are hardly surprising. However, this seems to be the harshest treatment the Templars received in other parts of Christendom. In England, the Templars were reluctantly rounded up and even after Clement ordered that they be tortured, none were willing to comply. [17] On Cyprus, King Amaury was also reluctant to arrest the Templars because they had supported him in his coup against his brother, and even when he did, the Templars were confined to their own estates. In Venice the investigations into the Order were conducted by the state, while the Templars remained free. In Germany the Templars arrived at the council in Mainz armed and accompanied by the local barons who swore to their innocence and as a result were set free. In Aragon the Templars proclaimed their innocence while entrenched in their castles and although James II besieged the castles and arrested the Order, they were freed in 1312 and granted pensions.

Back in France, Clement demanded that the matter be turned over to the Church's authority and he suspended the trial in February of 1308. But Philip continued to garner public support against the Order and lobbied the pope to resume the trials. Clement finally capitulated in July, but insisted that the trials continue under the direction of the clergy.

In August of that year, Clement issued the bull Regnans in coelis, which called for a general council to be held on 1 October 1310 at Vienne in order to deal with the matter of the Templars and to that end the Order was instructed to send suitable defensores to the council. When the second series of investigations began in 1309, the Templars were unwilling to defend themselves, largely out of fear of further torture. Although de Molay initially volunteered to defend the Templars provided he had legal assistance, he later withdrew the offer stating that he would give his deposition to none but the pope.

The papal commission seems to have been sincerely interested in getting to the truth and was a stark contrast from the methods used by Philip's interrogators. A call was sent out requesting that those wishing to defend the Order should assemble at Paris and by February of 1310 some 600 Templars had expressed a desire to comply. [18] However, since the majority of them had previously confessed during the initial inquiry, Philip's camp came to the forefront arguing that the Templars had confessed at one trial, yet contradicted themselves at the other. By withdrawing their confessions, the French king argued that the Templars had become lapsed heretics and the only suitable punishment was death. On 12 May, fifty-four Templars were handed over to Philip's men and burnt at the stake in Paris. Similar executions took place elsewhere in France until finally those who remained alive did so by remaining silent.

The Council of Vienne

The general council that was to commence on 1 October 1310 didn't actually start until 16 October 1311. However, the reason for the delay was not papal procrastination, but rather the fact that the papal commissioners working in Paris were having a hard time getting confessions that matched. One witness would contradict another witness and sometimes even managed to contradict themselves, but despite the dubious depositions, the papal commission ultimately determined that the Templars were orthodox. Those who had acknowledged the unworthy aspects of the reception ritual were absolved of their sins and restored their privileges in the Church. [19] However, the determination of the commission was that the Order itself needed to be reformed and its Rule brought in line with orthodoxy. The commissioners believed that the Rule, which they had copies of, was fine, but that unwritten and unorthodox practices had

been attached to it. It was these observations that were to form the basis of the Council of Vienne.

Although the men who had gathered at the council were doubtful of the Order's guilt and seemed genuinely interested in hearing what its members had to say, Philip had no intention of allowing the Templars to speak and continued to apply pressure on the pope. On 20 March, the king assembled at Vienne with a sizeable army and two days later Clement held a meeting with a number of cardinals and his special commissioners, who voted by a four-fifths majority to dissolve the Order. The result of the meeting was the bull Vox in excelso, which was read publicly on 3 April. It was clear that Clement knew that the contents of the bull would be met with resistance and that those present would want to debate the matter; however, with Philip's army nearby and Philip himself sitting beside him in the council, Clement was not prepared to take any chances. Before the bull was read, a clerk rose and stated that anyone who spoke without permission would be excommunicated.

In the end it was the Templars' defamed reputation and not their alleged guilt that dissolved the Order. After fighting for Christendom for nearly two centuries the Templars were destroyed not by their enemy's sword, but by their benefactor's quill:

'Therefore, with a sad heart, not by definitive sentence, but by apostolic provision or ordinance, we suppress, with the approval of the sacred council, the order of Templars, and its rule, habit and name, by an inviolable and perpetual decree, and we entirely forbid that anyone from now on enter the order, or receive or wear its habit, or presume to behave as a Templar.' [20]

In the end, Philip had succeeded in destroying the Templars, but failed to acquire any of its properties, if that had ever been his true intention. If it were, Clement must surely have had the last laugh, for on 2 May 1312, the pope issued a second bull, Ad providam, which turned the Templars' property over to the rival Order of the Hospitallers:

'In order that we may grant them [the Hospitallers] increased support, we bestow on them, with the approval of the sacred council, the house itself of the Knights Templar and the other houses, churches, chapels, oratories, cities, castles, towns, lands, granges, places, possessions, jurisdictions, revenues, rights, all the other property, whether immovable, movable or self-moving, and all the members together with their rights and belongings, both beyond and on this side of the sea, in each and every part of the world, at the time when the master himself and some brothers of the order were arrested as a body in the kingdom of France, namely in October 1307.' [21]

Thus far we have seen that although Pope Clement V played a large part in the demise of the Templars, he was not, as some Masonic versions of the story claim, plotting alongside Philip from the beginning. However, this erroneous information pales in comparison to the notions of Masonic writers and ritualists who created the idea that the Templars who escaped or survived the persecutions outlined in this chapter fled to live secret lives as Freemasons.

In order to understand the falsity of such notions, we should understand something of what became of the Templars after 1312. Their Order was now dissolved, their possessions and properties had been turned over to the Hospitallers and the former members of the Order were certainly not getting any younger. In fact, at the time the Order was arrested in France, the average age of the members captured was 42 years of age; [22] however, by 1312, the average age was nearly 50. Given that life expectancy in the fourteenth century was far shorter than it is today, is it likely that these men, who had few good years left and who, for the most part, had been pacific in their station within the Order fled to some foreign land to start anew under the guise of stone masons as many Masonic theories linking the Templars and Freemasons suggest?

In the bull Considerantes dudum, issued on 6 May 1312, Clement made special provisions for those members of the Order who had been found innocent or had confessed and been reconciled with the Church. They were still regarded as being tied to their monastic vows and were forbidden from returning to secular life; however, they were permitted to live in the Order's former properties, now in possession of the Hospitallers and were to receive a pension derived from the assets transferred to their long-time rivals. [23] This was certainly known to have occurred in France, England and Aragon. In some cases the Templars of Aragon joined the Order of Montesa, as they did in Portugal with the Order of Christ, two Orders that were granted former Templar lands. These new Orders, although sanctioned by the Church, were under the control of secular rulers. But despite the fact that many former members lived out the remaining days of their lives in quietude, the popular contention is that these men laid the foundation stones of the Masonic order as we know it today.

Starting with a common theme that large numbers of Templars had escaped the arrests of 1307, post-dissolution theorists have put forth a variety of final destinations for the Order, ranging from America on one side of the Atlantic to Scotland on the other. In almost all theories the Templars managed to escape by sea on eighteen galleys that were waiting for them in the harbour of La Rochelle.

The source of this theory lies in the testimony of a serving brother named Jean de Châlons, who testified in 1308 that Gérard de Villiers had managed to receive advance warning of the arrests and escaped with fifty horses. De Châlons went on to state that he had heard that de Villiers had set sail with eighteen galleys. [24] What is often overlooked is the fact that de Châlons' testimony regarding the Templar galleys was not based on first hand knowledge; rather it was a recitation of a rumour and, given that the rest of his testimony was damning of the Order, it is doubtful that there was any truth to his claims. In fact after the dissolution of the Templars in 1312, the Hospitallers became more involved in naval warfare; however, at that time they are recorded as having only four galleys. [25] It therefore becomes less likely that these galleys existed among the Templars in the numbers suggested by either de Châlons or the modern authors who have used his testimony as the basis for entire books.

Sadly, it has been the Freemasons themselves who have been responsible directly or indirectly for much of the Templar mythos as it exists today. [26] As we learnt in Chapter 1, eighteenth century Freemasons including Dr James Anderson and Andrew Michael Ramsay were the first to put forth the notion that Freemasonry pre-dated the crusades and that those who took part in the holy war were themselves Freemasons. Although Ramsay did not tie a Masonic apron directly around the Templars' waists, he did connect the Freemasons with their rivals, the Hospitallers, and it was for this reason, Ramsay postulated, that Masonic lodges were dedicated to St John. However, it was the German Freemasons who picked up where Anderson and Ramsay left off, adding the Templar angle via the Rite of Strict Observance. This rite started in the late 1740s and was strengthened by the efforts of Karl Gotthelf, the Baron von Hund. It was the belief of the members of this order that the Templars had acquired magical powers and secret wisdom when they occupied the former location of the Temple of Solomon during the time of the crusades. This esoteric torch was

The port of La Rochelle in France, where many authors claim the Templars sailed off into the sunset aboard eighteen Templar galleys, effectively escaping Philip's persecutions in 1307. *IStockPhoto.com Jacques Croizer*

passed by Jacques de Molay, the last Master of the original Order, to his successor prior to de Molay's execution on 18 March 1314. [27]

But just who de Molay's alleged successor was depends upon the path of Templar Masonry that one wishes to follow. The French claimed that he passed the reins to John Mark Larmenius, who continued on in secret. [28] There was also the claim that the Templar torch was passed to Pierre d'Aumont, who had fled to Scotland, where the exiled Templars established Freemasonry. Scandinavian Masons drew their Templar lineage through the Order of Christ in Portugal, which was a real Order; however, the Scandinavian Freemasons added to the lineage by making the claim that de Molay's nephew had carried his ashes to Stockholm, buried them there, and latterly established the Swedish Templar Order. There was also the perennial favourite that after escaping the horrors of France the Templars fled to Scotland, where they assisted Robert the Bruce in the Battle of Bannockburn; an act of support, which resulted in the Bruce establishing the Order of Heredom on their behalf as a repayment. [29]

Of course, none of the accounts had a kernel of truth in them, but as the Masonic author Burton E. Bennett wrote in a 1926 article on the Rite of Strict Observance published in *The Builder*:

'These fabrications were made for the purpose of establishing an Order not only that nobles of all countries could join, but that all who joined would believe they became ennobled. Designing men took advantage of it to obtain both money and power through 'lost secrets', occultism and magic. It was an age that believed not only with personal contact with God, but also with the devil; and the supposed secrets of the Ancient Masons furnished the seed for all this tremendous growth.' [30]

But Bennett was not the first to condemn these theories. Albert Mackey in his *History of Freemasonry* wrote disparagingly of the theory adopted by von Hund's Strict Observance:

'Of this rubbish is the legend of Peter d'Aumont and his resuscitation of the Order of Knights Templar in Scotland. Without a particle of historical evidence for its support, it has nevertheless exerted a powerful influence on the Masonic organisation of even the present day. We find its effects looming out in the most important rites and giving a Templar form to many of the high degrees. And it cannot be doubted that the incorporation of Templarism into the modern Masonic system is mainly to be attributed to ideas suggested by this d'Aumont Legend.' [31]

But these theories about Scotland eventually took root in Scotland and were contained in the pages of the Chevalier James Burnes' 1837 book *The Knights Templars of Scotland*, which created a direct lineal descent between the Templars and the Freemasons that has been accepted as historical fact by Masons and non-Masons alike. In his book, *The Rosslyn Hoax*, Robert Cooper explained that Burnes invented the myth 'for his fellow Freemasons who were interested in creating a Masonic Order which mirrored their own attitudes and their own 19th century chivalric ideals'. [32] Burnes, in crafting his history of the Templars in Scotland, made use of the d'Aumont connection, stating that he along with other refugee Templars 'continued to carry on the mysteries of the Order'. [33]

Before digging into the real origins of Masonic Templarism, it would be wise to take a brief interlude to examine the original Templar ceremony of reception to see if it contains any of the mysteries of the Order alluded to by Masonic writers of the nineteenth century.

References for Chapter 4

1. *The Trial of the Templars*, Malcolm Barber, p.45.

2. The Order of the Temple consists of three portions in Canada: Novice, Installation and Consecration. Although all three portions can be conferred in one evening, it is more common to confer each on separate occasions or to conduct the Novice and Installation segments on one occasion and the Consecration ceremony at another time.

3. The Second Historical Sketch, taken from the Installation portion of the Order of the Temple as conferred under the authority of the Sovereign Great Priory of Canada. 1996.

4. *Observations on the Orders of Knights Templar, and Knights of Malta*, Thomas Smith Webb, 1818. pp.227-228.

5. Barber. Op. cit. p.27.

6. Louis IX was captured during the Battle of Mansurah in 1250 and his ransom was paid in part by the Templars.

7. *A History of the Popes*, Charles A. Coulombe, p.287.

8. Ibid. p.287.

9. *The Knights Templar: A New History*, Helen Nicholson, p.201.

10. Barber. Op. cit. p.285.

11. Nicholson. Op. cit. p.215.

12. *The Last Templar*. Demurger, Alain. London, Profile Books. Op. cit. p.173.

13. Barber. Op. cit. p.46.

14. Ibid. p.46. Demurger. Op. cit. p.175. Barber references an additional twelve above the twelve mentioned in the official sources, while Demurger indicates that 40 Templars accompanied Gérard de Villiers, the former Master of France.

15. Demurger. Op. cit. pp.155-156.

16. Barber. Op. cit. pp.54-55.

17. Nicholson. Op. cit. p.226.

18. Demurger. Op. cit. p.177.

19. Ibid. p.178.

20. Vox in excelso, *A History and Mythos of the Knights Templar*. www.templarhistory.com/exels o.html

21. Ad providam, *A History and Mythos of the Knights Templar*.

www.templarhistory.com/provi dem.html

The bull goes on to state that properties outside of France in the Kingdoms of Castile, Aragon, Portugal and Majorca were exempted from the bull's decision.

22. Barber. Op. cit. p.54.

23. Considerantes dudum, *A History and Mythos of the Knights Templar*. www.templarhistory.com/consi der.html

24. Barber. Op. cit. p.101. *Supremely Abominable Crimes*, Edward Burman, p.225.

25. Nicholson. Op. cit. p.192.

26. Barber. Op. cit. p.317. Nicholson, *The Knights Templar: A New History*, p.240. Read, Piers Paul, *The Templars* p.303.

27. *The New Knighthood*, Malcolm Barber, p.318.

28. This claim would also be used by Bernard-Raymond Fabre-Palaprat when he launched his neo-Templar Order in 1804.

29. 'The Rite of Strict Observance', *The Builder*, Bennett, Burton E., October 1926.

30. Ibid.

31. *The History of Freemasonry*, Mackey, Albert G., p.262.

32. *The Rosslyn Hoax*, Cooper, Robert L. D., pp.245.

33. Ibid. p.300.

Templar Initiation – Then and Now

'Above all things, whosoever would be a knight of Christ, choosing such holy orders, you in your profession of faith must unite pure diligence and firm perseverance, which is so worthy and so holy, and is known to be so noble, that if it is preserved untainted for ever, you will deserve to keep company with the martyrs who gave their souls for Jesus Christ.'

Prologue to the Primitive Rule of the Templars

A Templar initiate is received into the Order in this nineteenth century romantic painting. The ceremony of reception was described in detail in the Templar Rule, but would later be misinterpreted after the arrests of 1307.
Author's collection

SETTING ASIDE the ridiculous notions about kissing buttocks and spitting on crosses that were supposed to have been an integral part of the Templars' ceremony of initiation, we are fortunate to be able to examine that ceremony as it was intended to be presented to men joining the Order in the thirteenth and fourteenth centuries. [1] This ceremony of reception, as it was called, became an integral part of the Templar Rule of Order, which evolved and expanded along with the Templar Order itself from the time the rule was first drafted at the Council of Troyes in 1129, until the Order retired from the Holy Land in the early years of the fourteenth century.

Although modern Masonic Templar rituals vary from country to country, the following account of the original ceremony will be of particular interest to members of the Order to illustrate the differences between the ceremony used by the medieval Templars and the elaborate ritual used by Masonic Templars.

The Initiation of a Medieval Knight Templar

Outside of combat in the field, the weekly chapter meeting was one of the few places that a Templar could find a little spice in his otherwise dull existence. It was within the tiled recesses of the chapter that members would gather to deal with the business of the Order – particularly the

transgressions of the brethren. These meetings were for members of the Order alone and even associate members were barred from the closed doors of the chapter meeting. [2] The utmost secrecy was to be exercised on all matters discussed in the chapter meeting and any brother who broke that silence by disclosing what was discussed could find himself expelled from the Order. A great deal was made of this secrecy during the trials that followed the Templars' arrest in 1307, but this secrecy was no different than that practised by other monastic institutions of the medieval era. However, unlike the other monastic Orders, such as the Cistercians, the Templars did not always have buildings set aside specifically for the purpose of holding chapter meetings and would use whatever building was most practical, often the chapel. [3] But whether the Templars held their chapter meetings in a specific room for the purpose or in their chapels, it was within the context of the chapter that new men were brought into the Order.

Similar to the process used by Freemasonry and many other fraternal organisations, the ceremony of reception began with the receptor asking the chapter if any brother had an objection to the postulant being admitted a member of the Order. [4] If there were no objections, the initiate was brought to a small chamber adjoining the chapter room. The receptor would then send two or three of the older members to interview him there. This aspect of the ceremony is not at all unlike the system used in Freemasonry to this day, where the candidate for admission is asked a series of questions outside the door of the Lodge Room; however, the questions asked are of a decidedly different nature.

As the men entered the chamber, the postulant, unaware of what was to come next, probably began to fidget, unsure of what was expected of him or what he could expect from the Order. That would soon change.

'Brother, do you request the company of the house?' he would be asked by one of the men.

'I do.'

Upon hearing the answer they were looking for, his interviewers would then inform him of the sufferings he could expect to endure by forever sealing himself to the Templar Order. The Templar way of life was

The Masonic Temple in Detroit, Michigan, built in the 1920s, is home to a beautiful modern Masonic Knights Templar asylum or meeting room. This room was designed to capture the feel of architecture that existed at the time of the Templars.
Stephen Dafoe

certainly a stark contrast from what he had previously known, for the Order of the Temple was a religious one and, as such, embraced a lifestyle that matched its holy mission. It could be expected that the new Templar would spend as much time on his knees praying as he would on his horse fighting. The details of this harsh and regimented lifestyle were often told from the personal experience of the men sent to talk to him; men who, having served the Order for a long period of time, had established a long track record with those sufferings. [5]

'Do you have a wife or a fiancée?' one would ask, as no married man could join the Templars as a full member.

'Have you made a vow or promise to any other Order?' another would query.

'Do you owe a debt to any secular man, whom you have not yet paid?'

'Are you in good health?'

'Do you have any secret illness?'

For each question, the would-be Templar was to answer a clear and prompt no; an affirmative answer to any of his interviewers' questions could prevent him from being admitted to the Order, which he desired to join. With the questions satisfactorily answered, the men would leave the postulant to reflect upon what awaited him and return to the chapter to inform the receptor of what had transpired.

'Sire,' one of the men would begin. 'We have spoken to this worthy man who is outside and have indicated to him the sufferings of the house as we were able and knew how to. And he says that he wishes to be a serf and slave of the house, and of all those things, which we asked him he is quit and free; there is no hindrance which means he cannot and should not be a brother, if it please God and you and the brothers.' [6]

After hearing from the committee, the receptor would again ask the chapter if any brother knew of a reason why the candidate should not be admitted, 'for it would be better now than later'. Hearing no complaint against the proposed brother, the receptor would then ask if he should be brought to the chapter on behalf of God.

'Bring him on behalf of God,' the brethren would chant in reply to the question.

Again the Masonic reader will no doubt see some similarity to the ceremonies used to initiate men into the Craft degrees.

Once again the interviewers were dispatched to the chamber where they would ask the initiate if he was still of the same mind as when they had spoken to him a few minutes before. If he was still willing to endure the hardships of the Templar way of life, he was to be instructed in how to approach the chapter, how to kneel, how to hold his hands clasped together and, most importantly, what words were expected of him before his potential brethren.

A corridor of Fountains Abbey in North Yorkshire, founded in 1132, shows just how close the Freemasons of Detroit came in capturing the medieval flavour. *Stephen Dafoe*

This carving found in Scotland's Rosslyn Chapel has created an incredible amount of attention in recent years for it appears, and has been claimed, to depict a man wearing a blindfold and a noose in the fashion of the Masonic ritual. While this carving has been used to suggest that the Templars were practitioners of Freemasonry, the ceremony of reception, as outlined in this chapter, makes no mention of blindfolds or nooses (referred to as a cable tow in the Masonic ritual). Additionally, Rosslyn Chapel was constructed in the mid-1400s, the carvings being added in the final stages of construction. The use of a blindfold and cable tow did not enter the Masonic ritual until the eighteenth century.
Author's collection

After the candidate, kneeling before the receptor, had humbly requested to be admitted to the Order, he would hear for the first time the words of the receptor:

'Good brother,' the receptor would begin, 'you ask a very great thing; for of our Order you see only the outer appearance. For the appearance is that you see us having fine horses, and good equipment, and good food and drink, and fine robes, and thus it seems to you that you would be well at ease. But you do not know the harsh commandments which lie beneath it: for it is a painful thing for you, who are your own master to make yourself a serf to others. For with great difficulty will you ever do anything that you wish: for if you wish to be in Acre, you will be sent to the land of Tripoli or Antioch, or Armenia; or you will be sent to Apulia, or Sicily, or Lombardy, or France, or Burgundy, or England, or to several other lands where we have houses and possessions. And if you wish to sleep, you will be awoken; and if you sometimes wish to stay awake, you will be ordered to rest in your bed.' [7]

Of course for the sergeants, who were the members of the Order who were not of noble birth, there was a further instruction that he might be called upon to do the basest of chores that the Order may require and whether he was called to work in the kitchen or the pigsty he would be obligated to follow the commands given him. [8]

It is here that any comparison between the life of a Templar and the life of a Freemason ends, although it may seem silly to point the differences out. While the Freemason has an obligation to support his lodge and the Craft, at no time is that obligation expected to interfere with his private or public avocations. Such was not the case with the men who joined the Knights Templar. From the day they entered the house until the day they died or were dismissed, every aspect of their life was dictated by the greater needs of the Order. The Templar would wake when he was told and go to sleep when he was told; he would eat what he was given and refrain from eating what he was not permitted to have. If the Templar had a favourite sword or horse, he could be deprived of them for no greater reason than the Master saw fit to give them to another brother of the Order. All of these hardships, the Templar was to accept without recourse or debate.

'Now decide, good gentle brother, if you could tolerate these hardships,' the receptor would continue.

'Yes I will tolerate them all if God pleases,' the candidate would reply.

Upon hearing the postulant's affirmative reply indicating his dedication to the Order, he was then informed that his admission to the Temple was not to be out of a desire for riches, nor to obtain honour; rather there were but three reasons for his seeking admission: to put aside the sin of the secular world, to do the work of the Lord and to be poor, undertaking a life of penance for the salvation of his soul. [9]

Again he was asked if he was willing to abide by what he had been told, after which he was sent outside the chapter where he was to 'pray to Our Lord that He may advise you'. While the initiate was outside the chapter room, the receptor would, for a third time, ask the brethren if there were any objections to his being admitted. Upon hearing no objection the receptor would ask for the second time if he should be brought forward on behalf of God.

'Bring him on behalf of God,' the brethren would once more chant.

One of the interviewers would once again be sent to bring him back to the chapter and once again the postulant would kneel before once again asking with humility to be admitted to the Order.

'Have you considered well, good brother, that you wish to be a serf and slave of the Order and leave behind your own will forever to do another's?' the receptor would ask.

'Sire, yes if it please God,' the candidate would once again reply.

Although the candidate had given his word several times, the Templar ceremony took great steps to make sure that the postulate was telling the truth. The receptor would raise the chapter for a prayer to Jesus Christ and His Holy mother, after which individual brethren would recite the paternoster. Following the prayers, the chaplain would offer an additional prayer to the Holy Spirit. The candidate was then to kneel and receive the Gospels on his outstretched hands, [10] for it was certain that the prospective member would not perjure himself on the words of Christ.

The receptor would repeat the questions the candidate had already been asked in front of the brethren, explaining the punishment he could face should it later be found that he had lied in answering any of them. He was also asked if he was excommunicated.

The status of excommunicated knights is a somewhat confusing issue. In the French translation of the Rule, drafted during the administration of Robert de Craon, the second Grand Master of the Order, the Templars were instructed to recruit wherever excommunicated knights were gathered. [11] However, in the original Latin Rule of 1129, it specifically mentions non-excommunicated knights. Historian, Judith Upton-Ward argued that this deliberate change to the Rule is an indication that as early as 1135-1147 the Templars had begun to widen their recruiting net by relaxing admission standards. [12] This is further supported by the fact that the original Latin Rule speaks of a probationary period, which was dropped by the time of the French translation. The parallels to present-day Freemasonry – especially in North America – will no doubt be immediate to many readers.

After the receptor had finished with his questions, the floor was turned over to the old men of the house who were offered the opportunity to question the candidate. When all the questions had been asked,

A Templar kneels before a priest in this modern interpretation of the Templars' religious observances by historian and artist Gordon Napier. *Gordon Napier*

the receptor would once again admonish the potential Templar to ensure that he had told the truth in all things.

Another set of questions would follow, the answers to which were always a promise to 'Our Lord and Our Lady St Mary' and to be answered with the words, 'Yes sire, if it please God.' Did he promise to obey the commands of the Master of the Temple and his commanders? Would he promise to remain chaste for the rest of his life? Did he promise to remain without property or possessions for the duration of that life? Would he promise to uphold the fine traditions and good customs of the Order for the remainder of his days? Would he vow to help conquer the Holy Land of Jerusalem and all other lands held by Christians for as long as he had the strength and power to do so? And lastly, would he vow never to leave the house of the Temple? [13]

Once the questions were satisfactorily answered, the candidate could expect the moment he had waited for – admission to the Order of the Temple. The receptor would then place the mantle of the Order around the neck of the newly admitted member, fastening the laces while the chaplain recited from the Psalms, 'Ecce quam bonum et quam jocundum habitare fratres in unum.' [14] This psalm is better recognised in its English translation, and should be immediately recognised by Freemasons of the American Rite: 'Behold, how good and how pleasant it is for Brethren to dwell together in unity.' [15] The newly made brother was then raised by the receptor and kissed on the mouth, a process that was replicated by the chaplain. [16]

The receptor would then sit the new Templar before him and say, 'Good brother, Our Lord has led you to your desire and has placed you in such a fine company as in the Knighthood of the Temple, because of which you should be at great pains to ensure that you never do anything for which it would be necessary to expel you from it, from which God keep you.' [17]

The remainder of the ceremony involved a detailed explanation of the Templar Rule or Order. The new member was taught how to attend the Order's religious observances, communal meals and other aspects that formed the Templar way of life – a life which he had vowed never to leave.

Although Freemasons reading the previous account of the Templar ceremony of reception will no doubt see several similarities between the ritual used by the medieval Templars and that used by the modern Masonic Order, they must also admit that there are an equal, if not greater, number of differences as well. The simple fact of the matter is that the Templar ceremony of reception contained no references to the building of Solomon's Temple, no circumambulations, no blindfolds, rolled up trouser legs or any of the other ceremonial trappings that form an integral part of the degrees of Freemasonry as universally practised throughout the world. While it is true that the modern Masonic Templar ritual has some passing similarity to that of the original Templars, it cannot be denied that where similarities do exist they are but an imitation of the former.

Writing in the latter part of the nineteenth century, Lieutenant Colonel William James Bury MacLeod Moore who was Supreme Grand Master of the Sovereign Great Priory of Canada was adamant in his views that Templary of the Masonic variety was little more than an imitation of the Templars of old:

'Individual members of the Order in the last century, joining the Masonic fraternity, may have tended in some measure to the formation of the Masonic imitation degrees of Knight Templars and Knights of Malta, and also to the perpetuation of the traditional belief of a connection having existed between the Templars of the Crusades and the Ecclesiastical builders – who were said to be conversant with, and practised the occult sciences of the East, in the retirement of their cloisters.

'Such, then, appears to be the true and correct history of Modern Templary from the most careful research and reliable authorities, who reject this mistaken belief, false theory, and fables of its being, either directly or indirectly, a portion of the system of "Free and Accepted" Masonry.

'The Orders of Knighthood are quite distinct from Masonry, and there is no such thing as Masonic Knighthood, and any such claim is a childish fable. The honours of Knighthood can only be conferred by the Sovereign or the representative of the Sovereign; but our system does not pretend to be a Knightly Order; it only promulgates the reading and teachings of the Ancient Knightly fraternity.

'The ceremonies of the United Orders of the Temple and Malta in the Empire are intended to inculcate the cardinal doctrines of the Catholic faith, with a firm belief in the holy and undivided Trinity, the chief and indissoluble character of the Templar Order, without which in spite of all sophistry and special pleadings, no true Templary can exist. To speak of Templary as an Order of "Free and Accepted Masonry" is simply ridiculous.

'The Order of the Temple existed for centuries apart from Masonry, without any known connection further than that the Knights of old employed the ancient Craft as workmen, and our modern Craft Grand Lodges consider the Templar degrees as glaring innovations on "Symbolic" Masonry. Although the United Orders cannot claim a direct descent from the old Religious Military fraternities of the Middle Ages, their teachings and practices distinctly prove their chivalric origin, and are a revival of the principles and usages of the old Religious and Military Orders, which they correctly represent.

'Modern Templary, then, is only quasi Masonic, nothing more, from being allied to it as one of the additional degrees for about a century past, and it never obtained official recognition in England, save as an adopted degree by the York 'Grand Lodge of all England,' which became extinct about 1790, when York Masonry died out, and never united with the regular Grand Lodge of England.

'Close investigation has clearly proved that the alleged origins of Masonic Templary in the different countries where it exists are mere fictions. The fabrications of the last century, principally derived from the idle legends of the obsolete "Rite of Strict Observance," which built up a mass of childish fables, used to support the theories of the high grade Masonic system, that the test of history totally rejects.

'The assumption that Freemasonry is the offspring of the old Military Templars is equally untenable.' [18]

If Masonic Templarism is not the offspring of the Military Templars of old, but merely connected to Freemasonry as an allied degree originating in the mid-eighteenth century, as MacLeod Moore contended, from whence did it originate? In order to understand the true connection between the compasses and the cross, we will start with a more detailed look at a man whom many have claimed to be the father of the Templar grades – the Chevalier Andrew Michael Ramsay.

References for Chapter 5

1. The Templar ceremony of reception comprised articles 657-686 of the Templar Rule of Order.

2. *The Knights Templar: A New History*, Nicholson, Helen, p.137.

3. Ibid. p.137.

4. *The Rule of the Templars*, Judith Upton-Ward, Woodbridge, The Boydell Press, 2001, p.168 § 657.

5. Ibid. p.168 § 658.

6. Ibid. p.168 § 659.

7. Ibid. pp.168-169 § 661.

8. Ibid. p.169 § 662.

9. Ibid. p.169 § 663.

10. Ibid. p.170 § 668.

11. Ibid. p.22 § 12.

12. Ibid. p.13.

13. Ibid. pp.171-172 § 675-676.

14. Ibid. p.172 § 678. *The Trial of the Templars*, Malcolm Barber, p.254.

15. KJV Psalm 133. In American Masonic Lodges the Holy Bible is open at Psalm 133 during the First or Entered Apprentice Degree.

16. Although much would be made of this seemingly unusual practice, as well as the entire ceremony of reception itself, during the trials that awaited the Order in its final days, the papal commission found nothing unorthodox about the ceremony as written.

17. Upton-Ward. Op. cit. p.172 § 678.

18. William J. Bury MacLeod Moore quoted in *The History of the Knights Templar of Canada*, Robertson, John Ross. Toronto. 1890. Hunter Rose & Co. p.9.

The Chevalier Andrew Michael Ramsay, shown here in the regalia
of the Order of St Lazarus, is the man credited with creating
the Templar Orders in Freemasonry.
Author's collection

6 Ramsay and the Oration that made him Famous

'Had there never been a Chevalier Ramsay, or had he written the Travels of Cyrus and not pronounced an Oration, the developments of Ritual beyond Craft Masonry must have assumed other forms.'

Arthur Edward Waite

Right: François de Salignac de la Mothe-Fénelon was a close friend of Ramsay and a man who was the subject of one of Ramsay's biographies. Fénelon converted Ramsay to Catholicism while Ramsay was a guest in his home.
Jupiter Images

IT IS PERHAPS ironic that the man who is most often credited with giving birth to the Masonic Templar degrees was a man who would never have been a likely candidate for admission into the original Order – at least not in the capacity of one of nobly born white mantled knights.

Andrew Michael Ramsay was born, the son of a humble baker, on 9 January, (probably in the year 1681) in the south-western coastal town of Ayr, Scotland. [1] It was here that the young Ramsay attended grammar school until the age of 14, when he entered the University of Edinburgh and began his higher studies. Upon graduation, Ramsay took up employment with David, the 4th Earl of Wemyss as a tutor to his children. This would be the first of many such positions held by Ramsay in his lifetime.

In 1706, Ramsay left the employ of the earl and in 1707 took up a study of mathematics under Sir Isaac Newton's companion, Nicholas Fatio de Dullier. Ever the wander, Ramsay later took off for the Netherlands with the English auxiliaries during the time of the Spanish War of Succession. [2] In 1710 Ramsay left military service and travelled to Rijinsburg, where he became a guest of Pierre Poiret.

Although raised a Calvinist, Ramsay began to embrace the mysticism of Quietism, a Christian philosophy that swept through France and other parts of the Continent during the seventeenth century. This mystical philosophy taught that mankind achieved the highest form of perfection through self-annihilation and the absorption of the soul into the divine while one was still alive. Essentially the practitioner would still the mind, allowing God to act within it. Poiret was friends with the Archbishop of Cambrai, François de Salignac de la Mothe-Fénelon, a man who, despite his Roman Catholic teachings, was a defender of the Quietism movement. Through Poiret, Ramsay struck up a friendship with Fénelon and stayed with him until 1715, during which time Ramsay converted to Catholicism. [3]

In 1718, Ramsay once again became a tutor to the children of the nobility, this time working in the

Charles Edward Stuart, known as Bonnie Prince Charlie or the Young Pretender, was a pupil of Ramsay for a brief time. Much has been made of Ramsay's Jacobite connections due to his teaching the young man.
Jupiter Images

employ of the Comte de Sassenage. While living with the Comte de Sassenage, Ramsay became acquainted with several Jacobite exiles from Britain and Ireland, who initially had been loyal to the deposed King James II of England and Ireland (King James VII of Scotland) and, upon James's death, to his son James Francis Edward Stuart. This man was, by Jacobite reasoning, the legitimate heir to the throne and although recognised as such by Louis XIV of France, his attempt, in 1715, to regain his kingdom resulted in an even greater influx of Jacobite supporters immigrating to France.

Martin I. McGregor in his *A Biographical Sketch of the Chevalier Andrew Michael Ramsay* says that extant letters written to James Francis Edward Stuart by Ramsay show a clear indication that Ramsay had become a Jacobite supporter himself. [4] McGregor cites Ramsay's conversion to Catholicism at the hands of Fenelon as the reason for his turning Jacobite. Whatever his motivations for supporting the Jacobite cause, in 1722, Ramsay became involved in negotiations on a proposed taxation by the British

government on the assets of exiled Jacobites. Ramsay's services impressed Stuart who invited him to become the tutor of his son Charles Edward Stuart, who would come to be known as the Young Pretender. Although much has been made of the fact that Ramsay was tutor to Charles Edward Stuart, what is lesser known is this employment was short-lived. Ramsay left the Stuart's employ in November of the same year, failing in his task, largely due to the fact that the young prince was only three years of age. [5] However, one of the positive outcomes from Ramsay's brief connection with the Stuart household was that on 20 May 1723, he was proclaimed a Knight of St Lazarus, and on 24 May of the same year, he was granted a patent of nobility by his pupil's father, James Francis Edward Stuart, the Old Pretender. This patent was issued on the basis of Ramsay's alleged descent from the House of Dalhousie and the House of Mar on his paternal and maternal sides respectively. [6]

Despite his obvious connections with the Jacobite cause and his failure in his tutorage of the young Pretender, Ramsay was none the less invited to tutor the Duke of Cumberland by George Augustus, the future George II of England. However, Ramsay declined the invitation on the grounds that he felt his Roman Catholicism made the appointment inappropriate.

Ramsay spent the years between 1725 and 1728 in the home of the Duc de Sully, and it is during this period that he wrote and published *The Travels of Cyrus*, a book, which although largely comprised of the work of others, was none the less popular with French readers. This was not Ramsay's only venture into the world of literature, for in 1723 he published a biography of his old friend Fenelon.

Ramsay the Freemason

RAMSAY left the home of the Duc de Sully and France in 1728, travelling to Britain, where he stopped briefly in London before moving on to Scotland, where he became a guest of the Duke of Argyll at Inveraray. His time in Britain must have been a pleasant experience, as he was accorded many honours between 1729 and 1730. Ramsay was made a member of the Royal Society in December of 1729, admitted a member of the prestigious Gentleman's Club of Spalding in 1730 and in that same year the honorary degree of Doctor of Law was conferred upon him at Oxford. [7] This latter honour is particularly worthy of note, as Ramsay was the first Roman Catholic to receive the honour in nearly two hundred years. However, with respect to his later contributions to Templary, Ramsay was made a Freemason on 16 March 1729. Although some have held to the idea that Ramsay was never a Freemason, a report in the London Evening Post dated 17 March 1729 specifically identifies him as being initiated the night before:

'On Monday night last at the Horn Lodge in the Palace Yard, Westminster (whereof his Grace the Duke of Richmond is Master) there was a numerous appearance of persons of distinction; at which time the Marquis of Beaumont, eldest son and heir apparent to the Duke of Roxburghe; Earl Kerr of Wakefield, a peer of Great Britain; Sir Francis Henry Drake, Bart., the Marquis de Quesne; Tomas Powel of Nanteos, Esq., the Chevalier Ramsay; and Dr. Misanbin, were admitted members of the Ancient Society of Free and Accepted Masons.' [8]

Upon his return to France in July of 1730, he once again took up employment as a tutor, this time to the son of the Duc de Bouillon, a family tied to the Jacobite Court through marriage. When his pupil died, Ramsay took up employment with another noble family as the tutor to the Prince of Tourenne, a position he maintained until 1741. It was during this period of his life that he wrote another book – a biography of the Viscount de Turenne, one of France's greatest military commanders, who began his career during the Thirty Years War. It was also during this time that Ramsay married the daughter of Sir David Nairne, the undersecretary of James Edward Stuart, who awarded Ramsay the title of Knight and Baronet in honour of the matrimonial celebrations. If Ramsay was in fact born in 1681, he would have been 54 years of age when he married. Regardless of his advanced years, Ramsay sired two children; however, his son died in infancy and his daughter was struck down from smallpox at the age of nineteen.

Despite his matrimonial and employment obligations, Ramsay seems to have had time to spare for Freemasonry, although the precise details of his involvement in the Craft in France are few in number. Certainly he was a member of Louis l'Argent Lodge in Paris and held the office of Orator. Additionally Ramsay is said to have been Grand Orator; however, there was no formal Grand Lodge structure in France until 1743, so the position, if he truly held it, must have been confined to an informal union of the lodges then operating in and around Paris. [9] Regardless of the hierarchy of embryonic French Masonry of the 1730s, it is clear that Ramsay had elevated himself to a position of respect within French Masonic circles – a considerable achievement, given the fact that he had been initiated into the Craft less than a decade earlier. It was in his capacity of Orator that Ramsay prepared and delivered an address that would form the building blocks upon which chivalric Masonry would rise.

Despite his obvious connections with the Jacobite cause and his failure in his tutorage of the young Pretender, Ramsay was invited to tutor the Duke of Cumberland by George Augustus, the future George II of England. Ramsay declined the invitation.
Jupiter Images

Ramsay was the author of many books over the course of his life. One of his lesser-known works was the biography of the Viscount de Turenne, one of France's greatest military commanders. Ramsay authored the biography while tutoring the Prince of Tourenne.
Jupiter Images

Ramsay's Oration

MASONIC authors have written a great deal over the years about Ramsay's Oration, as it has come to be known, an address Ramsay is alleged to have delivered to a Grand Lodge meeting on 21 March 1737. However, it is important to understand that the vast majority of Freemasons who have tackled the subject did not have all the information to hand; until 1967 there was but one extant version of the address. Given that the vast majority of Masonic opinion was formed and written in the nineteenth and early twentieth centuries – well before the discovery of the Epernay or manuscript version – these writers were deprived of the valuable insights the two versions contain.

But lest we get ahead of ourselves, we should look at what is commonly known to Freemasons about the address. Certainly the most often quoted aspect of Ramsay's Oration is the passage we looked at in Chapter 1. For the benefit of the reader, we will reproduce it here:

'At the time of the Crusades in Palestine many princes, lords, and citizens associated themselves, and vowed to restore the Temple of the Christians in the Holy Land, and to employ

Prior to delivering his famed Oration, Ramsay wrote to André-Hercule the Cardinal de Fleury, chief minister to Louis XV, seeking approval for the text. De Fleury replied to Ramsay with the words, "The King does not wish it." Soon after, Ramsay seems to have removed himself from Freemasonry.
Jupiter Images

themselves in bringing back their architecture to its first institution. They agreed upon several ancient signs and symbolic words drawn from the well of religion in order to recognise themselves amongst the heathen and Saracens. These signs and words were only communicated to those who promised solemnly, and even sometimes at the foot of the altar, never to reveal them. This sacred promise was therefore not an execrable oath, as it has been called, but a respectable bond to unite Christians of all nationalities in one confraternity. Some time afterwards our Order formed an intimate union with the Knights of St John of Jerusalem. From that time, our Lodges took the name of Lodges of St John.'

As this passage has been the root and marrow of the majority of twentieth century writings on the Oration, the Freemason of today can be forgiven for not knowing much more about the address than this. However, there is far more to Ramsay's Oration in terms of content, motivation and response than these few words can provide. Perhaps the most interesting aspect of the address is that Ramsay felt the need to receive permission to deliver the address. On 20 March 1737, Ramsay wrote to Cardinal de Fleury, Chief Minister to King Louis XV:

'As I am to read my discourse tomorrow in a general assembly of the Order and to hand it on Monday to the examiners of the Chancellerie, I pray your Excellency to return it to me tomorrow before mid-day by express messenger. You will definitely oblige a man whose heart is devoted to you.' [10]

Although there is no record of a reply from the cardinal, Ramsay must have either received a note or learned of the response to his letter, for on 22 March, he sent another to the cardinal in a modified tone:

'I learn that assemblies of Freemasons displease your Excellency. I have never frequented any of them except with a view of spreading maxims which would render by degrees incredulity ridiculous, vice odious and ignorance shameful. I am persuaded that if wise men of your Excellency's choice were introduced to head these assemblies, they would become very useful to religion, the state and literature. Of this I hope to convince your Excellency if you will accord me a short interview at Issy. Awaiting the happy moment, I pray you to inform me whether I should return to these assemblies and

I will conform to your Excellency's wishes with a boundless docility.' [11]

This time Ramsay received a reply, but certainly not the one he had probably hoped for; his letter was returned to him, on the margin of which was penned the words, 'The King does not wish it.' [12]

From these correspondences we learn a few pertinent facts on Ramsay's Oration and possible motives. He had prepared an address to Parisian Freemasons, which he was to deliver on 21 March 1737. However, before he could do so the address was to be presented to censors for approval prior to publication. The content of Ramsay's first letter would seem to indicate that Ramsay was seeking the support of de Fleury in the cause of French Freemasonry; however, in the second, he seems to be doing a fair bit of back pedalling and covering his own behind – going so far as to express his willingness to disconnect from Freemasonry, should it be the cardinal's desire.

Although Ramsay does not seem to have suffered from his involvement with the Craft, Louis XV published an edict in 1738 prohibiting all royal subjects from association with Freemasonry. It is said that de Fleury also bent the ear of Pope Clement XII, urging him to take action. [13] On 28 April 1738, Clement issued the bull In Eminenti Apostolatus Specula, which not only condemned Freemasonry, but forbade Catholics from participation in it. As this was the first papal pronouncement against Freemasonry, the reader may be interested in reading an excerpt from it:

'Now it has come to Our ears, and common gossip has made clear, that certain Societies, Companies, Assemblies, Meetings, Congregations or Conventicles called in the popular tongue Liberi Muratori or Francs Massons or by other names according to the various languages, are spreading far and wide and daily growing in strength; and men of any Religion or sect, satisfied with the appearance of natural probity, are joined together, according to their laws and the statutes laid down for them, by a strict and unbreakable bond which obliges them, both by an oath upon the Holy Bible and by a host of grievous punishment, to an inviolable silence about all that they do in secret together. But it is in the nature of crime to betray itself and to show itself by its attendant clamour. Thus these aforesaid Societies or Conventicles have caused in the minds of the

King Louis XV (1710-1774) was the ruler of France and Navarre during Ramsay's day. It was Louis according to de Fleury's marginal note who did not wish Ramsay to address the Freemasons of Paris. *Jupiter Images*

faithful the greatest suspicion, and all prudent and upright men have passed the same judgment on them as being depraved and perverted. For if they were not doing evil they would not have so great a hatred of the light. Indeed, this rumour has grown to such proportions that in several countries these societies have been forbidden by the civil authorities as being against the public security, and for some time past have appeared to be prudently eliminated.

'Therefore, bearing in mind the great harm which is often caused by such Societies or Conventicles not only to the peace of the temporal state but also to the well-being of souls, and realizing that they do not hold by either civil or canonical sanctions; and since We are taught by the divine word that it is the part of faithful servant and of the master of the Lord's household to watch day and night lest such men as these break into the household like thieves, and like foxes seek to destroy the vineyard;

degree of certainty, proximity to the supposed date of Ramsay's Oration aside. Certainly, de Fleury's opposition to Ramsay's request can be argued to be a combination of religion and politics and may have played a role in helping sort out for the pope what the 'common gossip has made clear'. Politically speaking, if Jacobites were involved in Freemasonry, it was in de Fleury's best interest to deny any support to the Craft, given that he was trying to keep peace with England at the time. [15] On a religious basis, the cardinal would have been opposed to any group interested in spreading moral teachings outside the scope of the Roman Catholic Church, a fact that rings clear in the excerpt from the bull reprinted above. Oddly enough neither Clement's bull of 1738, nor Benedict XIV's of 18 May 1751, was published in France. [16]

We also cannot be certain if Ramsay's motives were to introduce Catholic teachings into the body of French Freemasonry. Certainly the content of the second letter to de Fleury would give an indication that such may have been the case. As Ramsay wrote, 'I am persuaded that if wise men of your Excellency's choice were introduced to head these assemblies, they would become very useful to religion, the state and literature.' Of course, as previously mentioned, Ramsay may have simply been back peddalling to avoid any possible repercussions from his involvement in Freemasonry.

From the content of the letters, which have been long-known, it has been concluded that Ramsay never delivered the Oration, his permission having been denied by the marginal note 'The King does not wish it.' However, as mentioned earlier, Masonic writers of the nineteenth and early twentieth centuries did not have the benefit of the Epernay version. This document was discovered in 1967 in the archives of Epernay, France – hence its name. Entitled Discourse de le Chevalier Ramsay given at St John's Lodge on 27 December 1736, [17] it gives a date anterior to the date indicated in Ramsay's correspondence with Cardinal de Fleury. [18] This date is, of course the feast of St John the Evangelist – a date recognised by Freemasons to this day, and the day chosen in 1813 to commemorate the formation of the United Grand Lodge of England.

The manuscript or Epernay version is similar to the Grand Lodge, or printed version except when it comes to the discourse on the origins of Freemasonry. In the former, Ramsay traces Freemasonry's lineage back to the Old Testament and in so doing, ties the history of the Craft to the history of the Jews. However, this idea was expunged from the manuscript version. [19] What seems possible, if not

in fact, to prevent the hearts of the simple being perverted, and the innocent secretly wounded by their arrows, and to block that broad road which could be opened to the uncorrected commission of sin and for the other just and reasonable motives known to Us; We therefore, having taken counsel of some of Our Venerable Brothers among the Cardinals of the Holy Roman Church, and also of Our own accord and with certain knowledge and mature deliberations, with the plenitude of the Apostolic power do hereby determine and have decreed that these same Societies, Companies, Assemblies, Meetings, Congregations, or Conventicles of Liberi Muratori or Francs Massons, or whatever other name they may go by, are to be condemned and prohibited, and by Our present Constitution, valid for ever, We do condemn and prohibit them.' [14]

Whether this bull was issued as a direct or indirect result of Ramsay's Oration cannot be said with any probable, is that the Epernay version was delivered in Masonic lodges by Ramsay as part of his duties as Orator and even Grand Orator. The Grand Lodge version was intended for presentation at, as the name implies, a meeting of the Grand Lodge (whatever form that may have taken in 1737) and the references to the Jews were removed from the document to please the censors, who would have the final say as to whether or not it was published. Although it has been claimed that the Oration was originally printed at The Hague for the installation of the Duc d'Antin on 24 June 1738, the first known publication was in the 1741 edition of the *Almanack de cocus*. [20] There is a long-standing claim among past Masonic writers that Ramsay's Oration was publicly burnt in 1739 by order of Pope Clement XII; however, McGregor claimed that the destroyed document was an anonymous defence of Freemasonry, issued in response to Samuel Pritchard's *Masonry Dissected*. [21]

Ramsay's Motivations

WHAT were Ramsay's motives for writing his Oration? It is certainly clear that Ramsay's Oration, whenever it may have been delivered and printed, connected the Craft with the crusaders, and although this idea was introduced in passing by Anderson in his *Constitutions*, Ramsay was the first to make the proclamation loud and clear. The question remains, why? It is important to understand that unlike the lodges in England, where Ramsay had been initiated, membership in France was largely reserved for the upper echelon of society. Although England had its share of the upper crust, French Freemasonry – in its early stages – was essentially a gentleman's club in which the members met to socialise and partake in innocent pleasures. [22] Clearly Ramsay was attempting to market Freemasonry to the French aristocracy, gentry and bourgeoisie, who would have had little interest in belonging to an order descended from the common working class – even if they were skilled tradesmen. This is supported by another excerpt from the Oration, which precedes the oft-quoted paragraph referenced earlier:

'The word Freemason must therefore not be taken in a literal, gross and material sense, as if our founders had been simple workers in stone, or merely curious geniuses who wished to perfect the arts. They were not only skilful architects, desirous of consecrating their talents and good to the construction of material temples; but also religious and warrior princes who designed to enlighten, edify and protect the living temples of the Most High. This I will demonstrate by developing the history or rather the renewal of our Order.' [23]

Before moving on to the degrees that arose from Ramsay's Oration, we should address one of the commonly held myths concerning his crusader connection. There have been many authors over the years who have asserted that Ramsay claimed that Freemasonry was directly connected with the Templars. As we have seen, he made no such claims in his address; rather, his connection was to that of the Knights of St John of Jerusalem, whom Ramsay claimed were the reason Masonic Lodges took the name of St John. Others have claimed that Ramsay's reference to the Knights of St John meant the Templars is equally false. Having gone to great pains to gain the support of the cardinal it is unlikely that he would have made mention of a group suppressed by the Roman Catholic Church.

The Rite de Ramsay and other Myths

ONE of the most prevalent myths concerning Ramsay is that he created the so-called higher degrees. Written a century after Ramsay wrote his address to Parisian Freemasons we find some interesting commentary on Ramsay's involvement in the creation of these degrees in an article on Royal Arch Masonry published in the pages of Charles Moore's *Freemasons' Monthly Magazine*:

'In the year 1840 [sic], the Chevalier Ramsay, a Scottish nobleman and a strong adherent of the Stuarts, gave his celebrated lecture in Paris, concerning the origin of Freemasonry, founding his system on the postulate that Freemasonry was a branch of Templary. This was the commencement of all the so-called higher degrees which soon after spread over the continent and for a time almost destroyed every vestige of the plain and simple system of English masonry. Ramsay visited England and brought with him from Paris a number of these new degrees. Among them was one that he termed the Royal Arch; these degrees he sought to engraft upon the English system, but they were rejected by the Grand Lodge. Very soon after, the Ancient Masons publicly announced that ancient Masonry consisted of four degrees and that the Modern Masons possessed only three. The former divided the Master's degree into two parts, the second of which was comprised of fragments taken from the then existing higher degrees of the continent, and in which we find portions of Ramsay's Royal Arch, of the Knights of the Grand Architect, of the Burning Bush, of the East or Sword, of the Red cross, the Scotch Fellow Craft, the Select Master, etc., and to this they gave the name of Royal Arch. Thus this degree is in reality of French origin, although as a whole first practised in England. Ramsay qualified the French Royal Arch as the ne plus ultra of Masonry; the Ancient Masons extolled theirs as "the summit and perfection of ancient Masonry".' [24]

Of course Ramsay had no part in the formation of the Royal Arch Degree (or any other for that matter), but that did not stop numerous Masonic writers, such as the author of the article above, from spreading myths about the man. Of course the author almost certainly got his ideas from earlier Masonic authors such as Oliver, Thory and Fessler, the latter of which was the originator of the myth. It was Fessler's belief that Ramsay grafted the Knight of St Andrew of the Thistle onto the Craft degrees; however, the Order of the Thistle had already existed since the time of James II [25] and had nothing to do with Freemasonry, Scottish claims notwithstanding. But where Fessler may have got the ball rolling, Thory caught it and ran with it. In his *Acta Latomorum* he wrote of Ramsay's contribution to the high grades:

'In that year [1728], the Scottish Knight Baronet Ramsay laid in London the foundations of a new Masonry which, according to him, originated in the crusades and whose invention he ascribed to Godfrey de Bouillon. He asserted that the St Andrews Lodge in Edinburgh was the head of the true Order of the Freemasons who were the scions of the knights of the Crusades. He conferred three degrees: the Ecossais, the Novice and the Knight of the Temple. Ramsay preaches a reform based on his discovery; this doctrine is rejected.' [26]

These degrees, the fabrication of Thory's fertile mind, were collectively known as the Rite de Ramsay or Rite de Bouillon. Given that Ramsay was not initiated until a year later, it is hardly possible that he could have brought to England a new form of Freemasonry before he was initiated into the old. As there is no record of his having returned to England again, it is equally unlikely that he could have done so after his famed Oration, although that would seem the most likely time for him to have done so. In fact, there is no

evidence that Ramsay ever took part in Freemasonry again between his Oration of 1736-1737 and his death, six years later in 1743. [27]

Ramsay's Legacy

LIKE other Masonic authors before him, Ramsay invented a history of Freemasonry; however, Ramsay's history – tailored to the French aristocracy as it was – provided the firewood for the bonfire of chivalric degrees, which arose in the years after his famed Oration. Although he did not create the high degrees of Freemasonry – more especially the ones that bear his name – he none the less played an important role by laying the groundwork for their creation. Writing in his *A New Encyclopaedia of Freemasonry*, Arthur Edward Waite spoke of the importance of Ramsay's contribution to high grade Masonry:

'Had there never been a Chevalier Ramsay, or had he written the Travels of Cyrus and not pronounced an Oration, the developments of Ritual beyond Craft Masonry must have assumed other forms. As it is, we have a Scottish Rite, now regnant everywhere, and an Éccosais Régime in Switzerland. We have also Grades by the score, even to the fourscore and a hundred, which are of this, that and the other, but all carrying the too familiar prefix. In a few sentences of a speech, the illustrious son of a baker, who became – under the auspices of the Catholic religion – a Knight of the Order of St Lazarus, created as by magic, and knowing nothing of his power as a wizard, all High Grade Masonry, all its Éccosais systems and all the glory of Mother Kilwinning. The historical Lodge of Kilwinning is an old Lodge, with an old record, an old story to tell: it would have been not less obscure than Mary's Chapel in continental Masonry, if the Oration had not converted it into a wilderness of emblematic building "withdrawn into a wondrous depth" of splendour. We should have had Masonic developments beyond the Craft because not all of them are referable to the Wand of Ramsay, but we should not have had the shining panoplies of chivalrous Grades: he is progenitor of all the cohorts. And Scottish Masonry is old, as age goes in Masonry: it would have held its honourable and important place among us, had Ramsay followed contentedly his father's trade in Ayrshire; but there would have been no Éccosais Masonry – a thing of beauty and of wonder in some of its developments, but of vanity and hollow pretence in others.'[28]

To further understand the development of the Templar Orders in Freemasonry, we will turn our attentions to some of the degrees to which Waite referred and to some of the Templar myths that they created.

References for Chapter 6

1. *A Biographical Sketch of the Chevalier Andrew Michael Ramsay*, McGregor, Martin I. Research Lodge of Southland No. 415. 14 August 2007. 28 January 2008.

www.freemasons-freemasonry.com/ramsay_biography_oration.html

2. Ibid.

3. Ibid.

4. Ibid.

5. Ibid.

6. Ibid.

7. Ibid.

8. Ibid.

9. Ibid.

10. Quoted in ibid.

11. Quoted in ibid.

12. Quoted in Ibid. Quoted in Kahler, Lisa. 'Andrew Michael Ramsay and His Masonic Oration.' *Heredom: Transactions of the Scottish Rite Research Society Volume 1*. Washington: Scottish Rite Research Society, 1992.

13. McGregor. Op. cit.

14. 'In Eminenti.' Papal Encyclicals Online. 28 April 1738. 28 Jan 2008. www.papalencyclicals.net/Clem12/c15inemengl.htm.

15. McGregor. Op. cit.

16. Ibid.

17. Ibid.

18. McGregor. Op. cit. Kahler. Op. cit.

19. Kahler. Op. cit.

20. McGregor. Op. cit. Kahler. Op. cit.

21. Ibid.

22. Kahler. Op. cit.

23. Quoted in Kahler. Op. cit. Quoted in McGregor. Op. cit.

24. Moore, Charles W. *The Freemasons' Monthly Magazine Volume XX*. Boston: Hugh H. Tuttle, 1861. p.372.

25. Bernheim, Alain. 'Ramsay and His Discours Revisited.' *Pietre Stones Review of Freemasonry*. 28 January 2008.

www.freemasons-freemasonry.com/bernheim_ramsay03.html

26. Quoted in Bernheim. Op. cit.

27. McGregor. Op. cit.

28. *A New Encyclopaedia of Freemasonry*: Waite, Arthur E., New York: University Books, 1996, pp.208-209.

Godfrey
de Bouillon

Bridging the Gap

'But it is one thing to write as a poet, another to write as a historian; the poet may describe or sing things, not as they were, but as they ought to have been; but the historian has to write them down, not as they ought to have been, but as they were, without adding anything to the truth or taking anything from it.'

Cervantes, *Don Quixote*

The French author Beranger claimed that the order of Freemasonry was instituted by Godfrey de Bouillon in Palestine in 1330, after the defeat of the Christian armies. Of course, de Bouillon had died in AD1100, shortly after the Christian capture of Jerusalem.
Author's collection

ALTHOUGH Claude Antoine Thory claimed that Ramsay brought the Templar degree to England in 1728 (a myth that has long been perpetuated), the fact remains that there is no trace of chivalric degrees in Freemasonry prior to Ramsay's Oration. That being said, there were certainly many non-Masonic chivalric orders in existence at the time. The Knights of Malta, Knights of the Holy Sepulchre and Knights of St Lazarus, being bestowed by the Roman Catholic Church and the Order of Christ, under the Portuguese crown. [1] However, even when Freemasons appropriated their names, the rituals they crafted bore little resemblance to those of the Orders whose names they mimicked. There were of course some similarities. For example, the Military Order of the Hospitallers of the Holy Sepulchre of Jerusalem required of its adherents a vow to protect the Church of God and upon being knighted, the member was 'made, created and constituted, now and forever', [2] words that will be familiar to many Masonic Knights Templar. Additionally, the Templars of old required that members of the Order – at least in so far as the white-mantled knights were concerned – were nobly born. This requirement was, at least initially, a prerequisite for admission into the Rite of Strict Observance, an order we will look at in due course. [3]

It may seem somewhat of a mystery that Masonic chivalry should revolve around a Templar wheel when Ramsay clearly identified their rivals, the Knights of St John, as being the link between the compasses and the cross. It is important to understand, however, the role the Templar played in the minds of eighteenth century Europeans. While it is certainly true that the Hospitallers had played a vital role in the crusades and continued to play an important role in matters of war, the Templars had the benefit of a far more mysterious legacy. This legacy made them a suitable candidate for Masonic usage. The mystery of the Templars was amplified in many popular works on the order published about their trials and tribulations – both figurative and literal – between 1685 and the mid-eighteenth century. Waite, in describing the mindset of the age, said:

'Advanced persons were ceasing to believe in the priest but were disposed to believe in the sorcerer, and the Templars had been accused of magic, of worshipping a strange idol, the last suggestion for some obscure reason being not altogether indifferent to many who had slipped the anchor of faith in God. Beyond these frivolities and the foolish minds that cherished them, there were other persons who were neither in the school of a rather cheap infidelity nor in that of common superstition, but who looked seriously for light to the East and for its imagined traditional wisdom handed down from past ages.' [4]

It was Waite's belief that many were drawn to the Templar degrees because it was believed that the Templars of old had discovered secret knowledge unavailable in the west. This lust for secret knowledge, combined with the appeal of an Order who, despite persecution and suppression, survived for centuries, made a combination that was appealing to eighteenth century Freemasons. It is interesting to note that before Ramsay's Oration, there were no theories of Templar perpetuation. Quite simply, in the eyes of seventeenth and early eighteenth century writers, the Order was created in Jerusalem, successful in its growth and battles, persecuted at its end by a greedy king and ultimately destroyed – in that precise order. And while opinion may have varied widely as to the justness of those events, no author suggested that the Templars of old continued in secret after the suppression. However, after Ramsay's Oration we see the emergence of Templar survival theories in the legends of the chivalric orders that followed.

Tilting at Windmills

ALTHOUGH we looked at many of the claims connecting Freemasonry to the time of the crusades in Chapter 1, it might be worth looking at another, written by the French Masonic author Beranger, to have a clearer picture of the myth:

'The Order of Masonry was instituted by Godfrey de Bouillon, in Palestine, in 1330, after the defeat of the Christian armies, and was communicated only to a few French Masons, some time afterwards, as a reward for the services which they had rendered to the English and Scottish Knights. From these latter true Masonry is derived. Their Mother Lodge is situated on the mountain of Heredom, where the first Lodge in Europe was held, which still exists in all its splendour. The Council General is always held here, and it is the seat of the Sovereign Grand Master for the time being. This mountain is situated between the West and the North of Scotland, sixty miles from Edinburgh.

'There are other secrets in Masonry which were never known among the French, and which have no relation to the Apprentice, Fellowcraft and Master Degrees, which were constructed for the general class of Masons. The high degrees, which developed the true design of Masonry and its true secrets, have never been known to them.

'The Saracens having obtained possession of the holy places in Palestine, where all the mysteries of the Order were practised, made use of them

for the most profane purposes. The Christians then leagued together to conquer this beautiful country, and to drive these barbarians from the land. They succeeded in obtaining a footing on these shores under the protection of the numerous armies of the Crusaders, which had been sent there by the Christian princes. The losses which they subsequently experienced put an end to the Christian power, and the Crusaders who remained were subjected to the persecutions of the Saracens, who massacred all who publicly proclaimed the Christian faith. This induced Godfrey de Bouillon, toward the end of the thirteenth century, to conceal the mysteries of religion under the veil of figures, emblems and allegories.

'Hence the Christians selected the Temple of Solomon because it had so close a relation to the Christian Church, of which its holiness and its magnificence made it the true symbol. So the Christians concealed the Mystery of the building up of the Church under that of the construction of the Temple, and gave themselves the title of Masons, Architects, or Builders; they were occupied in building the faith. They assembled under the pretext of making plans of architecture to practice the faith of their religion with all the emblems and allegories that Masonry could furnish, and thus protect themselves from cruelty of the Saracens.

'As the mysteries of Masonry were in their principles, and still are, only those of the Christian religion, they were extremely scrupulous to confide this important secret only to those whose discretion had been tried, and who had been found worthy. For this purpose they fabricated degrees as a test of those in whom they wished to confide, and they gave them at first only the symbolic secrets of Hiram, on which all the mysteries of Blue Masonry is founded, and which is, in fact, the only secret of that Order which has no relation to true Masonry. They explained nothing else to them as they were afraid of being betrayed, and they conferred these degrees as a proper means of recognising each other, surrounded as they were by barbarians. To succeed more effectually in this they made use of different signs and words for each degree, so as not only to distinguish themselves from the profane Saracens, but to designate the different degrees. These they fixed at the number of seven, the imitation of the Grand Architect who built the Universe in six days and rested on the seventh; and, also, because Solomon was seven years in constructing the Temple, which they had selected as the figurative basis of Masonry. Under the name of Hiram they gave a false application to the Masters and developed the true secret of Masonry only to the higher degrees.' [5]

Although the early Masonic writers, in connecting Freemasonry to the time of the crusades, all followed similar themes and ideas, Templar Masonry actually evolved into several different theories, each as erroneous as the next. Even more have been added to the pot in recent years, creating a veritable stew of incredulity; however, for the purpose of the present discussion, we will confine ourselves to four principal ones:

1. The theory that Freemasonry descended from the Templars who joined the Order of Christ in Portugal.

2. The theory that Jacques de Molay, while in prison in France, gave a charter to John Mark Larmenius proclaiming him de Molay's successor.

3. The theory that the Templars joined forces with Robert the Bruce and participated in the Battle of Bannockburn.

4. The theory that a group of knights, under Pierre d'Aumont, escaped the persecutions in France and fled to Scotland where they established Freemasonry.

The Order of Christ Theory

ONE OF the lesser-known Templar theories is that embraced in Scandinavian countries, which seeks to draw an origin for Freemasonry from the Order of Christ in Portugal. This Order was a legitimate Order of knighthood created by King Denis II after the Templars had been suppressed in France and was officially sanctioned by Pope John XXII on 15 March 1319 [6] through the bull Ad ea ex quibus. Another papal bull, Ad Providam (issued by Clement V on 2 May 1312) declared that Templar properties throughout Christendom were to be turned over to the Hospitallers; however, King Denis' response was that the Templar properties in Portugal never truly belonged to the Templars, but were granted to them for their usage. As such, the king took possession of them in the name of the Portuguese crown.

While it is certainly true that original Templars formed an integral part of this new Order, it is beyond all credible belief that the Templars taught their Portuguese counterparts the secrets and mysteries of Freemasonry. Notwithstanding the fact that the Templars were not practitioners of Freemasonry, those who subscribe to the Portuguese connection claim that the

The rotunda chapel of the Convento de Cristo in Tomar, Portugal, was constructed in the mid-twelfth century and passed to the Order of Christ, after the Templars were dissolved in 1312. IStockphoto.com Mel Bedggood

Order was active in the construction of castles and churches. As such, it is possible that the masons employed by the Order embraced some elements of their ceremonies, which were open to the public. [7] Regardless of the unlikelihood of this theory William Mosley Brown, in his *Highlights of Templar History* (published by the Grand Encampment of the United States in 1944) claimed that there was a strong belief among the founders of the *Ordre du Temple* that the Portuguese Order was in possession of Templar secrets. According to Brown, Philip, Duke of Orleans sent two Frenchmen to Portugal in search of the secrets sometime after 1705, but they were arrested before obtaining them. [8] However, it would be many years later in 1804 that the *Ordre du Temple* would seek recognition from the Order of Christ, a recognition that was ignored. [9]

There is another Templar perpetuation myth, which formed the traditional history of the Master of the Temple Degree, the eighth of the Swedish Rite series. In this legend, the rituals and treasures of the Templars were revealed to de Molay's nephew, a man named Beaujeu, just prior to the Grand Master's death. Beaujeu, together with nine knights disguised as operative masons, escaped France with de Molay's ashes. After landing in Stockholm, they buried de Molay's earthly remains and went on to create Freemasonry.

The Larmenius Charter

THE LARMENIUS Charter is a document originally in the possession of the aforementioned *Ordre du Temple* and forms the backbone of one of the most popular theories of Templar perpetuation. Although it makes no claims regarding Freemasonry, it has none the less been embraced by a number of Masonic writers over the years including the anonymous author of the Templar Text Book (see Appendix IV) published in 1859 and the Chevalier James Burnes, who clung to it strongly in his *Sketch of the History of the Knights Templar*, published in 1840. [10] Even the great American Masonic author Albert G. Mackey lent it some credit in his *Lexicon of Freemasonry*. [11]

As touched on earlier, this document derives its name from John Mark Larmenius, who the *Ordre du Temple* claim was

The heraldric arms and seal of the Order of the Temple – the group who claimed their Templar legitimacy from the Larmenius Charter. Taken from James Burnes' Sketch of the History of the Knights Templar. *Author's Collection*

the legitimate Grand Master of the Order after de Molay, the martyred Templar leader having bestowed authority to continue the Order in secret under Larmenius. Appended to the document are the signatures of 24 Grand Masters from Larmenius (1313-1324) to Bernard-Raymond Fabre-Palaprat (1804-1838). Although the list of alleged Grand Masters have been reprinted in a number of Masonic books, including the two listed above, the text above the signatures is worth repeating for those unfamiliar with it:

'I, Brother John Mark Larmenius, of Jerusalem, by the grace of God, and the secret decree of the most venerable and holy martyr, the Grand Master of the Soldiery of the Temple (to whom be honour and glory), confirmed by the common council of the brethren, being endowed with the Supreme Grand Mastership of the whole Order of the Temple, to every one who shall see these letters decretal thrice greeting:

'Be it known to all, both present and to come, that the failure of my strength, on account of extreme age, my poverty, and the weight of government being well considered, I, the aforementioned humble Master of the Soldiery of the Temple, have determined, for the greater glory of God and the protection and safety of the Order, the brethren, and the statutes, to resign the Grand Mastership into stronger hands.

'On which account, God helping, and with the consent of a Supreme Convention of Knights, I have conferred, and by this present decree do confer, for life, the authority and prerogatives of Grand Master of the Order of the Temple upon the Eminent Commander and very dear brother, Francis Thomas Theobald Alexandrinus, with the power, according to time and circumstances, of conferring the Grand Mastership of the Order of the Temple and the supreme authority upon another brother, most eminent for the

mobility of his education and talent and decorum of his manners: which is done for the purpose of maintaining a perpetual succession of Grand Masters, an uninterrupted series of successors, and the integrity of the statutes. Nevertheless, I command the Grand Mastership shall not be transmitted without the consent of a general convention of the fellow-soldiers of the Temple, as often as that Supreme Convention desires to be convened; and, matters being thus conducted, the successor shall be elected at the pleasure of the knights.

'But, lest the powers of the supreme office should fall into decay, now and forever let there be four Vicars of the Grand Master, possessing supreme power, eminence and authority over the whole Order, with the reservation of the rights of the grand Master; which Vicars of the Grand Master shall be chosen from among the elders, according to the order of their profession. Which is decreed in accordance with the above-mentioned wish, commended to me and to the brethren by our most venerable and most blessed Master, the martyr, to whom be honour and glory. Amen.
'Finally, in consequence of a decree of a Supreme Convention of the brethren, and by the supreme authority to me committed, I will,

declare, and command that the Scottish Templars, as deserters from the Order, are to be accursed, and that they and the brethren of St John of Jerusalem (upon which may God have mercy), as spoliators of the domains of our soldiery, are now and hereafter to be considered as beyond the pale of the Temple.

'I have therefore established signs, unknown to our false brethren, and not to be known by them, to be orally communicated to our fellow-soldiers, and in which way I have already been pleased to communicate them in the Supreme Convention.

'But these signs are only to be made known after due profession and knightly consecration, according to the statures rites, and usages of the fellow-soldiery of the Temple, transmitted by me to the above named Eminent Commander as they were delivered into my hands by the venerable and most holy martyr, our Grand Master, to whom be honour and glory. Let it be done as I have said. So mote it be. Amen.' [12]

Admiral Sir William Sidney Smith (1764-1840) was another of the famous names connected to the Knights Templar via the Larmenius Charter. Smith was the head of the order started by Bernard Raymond Fabre Palaprat in 1804. This illustration is found in the pages of Chevalier James Burnes' *Sketch of the History of the Knights Templar*. *Author's collection*

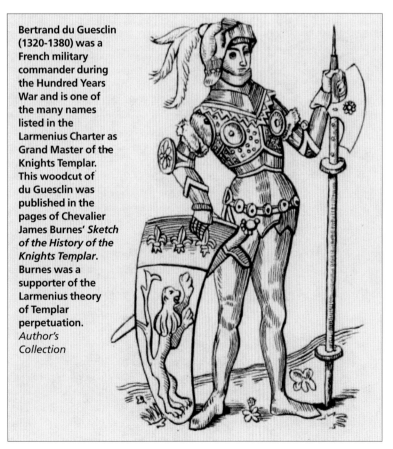

Bertrand du Guesclin (1320-1380) was a French military commander during the Hundred Years War and is one of the many names listed in the Larmenius Charter as Grand Master of the Knights Templar. This woodcut of du Guesclin was published in the pages of Chevalier James Burnes' *Sketch of the History of the Knights Templar*. Burnes was a supporter of the Larmenius theory of Templar perpetuation. *Author's Collection*

the derogatory comments about Scottish Templars may have been an anachronistic commentary on a modern problem, for, by this time, Masonic Templars had embraced a system of Templary whose legends and traditional histories were built upon a connection to Scotland.

The Robert the Bruce Legend

ONE OF the most enduring myths associated with the Templars in Scotland is the notion that the Templars played a prominent role in the Battle of Bannockburn on 24 June 1314 – and the prominence of that date to Freemasons, being the Feast of St John the Baptist, certainly has played no little part in its continuance. Essentially the theory is that the Templars who escaped the persecutions of 1307 fled to Scotland and aligned themselves to Robert the Bruce, who was, at the time, excommunicated by the Catholic Church for the part he had played in the murder of John Comyn at Greyfriars Church in Dumfries. It was these immigrant Templars, who just a few short months after the execution of their Grand Master, assisted the Bruce in routing the English at Bannockburn. Although no credible historian has ever offered the slightest bit of evidence to support the idea, the myth prevails to this day and forms the traditional history of the Royal Order of Scotland – an order the tradition claims was created by the Bruce in gratitude for the Templars' support during his struggles.

The Masonic writer Thory claimed that after the battle the Bruce created the Order of St Andrew of the Thistle. Later the Order of Heredom was added in recognition of the Scottish Masons who had formed a significant contingent in the battle. However, the Order of Knights of St Andrew of the Thistle couldn't have been created by Robert the Bruce in 1314, for it was started by James II more than a century later in 1440. [14] Nor is there any evidence to support the notion that the Templars ever formed a part of the Royal Order of Heredom. [15]

As to the unlikelihood that the Templars took part in the Battle of Bannockburn, the matter was dealt with in my last book, *Nobly Born*, and in intricate detail in Robert Cooper's excellent book, *The Rosslyn Hoax*. However, a single important point here may help to shred the myth. While it is true that the Bruce had been excommunicated, the persecutions of 13 October 1307 were not brought on by the pope, but rather by the King of France. As such, the Bruce's excommunicated status within the Catholic Church would afford the Templars no protection from the king.

Although a vast majority of Masonic scholars have concluded that the Larmenius Charter was a forgery, Waite was uncertain if it had been forged by the Duke of Orleans in 1705 or much later – perhaps by Palaprat. What remains important is that the document contains many historical errors, the least of which is that the Latin used in its construction is not the Latin that would have been common in de Molay's time. Additionally, it seems utterly beyond credulity that de Molay would have been able to summon a Chapter General while shackled in irons, both figuratively and literally. Finally, the document is written, as Brown remarked, in a 'code not unfamiliar to members of York Rite Freemasonry'. [13] As we saw in an earlier chapter on the original Templars, it has been a long-held belief that the Templars' transferred money using a coded cipher; however, the extant examples of such documents belie the notion, as they are penned in Latin.

But perhaps the most interesting aspect of the Larmenius Charter is the writer's commentary on the status of Scottish Templars, who he considers to be 'as beyond the pale of the Temple'. Many who subscribe to the authenticity of this document use the derogatory statements as proof of the validity of the document. However, if the document was created by Palaprat in the early 1800s – when Masonic Templary seems to have been in full swing –

It is worth noting that Anderson made mention of Robert the Bruce in his 1738 *Constitutions*, stating that the Bruce had employed the craft after the Battle of Bannockburn. [16] Although this seems to be the earliest Masonic reference to Robert the Bruce, the legend of the Templars involvement in the battle formed an integral part of the traditional history of the Royal Order of Scotland, formed sometime around 1741 – just a few years after Anderson's reference and Ramsay's Oration.

The d'Aumont Legend

ALTHOUGH the Bannockburn story plays a prominent role in the Templar Freemason mythos, the d'Aumont legend dwarfs it by comparison.

This legend tells that Pierre d'Aumont, the Preceptor of Auvergne, together with a number of knights fled from France to Scotland disguised as operative masons. On their arrival they created a new order to preserve the ancient traditions of their soon to be defunct Order. This new order, adopted the name Franc Maçons – Franc (meaning French and Free) and Maçons in homage to their disguise. Thus, the Franc Maçons became known as the free Masons when the new order later travelled to England. [17]

Disregarding for a moment the silly notion presented in the theory as to the etymology of the term Freemasons, let us unravel the story of d'Aumont, who the theory claims was Preceptor of Auvergne. While it is true that the Preceptor of Auvergne fled the arrests of 13 October 1307, his name was certainly not Pierre d'Aumont; rather, it was Imbert Blanke. Sometime after crossing into England, Blanke was arrested and later went on to play a role in the Templar trials of that country by defending his English Brethren. [18]

Although Blanke was accompanied by a number of brethren, the number of Templars that accompanied his mythical counterpart Pierre d'Aumont is suspiciously Masonic. For in addition to d'Aumont, we find two commanders and five knights. [19] On first reading, this arrangement may not seem like anything particularly noteworthy; however, the following phrase familiar to Freemasons may make things a little clearer:

'Three rule a lodge, five hold a lodge and seven or more make it perfect.'

In this sense, d'Aumont and the two commanders play a parallel in the myth to the Master and his two wardens, while the five knights represent the five masons who hold a lodge. Combined, the group form the seven or more who make it perfect. While this theory could easily be used to provide evidence of a Templar Freemason connection, it is my belief that the reverse is true and that von Hund's d'Aumont legend was carefully crafted to bear a Masonic symbolism. Although the above scenario is speculation on the part of the author, it is not out of the realm of possibilities, for later Masonic traditions connected Masonic symbolism to Templar themes.

In his short work *The Templar Orders in Freemasonry*, Arthur Edward Waite spoke of a ritual he had discovered called Le Chevalier du Temple, which he believed had been created sometime between 1768 and 1789. [20] Although the high degrees in Freemasonry were certainly in operation by this time, the Chevalier du Temple operated within the three Craft degrees. What is particularly unique about this ritual is that it does not paint a Templar perpetuation theory; rather, a number of surviving knights assembled and created Freemasonry to preserve the chivalry that had previously existed in their persecuted Order. The traditional history of the Order claimed that the originators of the secret combine required a period of seven years from its members to ensure that they were worthy. Three were spent as Apprentices, two as Fellowcraft and the final two as Master Masons. The obligation was taken in front of a black tomb representing that of the martyred de Molay. The lessons of the first degree related to the Canons of the Holy Sepulchre, the second to the Hospitallers of St John. The third degree, as would be expected, referred to the Templars, but particularly to the martyrdom of Jacques de Molay, who is the substitute for Hiram Abif. In the final degree, the part of the three ruffians is replaced with Clement V, Philip IV and the Prior of Montfaucon, the latter of whom had betrayed the Order to the king. Perhaps the most interesting aspect of the Master Mason Degree was the dual representation of the letters J.B.M., which Freemasons will recognise as the initials of the two pillars and the Master's word. However, in the rituals of the Chevalier du Temple, the letters stood for the initials of Jacques Burgundus Molay. [21]

Sadly, there is little information on this interesting Templar twist on the Craft rituals outside of the information provided by Waite. Given its late date, it certainly could not have been among the earliest and the lack of information on the Order would seem to indicate that its traditional history never gained the popularity of the d'Aumont legend.

It was Mackey's belief that the Templar Freemason

theories originated with Ramsay's Oration, which, in turn, gave rise to the d'Aumont theory of Templar perpetuation. Let us then close this brief interlude on some of those theories with the words of Mackey on the matter:

'The Chevalier Ramsay was the real author of the doctrine of the Templar origin of Freemasonry, and to him we are really indebted (if the debt have any value) for the D'Aumont legend. The source whence it sprang is tolerably satisfactory evidence of its fictitious character.

The inventive genius of Ramsay, as exhibited in the fabrications of high degrees and Masonic legends, is well known. Nor, unfortunately for his reputation, can it be doubted that in the composition of his legends he cared but little for the support of history. If his genius, his learning, and his zeal had been consecrated, not to the formation of new Masonic systems, but to a profound investigation of the true origin of the Institution, viewed only from an authentic historical point, it is impossible to say what incalculable benefit would have been delved from his researches. The unproductive desert, which for three-fourths of a century spread over the continent, bearing no fruit except fanciful theories, absurd systems, and unnecessary degrees, would have been occupied in all probability by a race of Masonic scholars whose researches would have been directed to the creation of a genuine history, and much of the labours of our modern iconoclasts would have been spared.

'The Masonic scholars of that long period, which began with Ramsay and has hardly yet wholly terminated, assumed for the most part rather the role of poets than of historians. They did not remember the wise saying of Cervantes that the poet may say or sing, not as things have been, but as they ought to have been, while the historian must write of them as they really were, and not as he thinks they ought to have been. And hence we have a mass of traditional rubbish, in which there is a great deal of falsehood with very little truth.

'Of this rubbish is the Legend of Peter d'Aumont and his resuscitation of the Order of Knights Templars in Scotland. Without a particle of historical evidence for its support, it has nevertheless exerted a powerful influence on the Masonic organisation of even the present day. We find its effects looming out in the most important rites and giving a Templar form to many of the high degrees. And it cannot be doubted that the incorporation of Templarism into the modern Masonic system is mainly to be attributed to ideas suggested by this D'Aumont legend.' [22]

The Baron of Templarism

THE D'AUMONT legend was the brainchild of the Rite of Strict Observance, promoted by Karl Gotthelf von Hund in Germany sometime between 1751 and 1754. [23] A decade earlier, a small number of German lodges had begun a practice of giving their Apprentices and Fellowcrafts the names of French Knights. Although the majority of these lodges were in Dresden, von Hund formed one in 1751 on his estate which comprised Unwürde and Kittlitz in the Lusatia, approximately 75 km east of Dresden. [24] It was from the close bonds of these lodges that von Hund's Rite of Strict Observance was created; however, in its early years the Rite was largely a local concern operating on von Hund's estate. [25] It would be another decade and a half before the order developed any wide-spread appeal.

Before looking at the Rite and its evolution, it is important that we address one of the claims made by Thory, which is as erroneous as his claims about Ramsay. It was Thory's contention that von Hund had taken his Templar degrees in the Chapter of Claremont, established by the Chevalier de Bonneville in 1754. However, given that von Hund doesn't seem to have been in Paris after he consecrated a new lodge there on 20 February 1743 and had already become active in his own Templar order by 1751, Thory's chronology does not stack up. Certainly von Hund's own claims were that he was initiated into Templary in 1743 after being introduced to it by Lord Kilmarnock after the two men met in Paris. It was claimed that von Hund had been initiated by a man referred to as the Knight of the Red Feather, who was supposed to have been none other than Charles Edward Stuart, the Young Pretender. This was the same man whom Ramsay had attempted to tutor some years prior.

The Rite of Strict Observance

IT HAS been claimed that the rite originated with C. G. Marschall von Bieberstein, who had founded two of the lodges, referred to earlier, that gave their initiates the names of French Knights. After von Bieberstein died in 1750, von Hund took over the embryonic rite. [26]

Under von Hund, the rite consisted of three degrees grafted onto those of the craft lodges: Apprentice, Fellowcraft, Master Mason, Scottish Master, Novice and Knight Templar. [27] The degree of Scottish Master concerned itself with preserving the lost word of Freemasonry which had been cut on a plate of pure metal, placed in a secure place and discovered once again many centuries later. This was, of course, nothing new and belonged to the Ecossais degrees that sprung up shortly after Ramsay's Oration. [28] The last two in the system were related to the Templars and concerned themselves with von Hund's d'Aumont legend. One of the most peculiar aspects of the Rite of Strict Observance was the obligation of its adherents to blindly obey the directives of the unknown superiors who ruled the order. These *Superiores Incogniti*, of course, issued their orders through von Hund. As mentioned earlier, it has been supposed that the Young Pretender was in fact the head of the order and the Knight of the Red Feather who had initiated von Hund; however, the lack of evidence would seem to indicate that this, too, is part of the mythos of the rite.

Sometime in 1762 a man going by the name Johnson appeared in Jena, where a Chapter of Clermont was working the Strict Observance system, claiming that he had authorisation from the Sovereign Chapter in Scotland to impart the true secrets of Freemasonry and, in so doing, straighten out the German lodges. Johnson, who was really named Leucht, had got hold of some Masonic papers on the craft and high degrees and convinced a number of Masons that he had obtained the necessary secrets to create the philosopher's stone, through which they could all become rich. [29] However, Johnson seems to be the only one who profited from his bogus claims. Although he bilked many German Freemasons out of their hard-earned money, it was eventually realised that he was a fraud and Johnson wound up dying in prison. Despite having gone along with Johnson's claims, von Hund and his rite did not seem to suffer greatly for it.

A decade later, in 1772, another man appeared with another angle on the rite. In that year a Lutheran theologian named Johann August Starck, who had created a group called the Clerical Knights Templar approached von Hund claiming that his order was superior. Starck's angle was that there existed among

Karl Gotthelf von Hund was instrumental in advancing the Rite of Strict Observance in Germany.
Author's collection

First, Second, Third Emblems of the entered Apprentice, Fellowcraft and Master Mason Degrees of the Rite of Strict Observance. Ferdinand Runkel, *Geschichte der Freimaurerei in Deutschland*, 3 vols. (Berlin: Verlag von Reimer Hobbing, 1932).
Courtesy of the Scottish Rite Research Society

the Templars of old a clerical branch of the Order who were in possession of the real occult secrets of the Templars. [30] Although the Clerical Knights Templar merged with von Hund's Rite of Strict Observance, the relationship was not long lasting and came to an end in 1778. [31] The mystical mumbo jumbo of the previous years must have caused some confusion in the temple, for the rite held a convention at Brunswick that ran from 23 May until 6 July 1775. [32] Despite its length, nothing seems to have come of it other than the members were more confused than before. On 15 August 1776, another convention was held, this time at Wiesbaden. Burton E. Bennett in his two-part article on the Rite of Strict Observance, published in the September and October 1926 issues of *The Builder* claimed that the convention had been suggested by a Baron von Gugumos, who had been at the previous convention in Brunswick. [33] Von Gugumos had claimed that the Strict Observance possessed none of the mystical secrets its members were looking for; rather these were possessed only by the true grand Master of the Order, the Patriarch of the Greek Church of Cyprus. Von Gugumos had promised the princes who were embers of the order that he could convince the patriarch to disclose the mysteries. As might be expected of superstitious people, many attended the convention and Gugumos

was only too happy to reinitiate the nobility into the real order and pocket a bit of cash from the sale of new regalia and paraphernalia. However, there were some who suspected he was a fraud; perhaps the Johnson episode had taught them a lesson. Whatever their motivations for doubting von Gugumos, they demanded that he perform the feats of magic he claimed to understand. As Bennett tells the story, Gugumos said he could only do so if they built a special shrine and if he travelled to Cyprus to procure the necessary altars and wands. As might be suspected, Gugumos left, but never returned.

Von Hund died on 28 October 1776, two months after the convention of Wiesbaden. On 28 April of the following year, representatives from the Strict Observance and the Grand Lodge of Sweden met together to promote the Duke of Sudermania, who was already Grand Master in Sweden to the position of Deputy Grand Master of the rite. To this end, a convention was held from 28 July to 27 August 1778 and the Duke was elected and installed. It was at this time that Starck's clerics withdrew from the Rite of Strict Observance. The Duke later resigned in 1780 and two years later the closing days of the Strict Observance began. From mid-July 1782 until the beginning of September 1783 a Convent of the Rite was held at Wilhelmsbad, during which it was resolved that the Freemasons were not the heirs and successors of the Templars of old, and soon after the rite came to an end.

However, it did not die out entirely, as it had become absorbed into the Rectified Rite. This rite was created in 1774 by Jean-Baptiste Willermoz, who had been initiated into the Rite of Strict Observance in 1773. [34] The rituals of the Rectified Scottish Rite, although built from the crude rituals of von Hund's Rite of Strict Observance, developed into eight degrees between 1775 and 1809. In addition to the three degrees of Craft Masonry, the rite consisted of Scottish Master, Esquire Novice, Knights Beneficent of the Holy City, Professed and Grand Professed. The rite, which like Masonic Templary requires its members to be Christian, is practised in France, Belgium and Switzerland to this day; however, the last two of its degrees are no longer worked in many lodges. [35]

Having examined the history of the Templars of old and their connection to Freemasonry, through poetic licence and historical fact, let us now turn our attention to how Templary evolved in the United Kingdom, the United States and beyond.

References for Chapter 7

1. *The Templar Orders in Freemasonry*, Waite, Arthur E. Morinville, Stephen A. Dafoe, 2006. pp.5-6.

2. Ibid. p.6.

3. Ibid. p.6.

4. Ibid. pp.7-8.

5. Quoted in Bennett, Burton E. 'The Rite of Strict Observance'. *The Builder* September-October 1926.

6. Brown, William M. *Highlights of Templar History*. Greenfield: Wm. Mitchell Printing Co., 1944. p.47.

7. Ibid. p.50.

8. Ibid. p.50.

9. Waite, Arthur E. *A New Encyclopaedia of Freemasonry*. New York: University Books, 1996. p.213.

10. Burnes, James. *Sketch of the History of the Knights Templars*. Edinburgh: Wm. Blackwood & Sons, 1840. pp.36-37. Burnes also devotes an appendix to the Latin version of the charter.

11. Mackey, Albert G. *Lexicon of Freemasonry*. Philadelphia: Barnes and Noble Books, 2004. pp.259-261.

12. Quoted in Brown. Op. cit. pp.51-52.

13. Ibid. p.51.

14. Mackey, Albert G. 'The Story of the Scottish Templars.' *The History of Freemasonry*. New York: Gramercy Books, 1996. p.259.

15. Ibid. p.259.

16. *The Rosslyn Hoax*, Cooper, Robert, London, Lewis Masonic, 2006, p.72.

17. Mackey. Op. cit. p.260.

18. *The Trial of the Templars*: Barber, Malcolm, Cambridge, Cambridge UP, 1996. p.46.

19. Mackey. Op. cit. p.260.

20. Waite, Arthur E. *The Templar Orders in Freemasonry*. Morinville, 2006. p.13.

21. Ibid. pp.14-16.

22. Mackey. Op. cit. pp.261-262.

23. Waite, Arthur E. *The Templar Orders in Freemasonry*. Morinville, 2006. p.9.

24. Bernheim, Alain, and Arturo De Hoyos. 'Introduction to the Rituals of the Rite of Strict Observance.' *Heredom: Transactions of the Scottish Rite Research Society Volume 14*. Washington: Scottish Rite Research Society, 2006, 47-104. p.49.

25. Ibid. p.57.

26. Bennett. Op. cit.

27. Bogdan, Henrik. 'An Introduction to the Higher Degrees of Freemasonry.' *Heredom: Transactions of the Scottish Rite Research Society Volume 14*. Washington: Scottish Rite Research Society, 2006. 9-46. pp.10-11.

28. Bennett. Op. cit.

29. Ibid.

30. Waite, Arthur E. *The Templar Orders in Freemasonry*. Morinville, 2006. p.20.

31. Bogdan. Op. cit. p.11.

32. Bennett. Op. cit.

33. Ibid.

34. Bogdan. Op. cit. p.11.

35. Ibid. p.13.

His Royal Highness, Albert Edward, Prince of Wales,
served as Grand Master of the Convent General from 1872-1895
and as patron of the Order until his death in 1910.
Drawn, lithographed and published by Edward J. Harty, 1875.

Templarism in the United Kingdom

'Modern Templary of the Empire can only be considered an imitation of the ancient Order, rather as appropriated than inherited, being a Christian association of Freemasons, who represent the traditions of the religious and military Orders of the Crusades, following as nearly as practicable their principles and customs, and strictly adhering to their teachings and Trinitarian doctrine.' [1]

Col William James Bury MacLeod Moore,
Grand Master of Canadian Templars *ad vitam*

As we have seen over the course of the previous chapters, the so-called high degrees of Freemasonry were created, in part, out of a desire to reunite the compasses of Freemasonry with the cross of Christianity. Anderson's *Constitutions of the Free Masons* published in 1723 and revised in 1738 had effectively opened the Craft's doors to men of other faiths and there existed a desire to return Freemasonry to its Christian roots. But regardless of religious faith, the men who joined the Craft in Britain were content to belong to a society of men who traced their origins back to the stone masons who built the Tower of Babel and Solomon's Temple. However, when Freemasonry was introduced on the Continent of Europe it was embraced by educated men of leisure who were not satisfied with belonging to an Order descended – according to legend – from common stone workers. As such, Ramsay in his Oration had offered a legend that would appeal to the bourgeoisie; one that connected the Craft not with rough-handed stone workers, but with the nobly born knights of the Crusades. This theory was embellished by von Hund and others through the Rite of Strict Observance to specifically identify the Knights Templar as the progenitors of Freemasonry.

Although the Great Masonic Congress held at Wilhelmsbad in 1782 had effectively closed the door on one chapter of the history of Masonic Templarism by declaring the story of a connection between the Templars of old and their modern Masonic counterparts a myth, it opened the door on a new era of Masonic Templarism. On the Continent, the dying embers of the Rite of Strict Observance gave rise to the Rectified Rite; [2] however, in Britain Templary took a different form. Although it is almost certain that the British regimental lodges would have worked with lodges under the Strict Observance before its demise, [3] there seems to be no major influence of that system upon the English working.

Early Traces of Templary in England

The earliest extant record mentioning the Templar degree in England comes not from a Masonic Lodge, but rather a Royal Arch Chapter. In the minutes of the Chapter of Friendship at Portsmouth dated 21 October 1778, it is mentioned that Thomas Dunkerley had advised the chapter that they were permitted to make Knight Templars if they so desired. [4] However, the degree was certainly known in Britain prior to this date. In his history of British Templary, Col William James Bury MacLeod Moore claimed that 'Templarism was first introduced into the British Empire in the Masonic lodges known as the "Ancients" under the Duke of Atholl who was also Grand Master of Scotland…'. [5] From 1751 until 1813 there was a bitter rivalry between two of the Grand Lodges operating in England, the Antients and the Moderns, the latter of which was actually the older of the two, having been formed in 1717. While the Moderns adhered to a three-degree system, the Grand

The Grand Conclave of 1791

On 24 June of that year a Grand Conclave was held in London and Thomas Dunkerley, who had granted permission to the Portsmouth Chapter to confer the Templar degree in 1778, was elected Grand Master. The new body was given the long-winded title Grand Elect-Knights Templar Kadosh and Holy Sepulchre of St John of Jerusalem, Palestine, Rhodes and Malta. [8] At the inaugural conclave, a set of statutes was drafted and adopted in the preamble of which we read of the motivating factor behind the movement:

'The flourishing state of Symbolic MASONRY, under the protection of his Royal Highness the PRINCE OF WALES, Grand Master; and the great increase of Royal Arch Chapters, patronised by his Royal Highness the DUKE OF CLARENCE; having animated the masonic KNIGHTS TEMPLARS of ST. JOHN OF JERUSALEM, &c. with a desire to revive their ancient, royal, exalted, Religious and military order; they confederated and unanimously selected their brother and knight companion, Thomas Dunkerley, of Hampton Court Palace, in the county of Middlesex, Grand Master of the confraternity, under the patronage of his Royal Highness PRINCE EDWARD, T.H.E.' [9]

This was not the first time that Dunkerley had presided over a Templar body in England. On 1 January of that year he had assumed the Grand Mastership of the Baldwyn Encampment at Bristol, having taken over from the encampment's previous Grand Master Joshua Springer. [10] Before examining the advancement of Templar Masonry in England under Dunkerley's administration and beyond, we should take a moment to understand a bit about the man and the encampment that he first presided over.

The First Grand Master

Thomas Dunkerley was born on 24 October 1724, [11] the illegitimate son of King George II, a fact he did not become aware of until after the death of his mother. [12]

In 1754, at the age of thirty, Dunkerley was initiated into the Craft in Lodge No. 31, which at that time met at the Three Tuns in Portsmouth [13] and received the Royal Arch degree in the same year and city. He must have been a competent Freemason, for within six years of his initiation, Dunkerley was granted a patent to inspect the condition of the craft wherever he happened to travel. By vocation,

Thomas Dunkerley was the Grand Master of the Knights Templar from 1791-1795. *Portrait in oils by Thomas Beach, courtesy of Loyal Lodge No. 251, Barnstaple.*

Lodge of the Antients generally permitted its lodges to confer other degrees outside those of Apprentice, Fellowcraft and Master Mason – Royal Arch, Knight Templar and Rose Croix included. [6] However, the Antients were not the only English Grand Lodge that allowed the conferral of the degree. The Grand Lodge of All England at York, another of the eighteenth century rivals and one that was formed in 1725, is known to have conferred the degree in its lodges in 1779 and may have done so before this date. [7]

But all of these examples of the presence of a Templar ceremony are within the confines of a Masonic Lodge or Royal Arch Chapter. However vague the development of Chivalric Masonry may have been over the years following 1778, when it is first referenced in the minutes of the Chapter of Friendship at Portsmouth, the picture becomes substantially clearer from 1791 onwards.

Dunkerley was a navy man, having joined at the age of ten. [14] Over a span of two-and-a-half decades, he rose to the rank of gunner and schoolmaster, but ascended no higher. It was through his early life as a sailor that Dunkerley arrived in Canada where he became Quebec's first Provincial Grand Master in 1760. [15] Seven years later Dunkerley received an appointment as Provincial Grand Master for Hampshire. This was in 1767, the same year that Dunkerley's royal parentage was made known to King George III, the grandson of Dunkerley's natural father. [16] As a result, Dunkerley was granted a pension and given a suite of apartments at Hampton Court Palace. In 1770, perhaps as a result of his new social status, Dunkerley began a study of law and was called to the bar in 1774. However, he does not seem to have done much in the legal profession, [17] preferring perhaps his involvement in Freemasonry. Dunkerley certainly was an active Freemason, for in 1793, he was presiding over no fewer than eight craft provinces and eighteen for the Royal Arch. [18]

Baldwyn Encampment – The Templars of Time Immemorial

GIVEN Dunkerley's vast experience in Freemasonry, it should come as no surprise that he should ascend to the Grand Mastership of England's oldest Templar body.

The origin of Baldwyn encampment is somewhat hard to pin down. Certainly, it has been said that it has existed since time immemorial, and enjoys that status among English Templary to this day. However, the term is often confusing to those outside the Craft, as well as to a goodly majority of the initiated. Generally speaking, the term simply means that the Masonic body received its warrant or existed prior to the formation of the governing Grand Body. This is certainly true with respect to Baldwyn, and, as such, it is permitted to confer ceremonies and maintain observances that those who followed the Grand Body do not enjoy.

Over the years it has been supposed that this encampment traced its lineage to the time of the original Templars; [19] however, it is unlikely that any member of the body today would subscribe to that belief. [20] Rather, Baldwyn can trace its lineage back to 1780, and perhaps even as early as 1772, through two documents. The first is a Charter of Compact dated 20 December 1780, [21] while the second is a reference in a Bristol newspaper dated 25 January 1772. [22] Frederick Smyth in his excellent history of

the Grand Priory of England argued that the newspaper reference, which indicated that a young recruiting party had spent 'the evening under the Rose with the Knights Templar,' does not offer proof that any formal Masonic meeting took place. [23] It was Smyth's belief that it was highly unlikely that junior military officers would have been likely candidates for the chivalric degrees. As we will see in the next chapter on Templarism in the United States, a similar situation existed in Boston with respect to social standing.

Regardless of which date is correct for the formation of Baldwyn Encampment, one of the most striking features about the body with respect to its approach to Templarism is that it was and is the practitioner of a Rite of Seven Degrees, although in reality nine:

The Craft Degrees, preferably taken in a Bristol Lodge
The Royal Arch, preferably taken in a Bristol Chapter
Knights of the Nine Elected Masters
Scots Knights Grand Architect
Knights of the East, Sword and the Eagle
Knights of St John of Jerusalem, Palestine, Rhodes and Malta, and Knights Templar
Knights of the Rose Croix of Mount Carmel [24]

Although it may seem peculiar to North American Masons – particularly those of the Ancient and Accepted Scottish Rite – to see the Rose Croix Degree, the 18th degree of that Rite, being practised as a part of Templar Masonry, it is important to understand that prior to 1845, when the Supreme Council was established in England, the degree was a common part of the Templar system in England. In fact, the degrees of Rose Croix of Heredom and Kadosh followed that of the Temple in the ritual hierarchy. MacLeod Moore said the Templar degree at that time stuck to actual history of the Order, while that of Rose Croix taught the truths of the Christian faith; the Kadosh degree, the final in the series, was designed to remind initiates of the martyrdom of Jacques de Molay and the persecution of the Templars of old. [25]

It was under this system of degrees that Dunkerley served as Grand Master and the Order seems to have thrived under his administration. Unfortunately, the Masonic historian has been robbed of many of the precise details regarding Dunkerley's brief term as Grand Master, as many of the records of his time were destroyed in a house fire in 1820. [26] However, what remains in the various scattered remnants of letters would seem to indicate that he was as studious in his dedication to Templary as he was to his Capitular and Craft responsibilities. Dunkerley's Grand Mastership was brief; he died in 1795 at the age of seventy-one, having served as head of the Order for just four years.

Dunkerley was succeeded by Thomas Boothby Parkyns, the first Lord Rancliffe, a man who seems to have shown little interest in Freemasonry, despite having been granted some prominent positions within the Craft. In 1783, he was serving as Provincial Grand Master for Nottinghamshire, and within six years was also responsible for three other Masonic provinces. Additionally, Rancliffe served variously as Royal Arch Grand Superintendent for Leicestershire and Rutland, Grand Zerubbabel of the Royal Arch and Grand Commander of the Society of Antient Masons of the Diluvian Order or Royal Ark and Mark Mariners, a position also previously held by Dunkerley. [27] As Grand Master of the Templars, Rancliffe held but two meetings of the Grand body during his first year of office and thereafter but one meeting per year. Like Dunkerley before him, Lord Rancliffe's term of office was short-lived, as he died in 1800 at the age of 45.

Following Rancliffe's death, the degrees fell into abeyance and while part of this may be ascribed to Rancliffe's inattention to the Order he was elected to preside over or, as MacLeod Moore believed, the dispersion and death of many of the older members in England and Wales, [28] it is important to understand that there was another important contributing factor.

In 1799, the year prior to Rancliffe's death, Britain introduced the Unlawful Societies Act. This legislation was brought forth by Henry Thornton, the Member of Parliament for Southwark, [29] a wealthy banker and evangelical philanthropist. Although the Act of Parliament was a reaction to the events of the French Revolution, it none the less affected Freemasonry, an institution believed by the Abbé Barruel to have been directly responsible for the same. On the day the bill was to receive its second reading, the Prime Minister met at Downing Street with some rather prominent Masons of the day. Chief among them was the Lord Moira, the Acting Grand Master of the Grand Lodge of England and the Duke of Atholl, Grand Master of the Antients; a man who was also Past Grand Master of Scotland. [30] Because the proposed act disallowed the use of secret oaths in societies and required initiations to be conducted in a public meeting,

Freemasonry was put in a rather precarious position in terms of its continued existence. Fortunately, Lord Moira and the Duke of Atholl were able to convince the Prime Minister that the Craft was not a seditious society and, after some concessions on both sides of the fence, the Freemasons were exempted from the act [31] – or so they had hoped. When the bill came before the House of Lords in June of 1799, further concessions were made and because of the hasty manner in which the amendments were passed, only lodges that existed prior to the legislation were exempt. [32] As such, Grand Lodges could not issue warrants for new lodges; however, they were able to get around the situation by giving new lodges the warrant and number of pre-existing lodges. [33]

Although the general state of conservatism brought about by the Unlawful Societies Act certainly played a part in preventing Templary from gaining widespread acceptance among Freemasons, it would seem that the Grand Conclave was dormant prior to its passing.

The Grand Conclave of 1805

IN 1804, Robert Gill, the Deputy Grand Master of the Order, who took on the affairs of Templary in England after the death of Rancliffe, wrote a letter to the encampments stating that 'the Grand Conclave has been dormant for at least six years, to the great detriment of the Order and the Brethren Sir Knights Companions in general'. [34]

Gill's letter, dated 23 October 1804, went on to inform the Templars that Encampment No. 20, then meeting in London, intended to form another Grand Conclave. [35] On 14 February 1805, Gill wrote to the encampments once again, informing them that a Charter of Compact had been created and that the Duke of Kent, who had previously served as Grand Patron during Dunkerley's administration, consented to be elected to the position of Supreme Grand Master of the Order. [36]

Although the Order was in many respects revived from the ashes, the staturtes drafted during Dunkerley's term were nowhere to be found, perhaps owing to the period of abeyance or Rancliffe's inattentive administration. However, when a copy was later discovered the Duke of Kent returned to his former position as Grand Patron and approved of the election of Judge Waller Rodwell Wright as Grand Master. [37]

In 1809, a Charter of Constitution was drafted and approved, which revoked the Charter of Compact of 1805. This was not merely a shuffling of papers within Masonic Templarism, for the new Charter of Constitution stated that the original statutes of 1791 had been rediscovered and that the Charter and Constitutions issued in 1804 were in 'many respects inconsistent and repugnant to such Antient Constitutions and usages…'. [38]

Although the rise, demise and rebirth of English Templary had spanned a period of but 18 years, and was certainly within the living memory of its current members, the discovery and acceptance of the original statutes seemed to breathe new life into the Order. Under Waller Rodwell Wright's administration, which lasted until 1812 when he resigned to take on a judicial appointment in the Mediterranean, [39] the roll of the Grand Conclave expanded to include 48 encampments [40] – a considerable expansion from the seven who united to form the first Grand Conclave in 1791. However, two years before resigning his post in favour of his successor, the Duke of Sussex, there was a great concern among English Templars that chapters and lodges were still conferring the chivalric degrees. As a result, the Duke of Kent issued a proclamation to put an end to the practice. [41]

The next Grand Master of the Order, the Duke of Sussex, was the sixth son of George III, who had granted Dunkerley his pension and apartments in 1767. The duke was also the brother of the Duke of Kent, who had served briefly as Grand Master and previously and subsequently as Grand Patron of the Order. Additionally, the Duke of Sussex was elected first Grand Master of the United Grand Lodge of England. For the benefit of the reader who may not be familiar with this important aspect of Masonic history, the United Grand Lodge of England was formed on 27 December 1813 and brought to an end the rivalry between the Antient and Modern Grand Lodges, previously referred to. This unification was the direct result of the efforts of the Duke of Sussex and the Duke of Kent, two royal brothers figuratively and literally, both of whom served as Grand Master of the Templars in England.

As mentioned previously, the two grand bodies had different approaches to the conferral of degrees beyond the three Craft degrees. In the articles of union of 1813 we see that the newly formed Grand Lodge took a more favourable opinion of the degrees:

'It is declared and pronounced that pure Ancient Masonry consists of three degrees and no more; Viz. those of the Entered Apprentice, the Fellow Craft, and the Master Mason, including the Supreme Order of the Holy Royal Arch. But this Article is not intended to prevent any Lodge or Chapter from holding a meeting in any of the degrees of the Orders of chivalry, according to the constitutions of the said Orders.' [42]

For 191 years the United Grand Lodge considered the Royal Arch Degree to be the completion of the Master Mason Degree. However, the standing was changed on 10 November 2004 when the Supreme Grand Chapter authorised the removal of the connection in the ritual.

Of course, back in 1813 there were those who, despite the decision of the United Grand Lodge, maintained that no degree above that of Master Mason should be considered Masonic. It is a situation that has prevailed to this day among a small segment of Freemasons. However, two centuries ago, such sentiment was widespread and the problem was a great threat to Templary. Smyth in approaching the subject said the Duke was in an awkward position: there was a faction opposed to the Templar grades, the Templars were still relatively few

His Royal Highness, Edward, Duke of Kent and Strathearn served the Order as Grand Patron 1791-1805 and from 1807-1820. From 1805-1807, he was Grand Master of the Order. *Engravings by Roberts, published in 1820.*

in number and had survived the Unlawful Societies Act by remaining within a Masonic context, and perhaps, more importantly, as head of both orders, the duke didn't want to offend the members of either organisation. [43] As such, the duke seems to have taken the position that the best path to Templar survival was to lie low until things calmed down. [44] Ironically enough, it was the same approach that the original Templars are believed to have used to survive the persecutions of 1307-1314, or so those who subscribe to the Templar-Freemason theory would have us believe. However, in the Masonic persecutions of Masonic Templars in the years surrounding the formation of the United Grand Lodge in 1813, it seems this is precisely what the Duke of Sussex did.

For a period of more than 20 years there is but one extant reference to a meeting of the Grand Conclave and that occurred on 31 January 1820 [45] – seven years and four days after the Articles of Constitution had caused a controversy for the Templars. However, it is possible that other gatherings occurred as the records of the order had been destroyed in that same year when the house of Robert Gill, who had served the Order since Rancliffe's death in 1800, burnt down. But information after the loss of the Order's records indicate that little was going on in Templary,

for only three new encampments were authorised between 1824 and 1830 [46] and it would not be until 1833 or 1834 that a new encampment would be created. [47]

Grand Conclave in 1846

THE DUKE of Sussex remained at the helm of the Templar Order until his death on 21 April 1843; however, it would be a few years before his successor was duly elected in 1846. In the interim, John Christian Burckhardt served the Order as Acting Grand Master, having previously served as Deputy Grand Master since 1807. [48] Although he served the Order for many years, he did not see himself a candidate for the high office of Grand Master, being 70 years of age at the time. However, he did see fit to propose a suitable candidate for the job, Colonel Charles Kemeys Kemeys-Tynte. In fact, one of Burckhardt's final services to the Order before retiring from active service was to install the Colonel in his office on 3 April 1846.

At the time of his installation as Grand Master of the Grand Conclave, Kemeys-Tynte had been a member of the order for 28 years, having been installed as a Knight Templar on 15 March 1818 in London. [49] However, this was not his only connection with Templary, for he was also a member of the English branch of the non-Masonic Order of the Temple, [50] created by Bernard-Raymond Fabre-Palaprat in 1804. This Templar system claimed a direct lineage back to the original Templars through the Charter of Larmenius. In fact, the Duke of Sussex was also a member of this organisation, [51] now long-since defunct, but surviving as the Sovereign Military Order of the Temple of Jerusalem (SMOTJ) and its fractious offshoots.

Under Kemeys-Tynte's administration, the statutes of the Order were revived twice, in 1846 and 1853, and in 1851 he worked towards a standard ritual for the encampments. The motivating factor behind the ritual changes was the removal of the Rose Croix and Kadosh degrees, which had been enjoyed by the Templars of England for many years, but abandoned after the formation of the Supreme Council in 1846. [52] Additionally, Kemeys-Tynte began creating Provincial Commanderies in 1851, following the geography of the previously existing Craft and Capitular provinces.

On his death in 1860, Kemeys-Tynte was succeeded by William Stuart, who was installed in January of 1861. Although Stuart's Grand Mastership was brief, lasting only eleven years, an additional fifty encampments were added to the rolls of Grand Conclave. [53] Many of the new encampments were established abroad and these were largely due to the powers of the Provincial Commanderies that Kemeys-Tynte had started in 1851.

The Convent General

BEGINNING in 1867 there was a movement to unite the Templar bodies of England, Scotland and Ireland under a Convent General, and in 1869 the Prince of Wales, who had been initiated into Freemasonry and Templary in Sweden, agreed to serve as Grand Master. [54] On 7 April 1873, a year before his death, Stuart resigned from the Grand Mastership of England in favour of the Earl of Limerick, who assumed the new title of Grand Prior of England and Wales. [55] At the same time, the Duke of Leicester, previously the Grand Master in Ireland, took on the role of Grand Prior of Ireland. Although Scotland had taken part in the preliminary discussions, they withdrew from the convent.

MacLeod Moore says it was regrettable that Scotland withdrew, but lays the blame on their representative at the talks, who did not understand

the subjects being discussed and, being personally prejudiced against the proposal, reported back to Scotland his fears that Scotland's independence would be sacrificed to England's supremacy. [56] Of course, claims MacLeod Moore, nothing could have been further from the truth, for the treaty of amalgamation gave equal powers to Scotland, England and Ireland. [57]

Although Scotland took no part in the matter after withdrawing, Ireland and England pressed on and produced a draft for a new set of statutes, which in England were hastily accepted by the Grand Conclave in England. [58] The result was a flood of memorials opposing the changes to the structure of Templary.

Chief among the complaints against the revisions was the dropping of the word Masonic from the title of the order, a situation that the Templars believed would make the order subject to the Unlawful Societies Act, then still in existence. [59] Additionally, the Templars were opposed to the claim that the Masonic Templar order derived from the medieval Templars. [60] This should be particularly interesting to the reader, as it is a firm indication that prior to the Convent General Masonic Templary in England made no such claim, but perhaps more importantly, that the majority of Templars were opposed to the idea. Another of the changes opposed by the Templars was a change in nomenclature. Encampments were now to be called preceptories and commanders were now to be referred to as preceptors, but if the Templars of rank were opposed to the change in name, they were more opposed to the loss of that rank when their term of office was over. The abolition of past rank meant that after a man's term of office ended, he reverted to the rank he previously held. [61] Although it may have been argued that the opposition was due to having to change regalia from one form to another and back again, the truth behind the opposition was likely due to the loss of voting powers in Grand Conclave.

But of all the changes to Templary brought forth by the Convent General the one that received the greatest opposition was the introduction of a revised ritual, which was made mandatory in 1878, although it was largely ignored by Irish and English Templars. [62] But while the new ritual may have been rejected by England and Ireland it was embraced by Canada, then still answering to England. Writing during a time in which the Convent General still existed, MacLeod Moore provides us with a glimpse on how the ritual developed and offers commentary on the rituals that existed before it:

William Stuart served as Grand Master of the Order from 1861-1872 during the Convent General. *Portrait in oils at Mark Masons' Hall, London.*

'The changes made in the reformed ritual, now practised, are consequent upon the report of the Ritual Commission of the Convent General in 1873, which shows that they had examined the rituals of the ancient Templars founded upon the Benedictine Canons, the Scottish Ritual, very closely copied from it and the English Ritual from 1851, adopted in place of that of Dunkerley previously existing, which was full of Masonic inaccuracies and anachronisms, and also the Irish Ritual. When at a general meeting held in April 1873, under the presidency of the Great Prior of England and Wales, it was determined to reject all novelties and innovations by Masonic Templars of a recent date, and every paraphrase of ritual other than those already mentioned, certain resolutions were unanimously adopted as a basis, on which the new Ritual should be drawn up, in accordance with these conditions and suited to the three kingdoms, consistent with the nature and traditions of the Order. No novelty has been introduced, and every clause of it is to be found either in actual words or in substance in one of the other of the Templar Rituals examined. Both the English and Scottish rituals recognise the class of 'Novice' this is in accordance with ancient rule and practice.' [63]

Around 1889 when MacLeod Moore was penning the words reproduced above, the Covent General concept was beginning to burn out, largely due to the opposition previously mentioned. As a result, the governing body made an attempt to cut the preceptories some slack by easing back on their seemingly harsh rules. One of the steps was to restore the past rank status; however, it all proved too little and too late.

Great Priory from 1895

In May of 1894, a committee was struck with seven members from Ireland and England gathering together to find out what had gone wrong. It is fortunate that the practice of shooting the messenger had long since fallen out of favour because the report returned to the Great Priory the next year didn't pull any punches. Despite the criticisms, the committee suggested that the purpose of the Convent General had been a good idea and that Ireland should be invited to form a new agreement, in the hope that Scotland would also come on board. [64] On 19 July 1895, with but the stroke of a pen, the Prince of Wales

became the Sovereign of the Order in the United Kingdom, and England, Ireland and Scotland were united in independent harmony under his benevolent leadership. [65] The Prince of Wales continued in this capacity until 1901, when he assumed the position of Grand Patron – a position he held until his death in 1910.

As we have only mentioned the situations in Ireland and Scotland in passing, and then largely in the context of their participation – or lack thereof – in the failed Convent General of 1872-1895, we should spend some time in understanding the evolution of Templary in those countries, before crossing the pond to the United States and Canada, each of whom has its unique history.

Templary in Scotland

In the previous chapter we looked at two myths connecting the Templars of old with their Masonic counterparts in Scotland.

However, there are other Scottish Masonic Templar legends that were long accepted as fact by the Masonic Templars of that country and beyond. For many year Scottish Templars held to a belief that the order sprang from the Ancient Priory of Torphichen in Midlothian. During the Reformation, according to the tradition, the possessions of the combined orders of the Hospitallers of St John and the Templars were forfeited to the crown of Great Britain and Ireland. The basis for this forfeiture was that the oath of the preceptor was to defend and preserve the Roman Catholic religion and when the last Grand Prior, Sir John Sandilonds, converted to Protestantism, he surrendered the possession of his order to the government. After the dispersion of the order in 1564, many of the members joined a Masonic lodge in Stirling, which, in turn, gave rise to the knightly orders of Malta and the Temple being incorporated into the body of Masonry. [66]

This tradition is certainly not the official position of the Great Priory of Scotland today, for the Grand Body offers a date of 1745 as being the earliest reference to chivalric Masonry. In the bylaws of the Old Stirling Lodge, adopted in 1745, there is a reference to the fees for the various degrees:

'Excellent and Super-excellent, five shillings, and knights of Malta, five shillings.' [67]

Contemporary with this time and in the possession of the same lodge are to be found the Stirling Brasses,

At this time the chivalric degrees seem to have been extremely popular with Scottish Freemasons and Smyth references an interesting situation in the Ayr St Paul Lodge No. 204 SC, formed in 1799, in which only Knight Templars were permitted to hold office. [71] By the turn of the nineteenth century the high degrees became so popular in Scotland that it was deemed necessary for the Grand Lodge to issue an edict prohibiting its daughter lodges from holding meetings in any degree above that of Master Mason on the punishment of being stricken from the rolls of Grand Lodge. [72] Although some lodges did not follow the directive and continued to confer the high degrees, others, fearing Grand Lodge reprisals, applied to the Early Grand Encampment of Ireland for charters.

In 1805, a charter was issued to form Edinburgh Encampment No. 31, and within a short period of time the encampment evolved into the Grand Assembly of Knights Templar in Edinburgh. Under Alexander Deuchar, this group applied to and in 1811 was granted a charter from the Duke of Kent, which established the Royal Grand Conclave of Scotland. [73] It is uncertain why Deuchar applied to England for status rather than Ireland; however, whatever his motives may have been, he was unsuccessful in uniting the Scottish Templars under the banner of a Grand Conclave. There were a large number of Templars centred around Ayrshire – the birthplace of Chevalier Ramsay – who were in possession of Irish warrants. In 1826, these Templars formed the Early Grand Encampment of Ireland under the direction of Robert Martin.

Although the Royal Grand Conclave suffered some setbacks in the early 1830s, it began to experience growth under the influential Grand Masterships of Sir David Milne (1836-1845), George Augustus, the sixth Duke of Atholl (1845-1863) and John Whyte Melville (1865-1883). A peculiar situation arose in this Grand Body during the administration of David Milne, which will be of particular interest to North American Shriners, who have heard rumblings of similar things in recent years. In 1844, a proposal was made to admit non-Masons into the order. The proposed fee structure was to be ten guineas for non-Masons, seven for Masons and only four for Royal Arch Masons. [74] Although it seems to have been infrequently exercised, the proposal was none the less passed and continued to be the situation until 1856, when the prerequisite of the Royal Arch degree became one of the items in the newly revised statutes. [75]

By contrast, the Early Grand Encampment saw

upon which are engraved Knights of Malta and Night [sic] Templar. [68]

The next reference to the existence of the chivalric degrees comes from the records of the Lodge of Scoon and Perth, dated December of 1778, in which we find reference to the conferral of the 'six sundry steps of Masonry' on the officers of St Stephens Lodge in Edinburgh. The degrees listed were that of Excellent, Super Excellent Mason, Arch and Royal Arch Mason and Knights of Malta. [69]

In October of 1779, the Grand Master of Lodge Mother Kilwinning, Archibald the Earl of Eglintoune, issued a charter to a lodge in Dublin called the High Knights Templar of Ireland Lodge. [70] This lodge, as we will see in due course, evolved into the Early Grand Encampment of Ireland and over the span of twenty-some years began issuing charters to form encampments in Scotland.

little growth during its first half century of existence, but began to experience growth in the later quarter of the nineteenth century. The two Templar Grand bodies coexisted until the first decade of the twentieth century. [76] In 1905, the Early Grand Encampment approached the Royal Grand Conclave, now called the Chapter General, with an eye towards a merger; however, little came of it. [77] Although the merger talks did result in the Chapter General changing its name to the Great Priory of Scotland, it was not until 3 April 1909 that the Early Grand Encampment, then under Arbuthnot Murray, closed up shop and merged with the Great Priory. [78]

Depiction of the Templar regalia and costume as it existed from 1850-1875.
Gordon Napier

Templary in Ireland

As we have already seen, the Mother Kilwinning Lodge of Scotland granted a charter in 1779 to form the High Knights Templar Lodge of Kilwinning in Dublin. This charter was granted to Hugh Cunningham for Craft working – all the Mother Lodge was actually sanctioned to warrant. [79] However, the lodge seems to have little understood this, assuming that the warrant authorised them to confer the high degrees. [80]

But prior to this date there exists evidence – although far from conclusive – to show that the degrees were already being worked in Ireland. The Rules of the High Knights Templars of Ireland, adopted in 1788, make mention of the then existing members, one of whom was a man named Edward Gilmore, who presumably was received into the order in 1765. [81] However, in the absence of any lodge minutes acknowledging the conferral of the degree or a certificate supporting the same, it cannot be said with any degree of certainty that Gilmore received the degree at that time.

However, it was the opinion of J. L. Carson that the Templar degree was being worked in Ireland as early as 1758. In his article on the history of Irish Masonry, published in the January 1916 issue of *The Builder* Carson informs us:

> 'In Ireland the Royal Arch was known as early as 1743, and the degree of Knight Templar in 1758. Tradition and generally accepted Lodge gossip leads us to believe both these degrees were worked in connection with Blue Lodges or as distinct organisations long previous to these dates. Many, if not all the Regiments stationed in Ireland having Military Warrants, adopted these degrees and worked them without let or hindrance under their ordinary Blue Lodge [Craft Lodge] Warrants, thus creating what were called "Black Warrants"; hence we account for the spread of the Royal Arch and Templar degrees as well as those of Blue Masonry, wherever these regiments were drafted.' [82]

Let us then set sail across the pond with those regimental lodges, where we will discover the earliest documented instance of the conferral of the Templar degree.

References for Chapter 8

1. MacLeod Moore, William James Bury. 'British Templary: a History of the Modern or Masonic Templar Systems with a Concise Account of the Origin of Speculative Freemasonry and Its Evolution Since the Revival A.D. 1717.' *History of the Ancient and Honourable Fraternity of Free and Accepted Masons and Concordant Orders*. London, The Fraternity Company, 1902, pp.769-770.

2. Ibid. p.771.

3. *Brethren in Chivalry*: Smyth, Frederick, London, Lewis Masonic, 1991, p.15.

4. Smyth. Op. cit. p.17.

5. MacLeod Moore. Op. cit. p.771.

6. Smyth. Op. cit. p.17.

7. Ibid. p.17.

8. MacLeod Moore. Op. cit. p.771. Smyth. Op. cit. p.23. Smyth gives the name as Grand Conclave of the Royal, Exalted, Religious and Military Order of H.R.D.M. Grand Elected Masonic Knights Templars, K.D.S.H. of St John of Jerusalem, Palestine, Rhodes, etc.

9. Quoted in Smyth. Op. cit p.118.

10. Smyth. Op. cit. pp.24-26.

11. Mackey, Albert G. *Encyclopaedia of Freemasonry and Its Kindred Sciences* Volumes I Comp. William J. Hughan. Chicago: The Masonic History Company, 1927, p.223.

12. Ibid. p.223. Smyth. Op. cit. p.24.

13. Mackey. Op. cit. p.224.

14. Mackey. Op. cit. p.223.

15. Smyth. Op. cit. p.24.

16. Mackey. Op. cit. p.223.

17. Ibid. p.224.

18. Smyth. Op. cit. p.24.

19. MacLeod Moore. Op. cit. p.789. Mackey. Op. cit. p93.

20. Smyth. Op. cit. p.124.

21. Mackey. Op. cit. p.93. Smyth. Op. cit. pp.125-126.

22. Mackey. Op. cit. p.93.

23. Smyth. Op. cit. p.125.

24. Ibid. p.127.

25. MacLeod Moore. Op. cit. p.774.

26. Smyth. Op. cit. p.28.

27. Ibid. p.30.

28. MacLeod Moore. Op. cit. p773.

29. Prescott, Andrew. 'The Unlawful Societies Act of 1799.' Centre for Research Into Freemasonry. Second International Conference of the Canonbury Masonic Research Centre. University of Sheffield, Sheffield. 4 November 2000. 28 January 2008. www.freemasonry.dept.shef.ac.uk/?q=book/print/46&PHPSESSID=eed5bdedf9947288165c3d626d29cf2c.

30. Ibid.

31. Ibid.

32. Ibid.

33. Ibid.

34. Quoted in Smyth. Op. cit. p.31.

35. Ibid. p.31.

36. Ibid. p.32.

37. Ibid. p.35. MacLeod Moore. Op. cit. p.773.

38. Quoted in Smyth. Op. cit. p.119.

39. MacLeod Moore. Op. cit. p.773.

40. Smyth. Op. cit p.37.

41. Ibid. p.37.

42. Quoted in Ibid. p.40.

43. Ibid. p.41.

44. Ibid. p.41.

45. Ibid. p.41.

46. Ibid. p.42.

47. Ibid. p.42. There is an indication that a Coteswold Encampment of the Seven Degrees was established at Cheltenham in 1833; however, there is little evidence to support it. Royal Sussex Encampment was formed in 1834 at Torquay.

48. Ibid. pp.42-43.

49. Ibid. p.49.

50. Ibid. p.49.

51. Ibid. p.41.

52. MacLeod Moore. Op. cit. p.774.

53. Smyth. Op. cit. p.51.

54. MacLeod Moore. Op. cit. p.774.

55. Ibid. p.774.

56. Ibid. p.774.

57. Ibid. p.775.

58. Smyth. Op. cit. p.56.

59. *The History of the Knights Templars of Canada*: Robertson, John R. Toronto: Hunter, Rose & Co., 1890. p.129.

60. Smyth. Op. cit. p.57. Robertson. Op. cit. pp.128-129.

61. Ibid. p.57.

62. Ibid. p.61.

63. MacLeod Moore. Op. cit. p.781.

64. Smyth. Op. cit. p.62.

65. Ibid. p.62.

66. MacLeod Moore. Op. cit. p.789.

67. Quoted in 'The Historical Background of the Order.' The Great Priory of Scotland. 30 January 2008. 31 January 2008. www.greatprioryofscotland.com/history.htm

68. Ibid.

69. Ibid.

70. Ibid.

71. Smyth. Op. cit. p.21.

72. The Great Priory of Scotland. Op. cit.

73. Ibid.

74. Smyth. Op. cit. p.54.

75. Ibid. p.54.

76. The Great Priory of Scotland. Op. cit.

77. Ibid.

78. Ibid.

79. MacLeod Moore. Op. cit. p.790.

80. Ibid. p.790.

81. Smyth. Op. cit. p.19.

82. Carson, J. L. 'Irish Masonry.' *The Builder* January 1916.

Modern depiction of a Templar helm, shield and sword.
Stephen McKim

Paul Revere was the second American to be made a Knight Templar.
He is recorded as having taken the degrees on 11 December 1769.
Portait of Paul Revere by John Singleton Copley c.1768-1770

Templarism in the United States

'The popular theory under which so many writers view the origin and history of Templar Masonry would trace it back by some mysterious line of connection to the Order of Malta which was dissolved in 1798, or back to the Order of the Temple, which ceased to exist in 1313, and the latter theory, even at this day, has many advocates. A better and truer theory is to credit the whole system of Masonic Templary to the inventive genius of the ritual makers of the eighteenth century.'

Sir Knight Theodore Sutton Parvin, Past Grand Recorder of Iowa

Right: **Boston's famous Green Dragon Tavern – home to revolutionary figures, was also the home of St Andrew's Lodge and Royal Arch Lodge, where William Davis, Paul Revere and Joseph Warren were made Knights Templar between 1769-1770.** *Author's collection*

PRIOR to the American War of Independence, we see no separate Templar bodies operating in what would become the United States of America. This isn't to say that Templary didn't exist in the colonies; on the contrary, for the earliest recorded instance of a Templar ceremony being conducted in the United States, or anywhere for that matter, in a truly Masonic setting, was at Boston in the summer of 1769. However, prior to the American Revolution it would seem that whenever Freemasons were initiated as Templars it was under the warrant of an existing Craft or Royal Arch lodge and not under the auspices of any distinct Templar body, as is the case today. Although evidence exists to support the emergence and proliferation of specific Templar bodies shortly after the American Revolution, the details are often sketchy and particularly prone to jurisdictional Masonic pride as well as a general misunderstanding of under whose authority the degrees were actually being conferred.

The first American to be created a Knight Templar was a man named William Davis, who received the four steps of Excellent, Super Excellent, Royal Arch and Knight Templar in Boston's St Andrew's Royal Arch Lodge [1] on 28 August 1769. [2]

Although St Andrew's Lodge No. 81 was established in Boston under a Scottish Warrant on

30 November 1756 (St Andrew's Day), the Royal Arch Lodge of the same name did not receive its warrant until 18 August 1769, just ten days prior to Davis being made a Royal Arch Mason and Knight Templar. [3] Both Masonic lodges met in the famed Green Dragon Tavern, so named for the tarnished copper dragon that was a prominent decoration outside the building.

It has been suggested that Royal Arch Masonry was brought to Boston by regimental lodges – particularly Glittering Star No. 322, operating under the Grand Lodge of Ireland and British Army Lodge No. 58, operating under the Grand Lodge of England. However, the records of St Andrew's Lodge show that six years prior to the arrival of the regimental lodges, a letter was sent to the Grand

Lodge of Scotland requesting a warrant to start a Royal Arch Lodge. [4] This letter of 29 October 1762 is strong evidence to suggest that there existed not only a desire among Bostonian Freemasons to confer the Royal Arch degree on other Masons but also that there must have been Royal Arch Masons capable of doing so. This argument is supported by the fact that the 1762 request to form a Royal Arch body, which was denied by Edinburgh, stated that 'a sufficient number of us have arrived at that sublime degree'. [5] How or where the Boston Freemasons had received the degree is unknown, as the regimental lodges, that are believed to have introduced the degree, did not arrive in the area until the autumn of 1768. [6] It is possible that some had received the degree in Virginia, as it was being practised in Fredericksburg Lodge as early as 1753. [7] But assuming for a moment that the Freemasons of Boston had received the Royal Arch degree as they said, they made no such claims with respect to having been made Knights Templar. Quite simply, there is no extant record of the degree having been conferred before Davis received it and the several preceding ultra-degrees of Freemasonry one summer's evening in 1769.

But who was this William Davis and what made him worthy of being the first Mason to be created a Knight Templar? Certainly he is best remembered to history as a revolutionary war hero who participated in the Battle of Bunker Hill in 1775 and the Siege of Yorktown in 1781. In fact, it was Davis who suggested the barrel defence used during the Battle of Bunker Hill on 17 June 1775: essentially barrels filled with earth and stone were rolled down the hill on the enemy. [8] This famous battle, one of the earliest in the American War of Independence, became the foundation stone for a patriotic Masonic side order known as The Sword of Bunker Hill, which was founded by an Illinois Freemason named Frank G. Taylor in 1912.

However, Davis' Revolutionary War efforts began several years after he received the four steps in St Andrew's Royal Arch Lodge. It is important to understand that the Freemasonry of Davis' day –

certainly in Boston – was substantially different than the Craft of today in many ways. Chief among those differences was the fact that Freemasonry did not open its doors to the common man. [9] While on the surface, the Craft promoted a universal system of equality among all men, that equality was reserved for men of similar social standing. As the owner of an Apothecary on Boston's Prince Street, Davis certainly would have met the then existing societal requirements to be made a Freemason. [10]

William Davis was born at Boston on 13 June 1724 – a year after Dr James Anderson wrote *The Constitutions of the Free-Masons*, in which he connected the Craft, albeit in passing, with the 'warlike knights' of the crusades. Although it is not known exactly when Davis became a Freemason, he seems to have been an active one. He was recorded as Master of St John's Lodge in Boston on 26 December, 1750 and latterly served as Master of British Army Lodge No. 58, [11] one of the lodges believed to have introduced Templarism to the United States. It is therefore not surprising that in the minutes of the meeting in which Davis was created a Templar we find, in addition to three members of the St Andrew's Royal Arch Lodge itself, two members of Lodge 58 as well as three from Lodge 322 – the other regimental lodge operating in Boston at the time. [12]

According to Masonic author Michael Kaulback, Davis was also a member of St Andrew's Lodge, having joined in 1757. [13] It was here that he became more closely acquainted with Paul Revere and Joseph Warren, the former immortalised in the poetry of Longfellow, [14] the latter killed at the Battle of Bunker Hill. While Warren and Revere's contributions to America's independence from Britain are well known, what is less commonly known is that they were the second and third men to be created Knights Templar in the United States. Revere received the same 'four steps' as Davis on 11 December 1769 and Warren was initiated into them the following year on 14 May 1770. [15] Like Davis, both Revere and Warren were active Freemasons throughout their lives.

Revere was initiated in St Andrew's Lodge in 1760 and after serving as secretary, ultimately took on the chair of Master of the lodge. [16] However, the high office in his mother lodge was not the pinnacle of his Masonic career, for he was elected Grand Master of the Grand Lodge of Massachusetts in 1794 and during his three-year term, nearly doubled the number of lodges in the state. [17]

Like Revere, Warren was also initiated in St Andrew's Lodge, having taken his first and second degrees in the autumn of 1761; however, it was not until 28 November of 1765 that he would take the Master Mason degree. Four years later, Warren received a commission from the Grand Master of Scotland, the Earl of Dalhousie, as Provincial Grand Master of Masons in Boston. The new Grand Lodge was inaugurated by St Andrew's Lodge, Lodge No. 58 and Lodge No. 322. [18] Warren was installed on 27 December 1769 and Davis, who had signed the original petition sent to Scotland, was present at the ceremony. [19] In his capacity as Provincial Grand Master, Warren appointed Captain Jeremiah French and Captain Ponsonby Molesworth as Grand Senior and Junior Wardens respectively. [20] Both of these men were members of Lodge No. 322 and it is possible that they took part in Warren's initiation as a Knight Templar in 1770. Like Revere, Warren also ascended to the chair of Grand Master, having received a commission in 1772 from the Grand Master of Scotland, the Fifth Earl of Dumfries to serve in the capacity of the rather lofty title of Grand Master for the Continent of America. [21]

Although there is some evidence to support the idea that the Royal Arch degree had been conferred prior to the arrival of the British regimental lodges in 1768, the emergence of a Templar degree seems to have followed closely on their heels and was conferred – at least initially – on men who had clear connections to the same. Davis had served as Master of British Army Lodge No. 58 and Warren had promoted members of Lodge No. 322 to high offices within the Provincial Grand Lodge system.

However, circumstantial evidence does not alone prove that the Templar degree was introduced by the regimental lodges, but whatever its origins it certainly wasn't a frequent ceremony. Between 1769, when Davis became the first to receive the degree, and 1794, when any mention of the Templar ceremony in the lodge records ends, St Andrew's Royal Arch Lodge initiated approximately 50 men – or just two per year. [22]

A little over a decade after Davis became the first Templar in the United States, we find in the records of Kilwinning Lodge in Ireland (warranted 8 October 1779) that its Masonic warrant was used to authorise the conferral of the degrees of Royal Arch, Knight Templar and Rose Croix. [23] However, it is important to understand that the Rose Croix is not the same as the Red Cross ceremony used in North America Templary today. Frederick Speed, a Past Grand Commander of Mississippi, writing in the later part of the nineteenth century, claimed that although the Scottish Kilwinning Lodges never conferred any degrees outside of St John's Masonry, both the St Andrew's Lodge in Boston and Kilwinning Lodge of Ireland derived their charters from Scotland. [24] Quoting the eminent Masonic scholar Theodore S. Parvin, Speed tells us that the regimental lodges were the most likely source for the Templar degree:

'Numerous military lodges were warranted by both the "Ancient" and "Modern" Grand

Paul Revere and General Joseph Warren were the second and third initiates into Templar Masonry in the United States.
Jupiter Images

Lodges of England, and the Grand Lodge of Scotland and Ireland. One distinguished regiment had a lodge connected with it, chartered in turn by both of the English Grand Lodges, and subsequently by those of Scotland and Ireland. It also had connected with it, under the same warrant, two chapters holding under the authority of the Grand Lodges of England and Ireland. In 1766 [1768] there were two military lodges stationed at Boston: No. 58 on the register of England, connected with the Fourteenth Regiment, and No. 322 register of Ireland, attached to the Twenty-ninth Regiment.' [25]

It was Parvin's belief that the Templar degree was brought to Boston by these regimental lodges. However, if they were not practised by their mother lodge, where did they acquire them? Kaulback supposed that Lodge No. 58, which was a 'Modern' Lodge, and therefore unlikely to have possession of the higher degrees, learnt of the Templar grade between 1766 and 1768, when they were stationed at Halifax, Nova Scotia with Lodge No. 322. [26]

Frederick Smyth in his history of the Great Priory of England referenced a little-known history of Lodge Glittering Star written by a Canadian Mason named R. V. Harris in which the author suggests that Lodge No. 322 was conferring the degree as early as 1765 when it was stationed in Nova Scotia. [27] However, prior to their arrival in Halifax, Lodge No. 322 was stationed in Ireland (1759-1765). [28] The degree of Knight Templar was certainly known in Ireland in the years following its introduction in the United States; however, it is believed to have existed on the Emerald Isle as early as 1740. [29]

Despite any modern-day romantic notions that the original Templars sailed from Scotland to North America to bury their vast treasure on Oak Island, it seems that the most likely candidate for the emergence of Masonic Templary in Nova Scotia and latterly Boston were the military regiments who sailed the Atlantic many centuries later.

The First Encampments

As FREEMASONRY began to evolve following the American War of Independence, we see the so-called higher degrees, which heretofore had been conferred sporadically within Craft and Royal Arch Lodges, begin to be worked under specific bodies. In 1795 the Grand Chapter of Pennsylvania was formed and by 1797 there emerged the General Grand Chapter, formed on 24 October 1797. However, with respect to Templar Masonry, we see no unified governing body until 1797 when the short-lived Grand Encampment of Pennsylvania was formed. But prior to that first Grand Body, we see the emergence of encampments of Knights Templar in Boston, Providence, Philadelphia, New York City, Baltimore and even as far south as Charleston, South Carolina. As is to be expected, jurisdictional Masonic pride has caused several to make the claim that they were the first – records and proof often notwithstanding.

The earliest candidate for the honour of being the oldest encampment of Knights Templar in the United States is not to be found in Boston, Massachusetts, as one might reasonably expect, but in Charleston, South Carolina. Those who support the South Carolina claim point to the existence of a Masonic diploma dated 1 August 1783, on which are found four seals.

Across the top of the diploma from left to right are found four circular devices drawn in pen. The first is a star of seven points containing the Latin motto *Memento Mori* or *remember that you are mortal* as well as the Ineffable Name in the centre. In the second illustration is found an arch resting on two pillars, in the centre of which is a keystone with the All-seeing eye. Beneath the arch is found a sun and the motto on the seal is *Holiness to the Lord*. The third illustration depicts a brazen serpent on a cross, erected on a bridge. The motto written on this seal is *Jesu Salvator Hominum* or *Jesus Saviour of men*. In the final illustration there is found a skull and cross-bones surmounted by a Latin cross. The motto on the seal, *In Hoc Signo Vinces* or *in this sign, you will conquer*, will certainly be recognisable to current American Templars.

The text of the diploma is as follows:
'We, the High Priest, Captain Commandant of the Red Cross, and Captain General of the most Holy and Invincible Order of Knights Templars of St Andrew's Lodge No. 1, ancient Masons, held in Charleston, South Carolina, under charter from the Grand Lodge of the Southern District of North America, do hereby certify that our trusty and well-loved brother, Sir Henry Beaumont, hath passed the Chair, been raised to the sublime degree of an Excellent,

Super Excellent, Royal Arch Mason, Knight of the Red Cross, and a Knight of that most Holy, Invincible and Magnanimous Order of Knights Templars, Knights Hospitallers, Knights of Rhodes, and of Malta, which several Orders are above delineated; and he, having conducted himself like a true and faithful brother, we affectionately recommend him to all the Fraternity of ancient Masons around the globe wherever assembled. [30]

'Given under our hands, and seal of our Lodge, this first day of August, 5783, and of Malta, 3517.

'GEO. CARTER, Captain General
THOS. PASHLEY, Ist King.
Rd. Mason Recorder.'

While this diploma, now in the possession of the Grand Encampment of Knights Templar, indicates that the Templar degree was being worked in Charleston as early as 1783, it does not prove that the degree was conferred by a Templar body. In fact, it shows the opposite. Speed, in examining the diploma, discovered that the seal was that of Lodge No. 40:
'This lodge [No. 40] was formerly St Andrew's Lodge, No. I, of Pensacola, Florida, established by James Grant, Provincial Grand Master of the Southern District of North America, which embraced East and west Florida; and its Registry number in Scotland was 143. It appears to have worked at Pensacola until about the close of the Revolution, when, as Florida became again a Spanish Province, Pensacola was deserted by many of its inhabitants, who had been British subjects, they removing to Charleston, South Carolina. This removal was mostly in 1783, and the year before, and with them it seems St Andrew's Lodge was also removed; and it applied for, and, in July, 1783, received a charter from the Grand Lodge of Pennsylvania, as No. 40 on its Registry.' [31]

Speed was of the belief that the existence of the South Carolina diploma does not prove that St Andrew's Lodge No. 1 was acting as a Templar body. Like the similarly named lodge in Boston – the first to confer the Templar degree on American soil – the Charleston body was a Master's lodge that conferred the degrees under a Craft or Royal Arch lodge warrant. It would not be until 1804 – possibly a little

dated 1802. [33] Boston was also able to trace its history back to 1802; however, only as a Council of Knights of the Red Cross. It was not until 1805 that it was organised as a commandery of Knights Templar. [34] Despite being the birthplace of the Templar grade in America, it cannot lay claim to being the home to the oldest commandery or encampment. St John's Commandery No. 1 of Providence, Rhode Island, also traces its lineage back to the year 1802 and Speed was inclined to believe that the records of this commandery offer the oldest extant account of the election and creation of Knights of the Red Cross in a body not under the warrant of a Craft lodge. [35] Washington Commandery No. 1 of Hartford, Connecticut, claimed to originate in 1796; however, Speed found conflicting evidence in a variety of sources and concluded that they probably did not begin until 1801. [36] In New York City there were encampments working as early as 1795; however, masonic author Robert Macoy claimed that outside sources indicate that Knights Templar were scheduled to lead the St John's Day procession of 1785. [37]

The situation in Pennsylvania gives us a date of 1793 for the formation of Commandery No. 1 at Philadelphia; however, this and subsequent Templar bodies were still acting under a Craft lodge warrant. [38]

The First Grand Encampment

IN 1797, the Masonic Templars of Pennsylvania became the first to move towards uniting under a common chivalric banner. To this end on 12 May 1797, sixteen representatives (four from each of

Templar diploma dated 1 August 1783 and issued in South Carolina is the oldest extant Templar document in the United States.

Author's collection

earlier – that Charleston Masons organised themselves as a Templar encampment. Even then it was a self-created body that did not receive a warrant until 1823, when it aligned itself with the General Grand Encampment of the United States. [32]

In studying the extant records of the other contenders for the claim of being the oldest encampment in the United States, Speed found that Maryland could trace its lineage back to a diploma

Pennsylvania's four encampments) assembled to discuss the possibility of forming a Grand Encampment of Knights Templar. [39] A week later on 17 May, the delegates adopted a constitution to govern the Templars in the state and the Grand Encampment of Pennsylvania was born.

What is particularly interesting about the four constituent encampments – Nos. 1 and 2 residing in Philadelphia and Nos. 3 and 4 in Harrisburg and Carlisle respectively – is that they were authorised to confer the Craft degrees. [40] Alfred Creigh, in his *History of the Knights Templar of the State of Pennsylvania* claimed that from its inception on 26 September 1786 until 16 May 1857, The Right Worshipful Grand Lodge of Pennsylvania subscribed to the belief that the Regulations of the Ancient York Masons authorised the conferral of the Christian Orders of Chivalry under a lodge warrant. [41] However, other sources indicate that this was not always the case, for on 15 September 1806 the Grand Lodge struck the word 'Knight Templars' from the bylaws of Lodge No. 101, citing that "no such being sanctioned by this Grand Lodge as a degree in Masonry'. [42]

Whatever the true relationship between the Grand Lodge and Grand Encampment may have been, there were those who took a dim view of the idea of Masonic Templarism – a concept that was still relatively new.

On 5 January 1805, Dr George Green wrote to the Grand Lodge complaining that although the Grand Lodge disavowed any cognisance of 'a society of people called Knights Templars' they none the less rented a room to them for their meetings and that the group was imposing on the Masons by drawing them into their society under the pretence that it was a high degree of Masonry. [43] It was not Green's only complaint against the Templars for on 17 October 1808 he wrote once again complaining that he was 'surrounded and borne down by the persecuting spirit of the Templars' and washed his hands of them. [44] In January of 1809, a report was made to Grand Lodge that the Templars owed five years in back rent, which was to be recovered from $100 the Templars had previously lent to the Grand Lodge. [45]

The Pennsylvania Grand Encampment's existence was brief and, although it was revived in 1814, it went dark again in 1824 as an outcome of the anti-Masonic excitement. [46] When the Grand Encampment re-emerged in 1852, it was under the authority of the Grand Lodge of Pennsylvania. However, in that same year the Grand Lodge solidified its position on its powers over concordant bodies stating:

'That Ancient Masonry consists of but three degrees Viz.: Entered Apprentice, Fellow Craft and Master Mason, including the degree of the Holy Royal Arch and this Grand Lodge claims no jurisdiction beyond the limits of Ancient Masonry.' [47]

It was at this time that the Grand Encampment of Pennsylvania aligned itself under the banner of the Grand Encampment of the United States.

The Second Grand Encampment and its evolution

BETWEEN the formation of the Grand Encampment of Pennsylvania in 1797 and the General Grand Encampment of the United States in 1816, there existed another Grand Encampment. This Grand Body, variously referred to as the Grand Encampment of Massachusetts and Rhode Island and the Grand Encampment of the United States, was formed in Providence, Rhode Island, on 13 May 1805 by Thomas Smith Webb. [48]

Although Webb is often erroneously referred to as the father of the American Rite, [49] he certainly is worthy of his prominent place within the history of American ritualism – having given the Craft its first

Thomas Smith Webb (1771-1819) is considered by many to be the founding father of the American Rite (erroneously referred to as the York Rite). Webb was instrumental in forming the Grand Encampment of the United States.
Author's collection

Henry Fowle is a lesser known American ritualist than his contemporary and companion Thomas Smith Webb. However, Fowle was none the less instrumental in the advancement of Templary in the United States during the early years of the nineteenth century.
Author's collection

printed ritual the *Freemason's Monitor* or *Illustrations of Masonry* in 1797. Webb was born at Boston on 30 October 1771 and educated by the age of fifteen. [50] The late Masonic scholar H. L. Haywood claimed that Webb was initiated into Freemasonry by special and legal dispensation at the age of 19; [51] others claim he entered the Craft at the age of 21. [52] Regardless of when he received his degrees, he had certainly become a Knight Templar by 1802, for in that year he established the St John's Encampment in Providence, Rhode Island. The reader will recall that it is this encampment that owns the earliest recorded instance of the election and creation of Knights of the Red Cross in a Templar body. Oddly enough, St John's Encampment did not receive its Charter of Recognition from the new Grand Encampment until 7 October of 1805 – five months after the Grand Encampment was formed. [53]

Another key player in the formation of the New England-based Grand Encampment was Henry Fowle, who formed and became the first Sovereign Master of Boston Encampment of Red Cross Knights in 1802 – the same year Webb founded St John's Encampment. Fowle's Council of Red Cross Knights organised itself into a Templar body in 1805, soon after the formation of the Grand Encampment of Massachusetts and Rhode Island. [54] Fowle was initiated into Boston's St Andrew's Lodge on 10 April 1793, and in 1795 received the degrees of Mark Master, Past Master, Most Excellent Master and Royal Arch Mason in St Andrew's Chapter (formerly St Andrew's Royal Arch Lodge). [55] This was the same Masonic body where Davis, Revere and Warner had been made Royal Arch Masons and Knights Templar in 1769 and 1770. Stanley C. Warner, a Past Grand Commander of Colorado in his 'A Short History of the Early Days of Templarism', published in the July 1922 edition of *The Builder* claimed that Fowle was made a Knight Templar on 28 January 1795 in St Andrew's Chapter. [56] However, the records of that body with respect to the conferral of the Templar degree end in 1794. Fowle himself makes no

mention of where he received the degrees, stating only that he had received the several Orders of High Priest, Knight of the Red Cross, Knight Templar and Knight of Malta several years prior to 1801 [57] and had spoken to several Masonic friends about the possibility of establishing them in Boston. This would seem to support the idea that the ceremonies has not only fallen into disuse in Boston subsequent to 1794, but also had begun to take on a different form than those possibly introduced by the military lodges in 1769.

It is not surprising to see that these two men, together with another prominent Mason and ritualist by the name of John Snow, were instrumental in the movement to form a General Grand Encampment of Knights Templar in 1816. This movement sought to unite the three then existing Grand Encampments of Pennsylvania, Massachusetts and Rhode Island, and New York, the last of which was organised on 18 June 1814.

On 11 June 1816, Webb and Fowle, representing the Grand Encampment of Massachusetts and Rhode Island, and John Snow, representing the Grand Encampment of New York, met with delegates from Pennsylvania to discuss uniting under one banner. After several days of back and forth discussion, it was determined that a union was not possible. The Templars of Pennsylvania reported:

> 'That it was impossible to carry their designs into execution without making a sacrifice upon the part of the Grand Encampment, and its subordinate encampments, which was considered unwarranted by every principle of Masonry, which was made sine qua non by the delegates from New England, who having seceded from the convention, it was of consequence dissolved.' [58]

Essentially the Templars of Pennsylvania wanted no part in mixing their pure form of Templary with the bastardised working of Thomas Smith, which they considered to be a 'New England Heresy'. [59] As is to be expected, there are two sides to the story. Henry Fowle told a different story altogether in his autobiography:

> 'Met in Convention but found the Knights here very adverse to a coalition as proposed,—not that they found the measure useless, impracticable, or wrong,—but the fact was that they were completely under the control of the Grand Lodge, that body having assumed an authority over all Masonic Bodies in that State, and exacted and received a portion of the fines,

not only of the Lodges, but also of the Chapters and Encampments. Several of the Grand Encampment were candidates for office in the Grand Lodge, and dare do nothing which would curtail her revenue, lest they should not be elected to office. As it respected the Orders of Knighthood, they were as ignorant as mules: we witnessed the reception of six candidates at one and the same time. After the ceremony was completed they asked Bro. [Thomas Smith] Webb what he thought of it. Webb asked if they wished him to be candid in his reply; they said, 'by all means.' 'Well,' said Webb, 'if I had not heard you tell them that they were Knights Templars I should not have believed it.' Their Grand Commander then desired Bro. Webb to request two of his party to step out with two of their and exhibit all the signs, grips and words of each degree from the Entered Apprentice to the Knight of Malta, inclusive. Bro. Webb requested Bro. [John] Snow and myself to gratify them. We accordingly stepped out with two of their officers, and having passed all the degrees, their Grand Commander asked his Grand Generalissimo: 'Well, Bro. H., what do you think of it: are you satisfied?' 'Yes, Most Eminent; that we know nothing,' was the reply. Hoping that something might turn up more favourable to our wishes, we continued to meet and argue with them for several days, until finding them totally incorrigible we gave them up and prepared for our return.' [60]

It is probable that neither Webb's version nor the Pennsylvania version of the Templar ceremonies was incorrect. Rather, then as now, Masonic jurisdictional pride dictated that the ritual used by any given jurisdiction is correct and that all others are impure.

The failure of Webb, Fowle and Snow to bring the Pennsylvania Templars onside in their plans to form a General Grand Encampment did not stop them from creating the body ten days later on 21 June 1816, nor did it stop Pennsylvania from ultimately aligning itself under her banner in 1857, as we have already seen.

One of the New York Templars who played a prominent role in the formation of the General Grand Encampment was Dewitt Clinton, a man who was certainly the best known outside of Freemasonry. Clinton had a long political career and was variously elected to serve as US Senator, Mayor of New York City and ultimately as Governor of New York State.

Clinton also took a run for president of the United States against James Madison in 1812. But Clinton also had a long and prosperous Masonic career serving as Grand Master of New York from 1806 until 1819, and from 1816 to 1826 as the General Grand High Priest of the General Grand Chapter, a body that had also been created with the hand of Webb and Fowle. It is therefore not surprising that we find Clinton, rather than Webb or Fowle, listed as the first Grand Master of the General Grand Encampment of the United States, the latter assuming a subordinate role to their well-regarded and experienced Brother Masons. The officers elected on 21 June 1816 were as follows:

Dewitt Clinton – General Grand Master
Thomas Smith Webb – Deputy General Grand Master
Henry Fowle – General Grand Generalissimo
Ezra Ames – General Grand Captain General
Rev Paul Dean – General Grand Prelate
Martin Hoffman – General Grand Senior Warden
John Carlisle – General Grand Junior Warden
Peter Grinnell – General Grand Treasurer
J. J. Loring – General Grand Recorder
Thomas Lowndes – General Grand Warder
John Snow – General Grand Standard Bearer
Jonathan Schieffelin – General Grand Sword Bearer [61]

DeWitt Clinton (1769-1828) was the first General Grand Master of the Grand Encampment of the United States. Clinton was a prominent American politician and Freemason, who had previously served as Grand High Priest of the General Grand Chapter of Royal Arch Masons and Grand Master of Masons in New York State.
Clipart.com

William Morgan, shown here as portrayed by the Anti-Masons and Freemasons, was an operative Mason who claimed to be a Freemason. In 1826, Morgan wrote a book exposing the rituals of the Craft degrees and subsequently vanished. It was alleged that Freemasons played a role in his demise, and the backlash against the fraternity nearly destroyed Freemasonry and Templarism in the United States.
Author's collection

admitted a member of a Royal Arch Chapter on the pretence of having previously received the Craft degrees. Morgan, despite Masonic mud slinging to the contrary, seems to have been – at least early on – a well-regarded member of the Craft as he was a frequent visitor and speaker to many lodges in the area. However, all of that changed when a petition was formed to start a new Royal Arch Chapter. Morgan's name was on the original document, but another was created which did not include his signature. Incensed that he had been snubbed by his Masonic Brethren, Morgan vowed to get even by publishing their secrets. Around the time his book was set to roll off the presses, Morgan's body was rolled over the bow of a boat from whence it sank to the bottom of the Niagara River. At least that was the story told by those who held to the belief that the Freemasons had killed Morgan; the Masons themselves have long denied the charges. As the Morgan Affair, as it came to be called, was the subject of a paper I wrote for Volume 15 of *Heredom: The Transactions of the Scottish Rite Research Society* (2007), I'll allow the interested reader to pick up the story there. What is important to the present discussion is that the backlash against the Craft as a result of Morgan's disappearance nearly caused the extinction of Freemasonry in the United States and even when it revived itself, it was never the same creature as it once was.

Templarism was not free from anti-Masonic persecutions of the day and to understand the effects the disappearance of William Morgan had on the Templars of New York State, and elsewhere, we need look no further than their own historical records, one example of which should prove sufficient for our present discussions.

Monroe Commandery No. 12 was formed on 13 July 1826 at Rochester, New York, near in time and place to where William Morgan had been abducted. Although the encampment seemed to grow in its first few years of existence, it, like many Masonic lodges, chapters and encampments, was laid low by the public backlash against all forms of Freemasonry. Thus, on 27 February 1829, the officers of the encampment met to discuss the possibility of surrendering their Charter. The following was the outcome of the meeting:

> 'WHEREAS, We, the officers and members of
> the Monroe Encampment, holden in the village
> of Rochester, in the county of Monroe being
> deeply impressed with our duty as both men and
> as Masons to use our best endeavors to restore
> harmony to the distracted community in which

Although the Constitution of the General Grand Encampment of the United States records but eight encampments and one Council of Knights of the Red Cross working under the three Grand Encampments it had jurisdiction over, the General Grand Encampment did not see tremendous growth over the next three decades. From 1816 until 1852, when Pennsylvania joined, the General Grand Encampment saw the addition of just six Grand Encampments under its banner. [62] However, the lack of growth was not caused by a lack of interest in Templary in particular, but rather by a general lack of interest in Freemasonry in particular.

The Morgan Excitement

ON 11 SEPTEMBER 1823, a disenfranchised Royal Arch Mason named William Morgan was abducted from the village of Batavia, New York, and never seen again. Morgan, who Freemasons have long argued was never regularly initiated into Freemasonry, was we live, and as it appears to us that by returning our Charter and abstaining from our regular meetings, that we will effect that very desirable object, therefore,

'*Resolved*, That we as citizens but more particularly as Members of our Ancient and Honourable Society, the first principles of which are to promote the harmony and good order of Society, deem it our duty to return our Charter of this Encampment to the Grand Secretary of the Grand Encampment of this State and that the Secretary be and is hereby instructed to return the same forthwith.' [63]

It was not until 1847, eighteen years after Monroe Encampment surrendered their Charter that the Templars of Rochester felt they could reassemble. In the winter of 1847-1848 Monroe petitioned the Grand Encampment of the State of New York for the return of their Charter and began anew as Monroe Commandery No. 12. [64] Similar dormant periods existed in other parts of New York State, as well as elsewhere in the country. The darkness of the Morgan excitement did not escape the Grand bodies and as we have seen, the anti-Masonic era ultimately led to the dormancy of the Grand Encampment of Pennsylvania. Although the Grand Encampment of New York continued its annual assemblies, there was little business to conduct and few Templars to conduct it. [65] Oddly enough, Genesee Commandery No. 10

moved from its headquarters in Leroy to Batavia, the village where Morgan had resided before his disappearance. This commandery continued to operate in Batavia for the next decade [66] and never surrendered their Charter during that time, despite conducting their affairs in the spiritual seat of anti-Masonry.

During the 1850s, when Freemasonry began to finally recuperate from the public backlash, an additional 10 Grand Commanderies were added to the list. [67] However, the next decade would see another period of relative dormancy as the nation and the Templars who formed a part of it split between Northern and Southern lines.

American North and South meets Masonic East and West

ONE OF the stories that Freemasons love to tell is the influence of Masonic principles on the field of battle. Nowhere is this theme carried to greater effect than in the romantic Masonic stories of brotherly love between the blue and grey uniforms of the American Civil War, and while there certainly were well-documented instances of fraternal compassion across the blood-soaked battlefields of that conflict, the presence of the compasses and the cross did not always transcend political and societal differences.

On the eve of the Civil War, Benjamin B. French, then Grand Master of the Grand Encampment of the United States, sent a circular to the constituent

This miniature replica of the Masonic Memorial Monument in the Gettysburg National Military Park tells the story of the unity of Freemasonry transcending the strife between North and South during the American Civil War. However, letters written by Templar leaders on opposing sides tell a different and less harmonious story.
Stephen Dafoe

bodies, which was also published in the May 1861 issue of Charles W. Moore's *Freemasons' Monthly Magazine*. From that publication we read of Grand Master French's desire for American Templars to do everything in their power to avert the impending conflict:

'CIRCULAR
'OFFICE OF THE GRAND MASTER OF KNIGHTS TEMPLAR OF THE UNITED STATES OF AMERICA
'BENJAMIN BROWN FRENCH,
'Grand Master of Knights Templar of the United States of America.
TO ALL TRUE AND PATRIOTIC TEMPLAR:
'BROTHERLY LOVE, PEACE, HONOR

'An awful fratricidal conflict seems to be impending. He alone rules the destinies of Nations can prevent it. He works through human instruments. I implore every Templar Knight on the continent of America, after humbly seeking strength and aid from on High, to exert all the means at his command to avert the dread calamity, which, to human vision, seems inevitable.

'Let each Templar to whom this may come remember how often we have stood at each other's side, and raised our voices in prayer for the prosperity of a common country and a common cause. Let all call to mind how the Knights of Virginia, mingling in fraternal brotherhood with those of Massachusetts, pledged themselves to each other, on Bunker Hill, only a few brief years ago; and when another year had passed away, the same noble bands stood together in the city of Richmond, in the State of Virginia, the birthplace of Washington, and with mutual vows bound their souls in everlasting covenant:! Let them remember these things, and, with hearts on fire with love for each other, and for their countrymen, go forth among those countrymen and implore the arbitrament of peace, instead of that of the sword.

'I ask no one to surrender a principle that has become dear to his heart; but I ask every one to labor and to pray that such counsels may take place between the contending parties, who have for so many years acted with a common impulse, as to restore harmony and kind feeling, and avoid the curse of having fraternal blood crying to Heaven from the ground, and bringing down its malediction on our children's children through all future time! Labor and pray that hostilities may be suspended until the mild counsels of peace can be appealed to, and that the appeal may not be in vain.

'Casting aside every political feeling, every political aspiration, and asking every Templar to do the same, let us, as one man, unite in one grand effort to prevent the shedding of fraternal blood, and to inaugurate here that blessed result which our Lord and Master initiated—'Peace on earth and good will to men.'

'Templars! You count, in this land, by tens of thousands. Each one has his influence in the circle about him. Never, no never, was there an opportunity to exert that influence in a more sublime purpose. Forward, then, to the rescue of your country from fratricidal war!

'But, if war must come—which dread calamity may God, in his infinite mercy, avert—then I call on every Knight Templar to perform that sacred duty, which so well becomes our Order, of binding up the wounds of the afflicted and comforting those who mourn.

'Dated at the City of Washington, on this eighteenth day of April, in the year of our Lord 1861, and the year of our Order 743.

'B. B. FRENCH, GRAND MASTER' [68]

French's circular had the opposite effect than he had hoped – at least from the Templars of Virginia. Nine days after French penned the note to American Templars, E. H. Gill, the Grand Master of the Grand Encampment of Virginia, offered his reply to what he saw as Northern rubbish. Gill's response was published in the June issue of *Freemasons' Monthly Magazine*, much to the disappointment of its editor, and reads as follows:

'OFFICE OF THE GRAND MASTER OF KNIGHTS TEMPLAR OF VIRGINIA
'Lynchburg, Va., April 27th 1861.

'Hon. B. B. French, Grand Master
'Grand Encampment Knights Templar of the United States

'M. E. Sir Knight—Your Circular of the 18th inst., relative to the "awful fratricidal conflict which seems to be impending" between the citizens of the North and the South, has been received; and as the people of the South are merely acting on the defensive in this conflict, those of the North regardless of that "Brotherly Love, Peace and Honor" alluded to in your circular, having trampled upon their constitutional rights, and being now about to invade their soil, their homes and their firesides, and to desecrate their altars, I am at a loss to understand why you should send such a circular to the Knights Templar of Virginia.

'Residing as you do in Washington, you cannot be ignorant of the fact, that Virginia has exhausted every honourable means to avert this conflict. "Casting aside every political feeling, every political aspiration," she has plead to prevent the "shedding of fraternal blood;' she has plead for 'Peace on earth and good will to men," and she has plead that her constitutional rights and those of her sister States of the South, should not be trampled upon; but her pleadings have been disregarded; and conscious of the justice of her cause, she now appeals to the "God of Battles," confident that Heaven will smile approvingly upon her efforts in resisting unto the death this Cain-like and marauding attack of the Vandals of the North; and I thank god, that the valiant Knights Templar of Virginia unanimously participate in this feeling of resistance, and are prepared to welcome their invaders "with blood-stained hands to hospitable graves," designated by no sprig of evergreen.

'For the reasons stated, I now, as the Grand Master of the Grand Encampment of knights Templar of the State of Virginia, give you notice, that the body is no longer under the jurisdiction of the Grand Encampment of the United States, and will no longer regard or obey any orders or edicts emanating from it, or its Officers.

'E. H. Gill, Grand Master.' [69]

Of course it was probably no matter of coincidence that Gill's letter was penned the same day that Virginia seceded from the Union. [70] But whatever animosities may have then existed between American Templars, they, like the country, eventually reunited. However, neither would be the same as it was prior to the Civil War.

Marching to the Beat of the Same Drummer

WHEN the craft re-emerged from the ashes of the anti-Masonic excitement, there was a strong effort to ensure that there was some uniformity to the rituals. To accomplish this end, two conventions were held in Washington and Baltimore in 1842 and 1843 respectively; neither succeeded in its aim. The best the efforts of those involved could produce was to make sure that lodges opened and conducted business on the Master Mason's Degree so that another Morgan wouldn't get past the tiled recesses of a Masonic lodge.

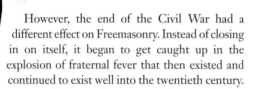

However, the end of the Civil War had a different effect on Freemasonry. Instead of closing in on itself, it began to get caught up in the explosion of fraternal fever that then existed and continued to exist well into the twentieth century. One of the peculiar aspects of this period in history, and one that would seem to be a direct result of the Civil War, was the penchant for marching in military formation. In this, the American Templars were certainly not alone, for other groups such as the Knights of Pythias (1864), Knights of Columbus (1882), the Grand Army of the Republic (1866) and scores of others began wearing the same style uniforms. This cookie-cutter costuming was in part a result of new fraternal organisations patterning themselves figuratively and literally after Freemasonry; however, part of the commonality of regalia was a direct result of the influence of the regalia houses themselves.

In her excellent paper 'Business and the Brethren: The Influence of Regalia Houses on Fraternalism', published in Volume 12 of Heredom, researcher Harriet W. McBride argued that 'for those returning soldiers who had belonged to a secret society before the war, a return to the lodge was one means of re-establishing pre-War social norms'. [71] While the Freemasons returning to their lodges may have been looking to reconnect with their pre-military lives, there was also a great desire to maintain a connection to the camaraderie experienced in the field of battle. As such, a spirit of militarism swept the nation during the 1870s that extended beyond those who had participated in the Civil War. Men who came of age after the war wanted to connect to

the shared military experience of those who had participated. [72] The regalia houses were only too happy to fill the need and supplied the growing number of fraternal members with a wide variety of uniforms, swords and other militaristic paraphernalia, all of which was prominently displayed in great public processions.

In this, the American Templars, like the original Templars on the field of battle, were certainly in the vanguard. There was perhaps no greater critic of the American Templars' penchant for parades than Col. William James Bury MacLeod Moore, the Grand Master of Canadian Templars *ad vitam*, who, just prior to his death in 1890, wrote:

'Imitation military public displays and processions of the Knights Templar body, so much indulged in on this Continent, quite unknown in the British Empire, are out of place, although harmless in themselves. They are entirely opposed to the true meaning and object of Christian Templary, entailing a great and unnecessary expenditure, and serving no other purpose but to pander the vainglory and self-gratification of the members who take part in them. Are all the poor and needy in the land provided for? Are there no more hospitals and schools required, to which the great outlay at those gatherings might and could be legitimately applied, instead of wasting the means in idle shows?' [73]

While MacLeod Moore's criticism of Templary as it was practised in the United States may seem harsh – particularly to American Templars – it is important to understand that, despite the close proximity to their American Fratres, the Canadian Templars' system was a decidedly different Order.

References for Chapter 9

1. St Andrew's Royal Arch Lodge later became St Andrew's Chapter.

2. 'The First Knights Templar in the United States', Kaulback, Michael AQC volume 107 1994. 'A Short History of the Early Days of Templarism', *The Builder* July 1922, Warner, Stanley C. National Masonic Research Society, Iowa. 1923. Warner quotes the minutes of St Andrew's Royal Arch Lodge as follows: 'The petition of Bro. William Davis coming before the lodge begging to have and receive the parts belonging to a Royal Arch Mason, which being read, was received and he unanimously voted in, and was accordingly made by receiving the four steps, that of Excellent, Super-Excellent, Royal Arch, and Knight Templar.'

3. *Brethren in Chivalry*, Smyth, Frederick. Lewis Masonic. London. 1991. p.89.

4. Kaulback. Op. cit.

5. Smyth. Op. cit p.89.

6. Smyth. Op. cit. p.90. Kaulback. Op. cit.

7. 'The High Degrees in the United States: 1730-1830', Morris, S. Brent. 1998 Blue Friar Lecture.

8. Kaulback. Op. cit.

9. *American Freemasons: Three Centuries of Building Communities*, Tabbert, Mark. New York, New York University Press, 2006, pp.37-38.

10. Kaulback. Op. cit.

11. Ibid.

12. Smyth. Op. cit. p.90.

13. Kaulback. Op. cit.

14. The revolutionary war hero was immortalised in Henry Wadsworth Longfellow's poem *Paul Revere's Ride*, written in 1861.

15. Kaulback. Op. cit.

16. Tabbert. Op. cit. p.37.

17. Ibid.

18. 'Military Lodges', *The Builder* October 1918, Lawrence, Dr G. Alfred. National Masonic Research Society. Iowa. 1918.

19. Kaulback. Op. cit.

20. Correspondence from Ron Gee, then Senior Warden of Lodge Glittering Star No. 322 (IC) to Gary Dreyfus. www.web.mit.edu/dryfoo/Masonry/Reports/glitter.html (accessed January 26 2008).

21. Lawrence. Op. cit.

22. 'A Short History of the Early Days of Templarism', *The Builder* July 1922, Warner, Stanley C. Iowa. 1922.

23. The Knights Templar of the United States of America, and Government by a Grand Encampment, Grand Commanderies, and Commanderies. The Ritual, and Ethics of American Templary. Division XVI of History of the Ancient and Honourable Fraternity of Free and Accepted Masons and Concordant Orders, Speed, Frederic, Boston. The Fraternity Publishing Company. 1902. p.703.

24. Ibid. p.703.

25. Speed. Op. cit. p.703. Speed is quoting Theodore S. Parvin, the first Grand Secretary of the Grand Lodge of Iowa.

26. Kaulback. Op. cit.

27. Smyth Op. cit. p.91.

28. Kaulback. Op. cit.

29. Smyth. Op. cit. p.91.

30. Speed. Op. cit. p.704.

31. Speed. Op. cit pp.704-705.

32. Speed. Op. cit p.704.

33. Ibid. p.707.

34. Ibid. p.707. *The Autobiography of Henry Fowle of Boston (1766-1837) With Notes and Appendices by David H. Kilmer*, Fowle, Henry, Maryland. Heritage Books. 1991. p.39. Fowle, a prominent Bostonian Mason, formed the Council of Knights of the Red Cross and was instrumental in the later formation of the Grand Encampment.

35. Speed. Op. cit. p.708.

36. Ibid. pp.710-711.

37. Ibid. pp.711-712.

38. Speed. Op. cit. p.707.

39. *History of the Knights Templar of the State of Pennsylvania Volume I*, Creigh, Alfred. Philadelphia. J. B. Lippincott & Co. p.47.

40. Ibid. pp.48-49.

41. Ibid. p.47.

42. Brown, William M. *Highlights of Templar History*. Greenfield: Wm. Mitchell Printing Co., 1944. p.76.

43. Ibid. p.76.

44. Ibid. p.77.

45. Ibid. p.78.

46. Warner. Op. cit.

47. Creigh. Op. cit. p.47.

48. Brown. Op. cit. p.74. The Convention began on 6 May 1805 and adopted a constitution on 13 May. On 15 May, Thomas Smith Webb publicly announced the formation of the Grand Encampment.

49. Among them Albert Mackey who wrote in his Masonic Encyclopaedia entry on Webb, 'No name in Masonry is more familiar to the American Mason than that of Webb, who was really the inventor and founder of the system of work, which, under the appropriate name of the American Rite (although often improperly called the York Rite), is universally practised in the United States.'

50. 'Thomas Smith Webb', Iowa Grand Lodge Bulletin Vol. LVI No. 9, 1955, Haywood, H. L. www.iowamasoniclibrary.org/webforms/Downloads/Thomas%20Smith%20Webb.pdf (accessed 27 January 2008).

51. Ibid.

52. Warner. Op. cit.

53. Ibid. p.74.

54. Fowle. Op. cit. p.39.

55. Ibid. pp.32-33.

56. Warner. Op. cit.

57. Fowle. Op. cit. p.35.

58. Speed. Op. cit. p.717.

59. Ibid.

60. Fowle. Op. cit. pp.49-50. This is taken from the printed version of Fowle's autobiography. The manuscript version for the event tells the same story in a slightly different tone.

61. Webb, Thomas S. *The Freemason's Monitor or Illustrations of Masonry*. Salem: Cushing and Appleton, 1818. pp.247-248. Webb reprinted the Constitutions of the General Grand Encampment in the 1818 edition of his work.

62. Warner. Op. cit.

63. Searing, Richard A. *History of Monroe Commandery No. 12 Knights Templars Stationed At Rochester New York 1826-1914*. Genesee, The Genesee Press, 1913. p.9.

64. Ibid. p.11.

65. Ibid. p.9.

66. Ibid. pp.9-10.

67. Warner. Op. cit.

68. Moore, Charles W. *The Freemasons' Monthly Magazine Volume XX*. Boston: Hugh H. Tuttle, 1861. p.211.

69. Ibid. p.226.

70. Virginia seceded from the Union on 27 April 1861 and on that same day West Virginia, wishing to remain part of the Union, seceded from Virginia.

71. McBride, Harriet W. 'Business and the Brethren: the Influences of Regalia Houses on Fraternalism.' *Heredom: Transactions of the Scottish Rite Research Society Volume 12*. Washington: Scottish Rite Research Society, 2004, 163-202. p.179.

72. Ibid. p.181.

73. MacLeod Moore, William James Bury. 'British Templary: A History of the Modern or Masonic Templar Systems with a Concise Account of the Origin of Speculative Freemasonry and Its Evolution Since the Revival A.D. 1717.' *History of the Ancient and Honourable Fraternity of Free and Accepted Masons and Concordant Orders*. London: The Fraternity Company, 1902. pp.741-794.

This cabinet card depicts an American Templar complete with his tuba. Marching with great fanfare became a unique staple of Templary in the United States and a tradition that has remained until the present time. The apron the man is wearing once formed an important part of the Masonic Templar regalia; however, the apron is no longer permitted in American commanderies with but a few exceptions. *Carson Smith collection*

Above opposite: This early twentieth century postcard depicts a group of Knights Templar parading down the street before a large audience. Little expense was spared for parades, which formed an integral part of the American Templars' triennial conclaves. *Carson Smith collection*

LT.-COL. WM. JAS. BURY MacLEOD MOORE, G.C.T.,

Supreme Grand Master,

SOVEREIGN GREAT PRIORY OF KNIGHTS TEMPLARS OF CANADA.

**Lieutenant Colonel William James Bury MacLeod Moore was the first
Supreme Grand Master of Knights Templar in Canada.
Engraving as it appeared in John Ross Robertson's 1890 edition of
The History of the Knights Templars of Canada.**
Author's collection

10 Templarism in the Dominion

'He had the air and manner of a soldier always, free from arrogance or self-sufficiency, being invariably a dignified, courteous, and affable gentleman…'

Albert Pike speaking of William James Bury MacLeod Moore

IT WOULD be difficult to understand the history of Templarism in Canada without first having a brief understanding of William James Bury MacLeod Moore, the man responsible for its growth and prominence in Canadian Freemasonry. Being predisposed of a great admiration and love for the man, as every Canadian Templar ought, it might be fitting to begin with a memorial compiled by Henry Leonard Stillson, editor in chief of *The History of the Ancient and Honourable Fraternity of Free and Accepted Masons and Concordant Orders*, the book in which MacLeod Moore's final words on the Christian Order he so greatly loved are to be found. Moore died shortly after penning his monograph on British Templary, which formed the twenty-seventh chapter of the aforementioned book.

'In 1888, a well-known Masonic editor wrote: "the name of Lieutenant-Colonel William James Bury MacLeod Moore, G.C.T., Supreme Grand Master, of the Sovereign Great Priory of Knights Templar of Canada, is one that will live when its possessor shall have passed to the 'Great Beyond.'" This is a sentiment which will strike a responsive chord in the breast of every reader as he peruses the pages following, the preparation of which closed the long life-work of the eminent brother, who has now passed to his reward, the summons coming even amidst his closing labours thereon. Of his presence and character, General Albert Pike, a life-long friend, says:

"He had the air and manner of a soldier always, free from arrogance or self-sufficiency, being invariably a dignified, courteous, and affable gentleman, vera simplicitate bonus, candid, frank, and sincere, altogether a man after the old pattern, and withal a most kindly, lovable man. Not smiled upon by fortune in the later years of his life, nor free from vexatious annoyances and heavy crosses; but he accepted these and all the ills of life, and the deprivations and disabilities of old age, with equanimity, as a wise man should; and to the last stoutly resisted any innovations in the Knights Templary of Canada, these seeming to him depravations that would vulgarise it."

'He received the three degrees of Craft Masonry in a single evening, on the 17th of August 1827, when only seventeen years of age, at a special meeting of Glenkindie Lodge held in the house of Master, Major General Sir Alexander Leith. In 1831, he was exalted to the Royal Arch Degree, and made Mark Master, and on October 29 1844 was installed High Knight Templar and Knight of Malta, in the Encampment attached to Lodge 242, in the old town of Boyle, County Roscommon, Ireland. He received the degrees of the AAS Rite in New York City, in the year 1863, and his subsequent record is mentioned in his monograph in his work. Grand Master Henderson (his successor) – who has also since passed to a better life – in a memorial circular, says:

"In 1849-50, when, as an officer in HM Majesty's 69th Regiment, he was stationed at Malta, he was mainly instrumental in reviving the Masonic Order of the Temple in that Island, and on his arrival in Canada, in 1852, he at once identified himself with Freemasonry, being most zealous in its advancement. Having ascertained that there were historic records extant of an old encampment at the city of Kingston, with a zeal and ardour truly his own he set about reviving it, and through his well-known influence with the Supreme Grand Conclave he obtained in the year 1854 a warrant for its revival under the name Hugh de Payens Encampment, and was gazetted the first Eminent Commander. To his exertions the revival of the Order in Canada is wholly due, and the twenty-seven preceptories now under the banner of the Sovereign Great Priory bear witness to the success of his efforts in the cause of the Order of the Temple. Such whole-souled devotion of his time and talents won prompt and deserving recognition at the hands of the preceptories, and the highest office in the gift of the Fratres was bestowed on him. He was unanimously elected Supreme Grand Master 'Ad Vitam,' which office he worthily filled up to the time of his death. He was honorary member of several preceptories, not only in his own, but also in foreign jurisdictions and in the year 1873, His Royal Highness, the Prince of Wales, as Grand Master of the Order of the Temple, conferred on him the distinguished honor of the Grand Cross of the Temple, – one of twenty-one, six of whom were royal personages."

'The Order of the Temple became the work of his life, and the Allocutions that form the basis of his contribution to this work, and which for so many years he sent forth, are mines of historic research and valuable information. He was a recognised authority in Masonic lore and especially in that of Templary.' [1]

Canadian Templary Before MacLeod Moore

WHILE the history of Canadian Templary cannot easily be separated from the name or touch of MacLeod Moore, the fact remains that he didn't simply pull chivalric Masonry out of his suitcase on his arrival in 1852. The Templar degrees were certainly known in Canada well before his arrival, and, as we saw in the previous chapter, there are traces of it to be found in Halifax, Nova Scotia, starting between 1766 and 1768.

That being said, the earliest extant record for the existence of Templary in Halifax comes to us from 1782 – thirteen years after William Davis was initiated in St Andrew's Royal Arch Lodge in Boston. As one might reasonably expect, the degrees were conferred under a Craft lodge warrant. From that record, reproduced in the pages of John Ross Robertson's *The History of the Knights Templars of Canada* we learn that on 20 September 1782:

'At a Chapter of Royal Arch Masons held under Warrant No. 211 on the Ancient Grand Registry of England at the 'Golden Ball,'

'Present:
'The Rt. Worshipful Br. KIRKHAM, H.P.; R.W. Br. JOHN WOODIN 1st K.; R.W. BR. EPHM. WHISTON, 2nd K.; R.W. Br. JOHN CODY, S: R.W. BR. JOHN WILLIS.

'Applications having been made by Brothers John George Pyke, John Clark and Joseph Peters, Past Masters of Regular Lodges of Free and Accepted Ancient York Masons, for further Light and Knowledge in the secret and hidden Mysteries of Free Masonry; and they on strict trial and due examination being found worthy, were by us installed and Instituted into the Sublime Secrets of Royal Arch Masonry. After which:

'An Assembly or Encampment of Sir Knight Templars being formed, the said Brothers J.G. Pyke, John Clark, and Joseph Peters, were Instituted and Dubbed Knights of the Most Noble and Right Worshipful Order of Sir Knight Templars.

'And the Lodge was closed in Peace and Harmony.' [2]

It is worth noting that this lodge was St John's Lodge No. 211 and still exists today as St John's Lodge No. 2 on the Grand Registry of Nova Scotia. The lodge was organised on 11 May 1780 by dispensation granted under the 4th Duke of Atholl, then Grand Master of the Antients [3] and received its warrant on 30 June of the same year.

From this initial record, penned two years after the lodge was warranted, until late in 1784, the lodge

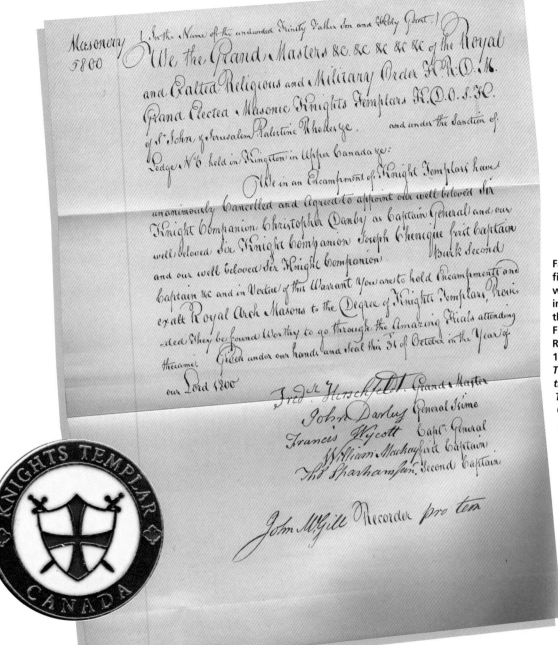

Facsimile of the first Templar warrant issued in Canada in the year 1800. From John Ross Robertson's 1890 edition of *The History of the Knights Templars of Canada.* Author's collection

Templar lapel pin depicting the emblem of the Sovereign Great Priory of Canada. Author's collection

seems to have held ten meetings in which Past Masters of Craft lodges were initiated into the Royal Arch degree and dubbed Knights Templar. [4] However, as was the case elsewhere at the time, these degrees were being worked under lodge warrants and not under separate Templar bodies. The earliest warrant for a Templar encampment was not to be found in Nova Scotia, but rather in Kingston, Ontario and was discovered by John Ross Robertson in the

archives of the Rev Dr Scadding of Toronto when Robertson was conducting research for his two-volume work *History of Freemasonry in Canada.* [5]

This warrant, dated 31 October 1800, is unique in its simplicity: printed on plain foolscap rather than parchment and completely devoid of gilded writing or seal to decorate it as was so often the tradition in Masonic warrants – and, as Robertson so diplomatically put it, the 'writing bore evidence that the schoolmaster was on a vacation.' [6] However poorly worded Robertson may have felt the warrant was, it none the less provided him and the student of Templar history with some valuable insights into the origin and evolution of the Order in Canada. The text of the warrant, reproduced within this book is as follows:

'In the Name of the Undivided Trinity: Father, Son and Holy Ghost.

'We the Grand Master, etc., etc., etc., etc., of the Royal and exalted Religious and Military Order, H.R.D.M., Grand Elected Masonic Knights Templars, K.D.O.S.K., of St John of Jerusalem, Palestine Rhodes, etc., and under sanction of Lodge No. 6, held in Kingston, in Upper Canada, etc.

'We in an Encampment of Knights Templars, have unanimously counselled and agreed to appoint our well-beloved Sir Knight, Companion Christopher Danby, as Captain-General; and our well-beloved Sir Knight, Companion Joseph Cheneque, First Captain, and our well-beloved Sir Knight, Companion _____ Burk, Second Captain, etc., and in virtue of this warrant you are to hold Encampments and exalt Royal Arch Masons to the Degree of Knight Templar: provided they be found worthy to go through the amazing trials attending the same.

'Given under our hands and seal, this 31st of October, in the year of our Lord 1800 (Signed.)

'Frederick Hirschfeldt, Grand Master.
'John Darley, Generalissimo.
'Francis Wycott, Capt. General.
'William Mackay, First Captain.
'Thos. Sparham, Junior, Second Captain.
'John McGill, Recorder pro-tem.' [7]

From the opening words of the warrant we can see that, from its early beginnings, Templary in Canada has always been Trinitarian Christian in nature. While this will certainly come as no surprise to Canadian Templars, it may seem unusual to members of the Order in the United States, many of whom are of the belief that admission into the Order requires only a willingness to defend the Christian faith. Such is simply not the case, and the Grand Encampment of the United States' promotional materials is somewhat conflicting in nature. On its website it makes the claim that:

'The Knights Templar is a Christian-oriented fraternal organisation based on the ancient organisation that was founded in the 11th century.' [8]

However, in the following paragraphs it states: 'Currently, Templar membership consists of people from all walks of life, including doctors, lawyers, clergy, businessmen and entertainment personalities, all of whom profess a belief in the Christian Religion.' [9]

The petition for membership is clearer in identifying the Grand Encampment's position: 'THE UNDERSIGNED further confirms, that insofar as his petition relates to his becoming a member of the named Commandery of Knights Templar, he is a firm believer in the CHRISTIAN RELIGION.' [10]

The preceding remarks are in no way intended to cast a negative view on Templary as it is practised in the United States. However, it is worth pointing out that the respective Grand Bodies of Canada and the United States approach the uniting of the compasses and the cross in a different manner. Some years back I was doing some research for an article for Templar History Magazine on the profession of faith, as I personally knew American Templars who were of the Jewish and Pagan faiths. When the subject was broached through a contact in the Grand Encampment, the response came back that the Grand Body wished the matter dropped. The validity of cross-jurisdictional orders aside, it became clear to me that what was being required in principle by the Grand Encampment was not always being followed in practice. However, in Canada our own petitions were a cause of concern between 2000 and 2002 under our Supreme Grand Master Larry J. Hostine. At that time Canadian petitions referenced the Holy and Undivided Trinity; however, Grand Master Hostine felt that these should be revised to read holy and Undivided Christian Trinity. His argument, and correctly so, was that he wanted to remove any potential misunderstanding in the minds of potential candidates and to this end, the wording of the applications were changed. [11]

What is important in the preceding digression is that it seems that the difference between the two countries in their admission requirements is long-standing, as it was a particular bone of contention with MacLeod Moore who wrote:

'The formula of reception into the Christian degrees of Knights Templary is totally distinct from and different in structure, creed and usages, from that of the Templar degrees based upon Freemasonry. The admission of members of the Hebrew persuasion and Unitarians, on this continent, is directly opposed to the teachings and constitutions of the Order strictly enforced in the British Empire, which require a test of belief in the Holy and undivided Trinity, without which no Templary can exist, all special pleading to the contrary notwithstanding.' [12]

The second thing that is of particular interest about the Kingston warrant is that the reference to the Royal and exalted Religious and Military Order, H.R.D.M., Grand Elected Masonic Knights Templars, K.D.O.S.K., of St John of Jerusalem, Palestine Rhodes, etc., follows closely the style adopted by the Grand Body of Dunkerley's day, which, as we saw in Chapter 8, was the Grand Elect-Knights Templar Kadosh and Holy Sepulchre of St John of Jerusalem, Palestine Rhodes, and Malta. Despite the similarity in nomenclature, this encampment does not seem to have received its warrant from the Grand Conclave in England.

Thus far we have seen that the early order in Canada was then, as now, Trinitarian Christian in nature and descended from England – by way of the Antients, in the case of Nova Scotia and patterned after the system used by Dunkerley, in the case of Kingston.

But the members of this new encampment also shed some light on the origins of Templary in Canada before the arrival of MacLeod Moore. For on the list we find the names of John McGill and Alexander McNabb, both of whom were members of the 1st American or Queen's Rangers, commanded by Col. Sir John Graves Simcoe. [13] This regiment arrived in Canada from England in 1790 and like the Irish and English regiments mentioned in the previous chapter, had a lodge attached to it. This lodge, Queen's Rangers Lodge met at Newark and in 1794 in York (now Toronto). The lodge disbanded in 1800 – the same year the Kingston encampment warrant was issued, and the lodge's charter was returned to England. [14] Although this in no way proves that the Queen's Rangers brought Templary to Kingston, it is not entirely out of the realm of possibility, as it is almost certain that it had been the regimental lodges that introduced the degrees south of the border.

We next hear of Templars in Kingston in 1824, when a warrant was issued by the Grand Royal Arch Chapter of Upper Canada on 12 February to form the St John of Jerusalem Encampment. [15] Although there are few remaining documents produced by this encampment, which was attached to St John's Lodge (now The Ancient St John's Lodge No. 3 GRC), they show that the encampment continued to operate until 1828. [16]

The text of the warrant of 1824 is particular interesting and bears repeating in full so that we can understand a couple of things about it:

'In the name of the Holy and Undivided Trinity, etc., Ziba M. Phillips, G.M.

'To all and every our Right worthy and loving brethren, Sir Knights Templars and Knights of Malta;

'I, Ziba M. Phillips, Esquire, Grand Master for the Province of Upper Canada, etc., etc.: Send Greetings, –

'Know ye, that by virtue of the authority and confidence reposed in me, as Grand Master of the Conclave of Knights Templar, Knights of Malta and of the Holy Order of the Priesthood, sanctioned by the Grand Royal Arch Chapter of Upper Canada, etc., etc.

'In testimony of the great esteem and confidence reposed in our Right Trusty and Well-Beloved Brethren, Sirs John Butterworth, William Chestnut, Thomas Ferguson, Robert Johnstone, Thomas Smith, George Millward, Joseph Dalay, Benjamin Olcott, Robert Walker, William Donaldson, James Meagher, Samuel Boyden and George Oliver, of the Town of Kingston, I do form them, my said worthy and well-beloved brethren, sir Knights into a regular Grand Encampment, or Grand Conclave, therein, when duly congregated, to exalt worthy Royal Arch Masons to the Sublime and Most Holy Degrees of Knights Templar, of Malta, and the Red Cross, according to the customs and usages of Knights of those degrees in all ages and nations round the globe. And I do hereby give to the above named Brethren Sir Knights full power and authority to nominate their successors, and invest them with their badges and empower them with their privileges whenever they shall think proper, according to the ancient custom, they the said Knights and their successors paying due respect to the

Supreme and General Grand Conclave at Malta, and to us, by whom these presents are granted.

'In testimony, whereof I herewith set my hand and affix the Seals of the Cross, at Kingston, this twelfth day of February, in the year of our Lord, 1824, and of Light 5824.

'(Signed)

'ZIBA M. PHILLIPS, G.M.
'Signed in the presence of Philip F. Hall, K.T., K.M., Grand Recorder P.T.' [17]

One of the first things that stand out in the warrant is the reference to the Red Cross degree. As we will look at this degree in detail later in this chapter, let it suffice to say that the degree was common among the Templars of the United States at the time, and the Grand Chapter of Upper Canada, established in 1818, followed the Royal Arch system of the United States.

Accepting the 1824 warrant at face value, one could be forgiven for assuming that this encampment received its authority from the Grand Chapter of Upper Canada by way of the Supreme and General Grand Conclave at Malta. Thus we have a Maltese origin for Templary in Canada. However, the problem is that there was no such body in existence in Malta, showing that Masonic myths were not confined to traditional histories alone. Oddly enough it was MacLeod Moore himself who was instrumental in Templary being introduced on the Island of Malta when he was stationed there in 1849-1850. Certainly the Grand Chapter of Royal Arch Masons existed, having been formed seven years previously in 1817 under Phillips. We can therefore conclude that neither the warrant of 1800 or 1824 derived its legitimacy from the then existing Grand Bodies in the United Kingdom. MacLeod Moore would change that status.

Canadian Templary Under MacLeod Moore

As WE learnt earlier, MacLeod Moore was transferred to Canada in 1852, where he was stationed at Kingston, Ontario. This was during the administration of Kemeys-Tynte as Grand Master of the Grand Conclave. Although he had been initiated into Templary in Ireland, he had served under the English system as Second Grand Captain and had been Eminent Commander of the Melita

Encampment on the Island of Malta. In fact, MacLeod Moore was the founder of the encampment. [18] Ever an active Freemason, MacLeod Moore immediately sought to connect with his Masonic Brethren and discovered that the Grand Conclave of England had no connection to Canada, though there once was an encampment in Kingston, which had gone dormant some years before.

He soon set himself to the task of reviving the defunct encampment, which had begun and received its warrant nearly a quarter century earlier in 1824. Although the encampment was no more, two of its former members – Samuel Boyden and Robert Sellers – were still alive and living in the area. [19] When MacLeod Moore was able to locate the warrant of 1824, he sent it to the Grand Conclave along with a petition signed by Boyden and Sellers, as well as a number of other Freemasons residing in the area. Just two years after his arrival in Canada Kemeys-Tynte issued MacLeod Moore a warrant, dated 10 March 1854, for the establishment of Hugh de Payens Encampment.

Although the United States can boast such Revolutionary luminaries as Paul Revere, William Davis and Joseph Warren as its earliest members, Hugh de Payens is not without its own notable early members. Among them were the Canadian statesman Sir Allan Napier McNab and two fathers of Confederation, Sir Alexander Campbell and Sir John A. MacDonald, the latter of whom was Canada's first Prime Minister. [20]

Within the first year there were three encampments operating in the Province of Canada: the aforementioned Hugh de Payens in Kingston, Geoffrey de St Aldemar in Toronto and William de la More, the Martyr in Quebec. Although MacLeod Moore was appointed the first Commander of Hugh de Payens Encampment, Kemeys-Tynte went a step further on 7 July 1854 by appointing MacLeod Moore Provincial Grand Commander for the Province of Canada. [21]

On 7 October 1855, the three encampments were called to a meeting held at Kingston by the new Provincial Grand Commander. Although no representatives came from Geoffrey de St Aldemar, this is likely due to the difficulties travelling between Toronto and Kingston, merely a three-hour drive by today's standards, but certainly a much longer journey by horse and carriage. In all 13 Templars attended this first Provincial Grand Conclave for the Province of Canada. It was directed by the Supreme Grand Conclave in England that Hugh de Payens Encampment in

Kingston would hold rank in the body and that their rank would be effective from 12 February 1824, the date of their original warrant. [22] As such, Hugh de Payens can trace its lineage back to 1824 and today enjoys a special status among Canadian Templary under the name Hugh de Payens Premier Preceptory No. 1.

Fraternal relations between Canadian and American Templars were formed quickly, with the General Grand Master of the United States officially recognising the Canadian Fratres at the second Annual Assembly of the Grand Provincial Conclave held in Kingston in 1856. It wouldn't be long before elements of American Templary would begin to creep into the Canadian system.

In 1859, MacLeod Moore authorised the encampments to confer the Malta degree, then common in the United States, but certainly, as we have seen, not unknown to the Canadian Templars – including MacLeod Moore himself, who had received the degree in Ireland 15 years previously. However, the introduction of the Malta degree was not a direct result of the influence of the American Templars. As MacLeod Moore said in a circular issued on 5 April 1859:

> 'The Eminent Commanders of Encampments under this jurisdiction are hereby notified that they are authorised to confer in their Encampments, on all regular Knights Templars, as an honorary degree, that of Masonic Knights of Malta. Until of late years the combined Orders of the Temple and St John of Jerusalem or Malta, were conferred in the English, and are still in the Scottish, Irish and United States Encampments.
>
> 'This Degree commemorates the union of a branch of the Ancient Military Order of St John, joining with the Templar Knights as Masons, during the latter part of the sixteenth century, and preserves and transmits the knowledge of their origin from the chivalric head of this Order of Knighthood, which obtained possession of the Island of Malta in 1530, and were known as Knights of Malta. They still exist in England as an incorporated body, unconnected with the Masonic branch.
>
> 'The proper form of reception can be obtained by Eminent Commanders and Past Eminent Commanders of the Order of the Temple (who have already received the degree) on application to this office, or that of the Provincial Grand

Chancellor, Frater Samuel Deadman Fowler, Kingston, Canada West.

> 'It is to be understood that in conferring this degree it is not to be mixed with the Templar ritual, our present venerated and esteemed Supreme Grand Master Frater C. Kemeys Kemeys Tynte, on his election, having only assumed authority over the Order of the Temple as a distinct body.
>
> 'Encampment Commanders will be pleased to make their own By-laws and Regulations for the government of this degree of Knights of Malta, always being guided by that of the Templar Order.' [23]

It is important to understand that at this stage of Templar development in Canada, the Malta degree does not seem to have been particularly held in high regard, and, as evidenced by MacLeod Moore's circular, was to be kept distinct from the Order of the Temple. Even lesser regarded was the Red Cross degree, then an integral part of the American Templar system, which, although authorised by the warrant of

1824, was first discussed at a General Assembly of the Provincial Grand Conclave held in Belleville in 1861. Before looking at MacLeod Moore's reaction to what he saw as a non-Christian degree, it is important to provide some understanding of the Order of the Red Cross to readers unfamiliar with it.

A Red Cross digression

IN THE United States and Canada, Masonic Templars are initiated into three, rather than two orders: the Red Cross, Malta and the Temple – the first of which is peculiar to the North American Templar system.

The ritual of the Order of the Red Cross, like many of the side degrees in Freemasonry, is essentially a morality play, in which the candidate plays the part of one of the characters in the play. With respect to the Order of the Red Cross, the play is divided into three sections or acts, in which the candidate takes on the persona of Zerubbabel, a character prominent in the Holy Royal Arch degree. Biblically speaking, Zerubbabel was a governor of Judah and the man responsible for bringing the Jews out of Babylonian captivity and for building the second Temple.

In the ritual's first act, Zerubbabel meets with the Jewish Sanhedrin, who are concerned that their plans to rebuild the City of Jerusalem and the Jewish Temple are constantly being thwarted by their enemies. A decision is made to send a representative to the Court of Darius, the King of Persia, in order to garner the monarch's support in their cause. Zerubbabel volunteers to make the journey, as he knows the Persian king personally.

During the second act, despite being provided the passwords to gain admission to a foreign land, Zerubbabel is captured after crossing a bridge into Persia and carried to the king in chains as a spy.

In the final act, the prisoner Zerubbabel informs the king that he is not a spy, but rather has come to Persia to request the king's support. Darius offers to grant Zerubbabel's request if he discloses the secrets of Freemasonry. Zerubbabel refuses to do so, but rather than be offended, the king – impressed with Zerubbabel's integrity – frees the prisoner.

The Masonic drama concludes with Zerubbabel being invited to take part in a royal debate as to which is strongest: wine, the king or women. When given the opportunity to enter the debate, Zerubbabel determines that, although all have power over the hearts and minds of men, in the end, truth is the most powerful.

The Old Testament does not record a meeting between Zerubbabel and Darius; rather the fifth chapter of the Book of Ezra tells us that a local governor named Tatnai and a Persian official named Shetharboznai sent a letter to Darius announcing that the Jews had begun construction on the Temple. [24] The premise upon which the Red Cross ritual is based seems to have been taken from a combination of the works of the Jewish historian Josephus and the Apocryphal Book of I Esdras, [25] in which the story of the debate and Zerubbabel's participation in the same is told.

However, as is often the case with Masonic degrees, the writers of the ritual have attached their own embellishments upon the story, in this case having Darius reward Zerubbabel by creating the Order of the Red Cross, an Order that simply did not exist.

As such, North American Freemasons have, as part of their Templar system, a ritual that has no foundation in historical fact serving as a prerequisite for two Orders which are based upon historical reality: those of Malta and of the Temple. Although American and Canadian Templars see the Order of the Red Cross as a bridge between the prerequisite Holy Royal Arch degree and the Chivalric orders, it is none the less a peculiar addition to a system that is entirely Christian in nature. This is not to be critical

The banner of the Illustrious Order of the Red Cross as used in Canada. Although not unknown in other parts of the world, the non-Christian degree does not form a part of the Templar Orders in Freemasonry outside of North America.
Stephen Dafoe

of the degree itself, for the Order of the Red Cross teaches the Freemason a valuable lesson about the value of integrity and truth; however, it would be better placed outside the Templar system as it is in other countries.

For example, in England the Red Cross degree falls under the governance of the Allied Masonic degrees, while in Scotland it is worked through the Royal Arch under the name the Babylonish Pass. In Ireland, the degree was originally called the Red Cross of Babylon or Daniel, but is now known as the Knight of the Sword and forms the first degree governed by an independent body known as the Grand Council of Knight Masons. This organisation was formed in 1923 by 21 members of the Great Priory of Ireland, who decided to take over the so-called green degrees after they fell out of favour in Irish preceptories. [26] There also exists a variation on the degree known as the Prince of Jerusalem, which is the 16th degree of the Ancient and Accepted Scottish Rite.

Even in those countries where the Order of the Red Cross is part of the Masonic Templar package, there seems to be a desire to explain the peculiar positioning of a non-Christian degree in a Christian system. In the closing words of the *Historical Lecture* found in the Canadian version of the Red Cross ritual, the candidate is told:

> 'The Illustrious Order of the Red Cross is not a pagan rite, nor is it a mere social observance. It is an Order founded upon Truth, and is a proper preparation for the solemnities of the Orders of Malta and of the Temple. As Judaism was a preparation for Christianity, so let the Illustrious Order of the Red Cross be a preparation for the Christian Orders of Malta and of the Temple, which are to follow.' [27]

MacLeod Moore's Thoughts on the Red Cross

ALTHOUGH the Order is an integral part of the Templar system in Canada today, it was not always so. MacLeod Moore originally granted encampments the right to confer the degree so that Canadian Templars could visit their American counterparts. In his annual address during the sixth annual assembly of the Provincial Conclave held in St Catherines in 1862, MacLeod Moore spoke of the degree and his thoughts on its pedigree:

> 'With reference to the preliminary Degree of Knight of the Sword and East, or Babylonish Pass, known in the United States as 'Red Cross,'

and of which their Grand Encampment insist that every Companion should be in possession before he can obtain admission to a Knights Templar Encampment, I pointed out to Committee of Grand Conclave sitting in February last [1861], the necessity of obtaining an authority to confer it under our Templar Warrants. The Grand Vice-Chancellor communicated to me that the Committee resolved, that in consequence of the Statutes of the Order being silent as regards this Degree, (though conferred by some old Encampments in England,) I was to use my own discretion in the matter. I have therefore, carefully examined the Ritual of the 'Red Cross' used in the United States, as also that of the 'Knight of the Sword,' East, and East and West, as given under the Templar Warrants of Ireland, and the Royal Arch Chapters of Scotland,–being in fact, the same Degree as that of the 'fifteenth' of the 'Ancient and Accepted Scottish Rite,' and 'sixth' of the French Rite; and consider the Ritual used in Scotland and Ireland the one best adapted for us, it appearing to be the original Degree from which that of the 'Red Cross' of the United States is taken; in the latter there seem to be few inconsistencies, and it has been altered from the

The jewels of a Canadian Masonic Knight Templar consist of three emblems on a single bar. The first, a green sash and red cross, represents the Illustrious Order of the Red Cross. The second, a black sash and Maltese Cross, represents the Order of Malta. The third, a red and white striped sash with a seven-pointed star, represents the Order of the Temple. The gold colour of the star indicates that the Templar belongs to a preceptory that is in excess of 100 years' existence.
Stephen Dafoe

original (although not in essentials) to suit their own peculiar mode of working.' [28]

Never afraid to add his personal opinions on what he saw as the ridiculous nature of American Templary, MacLeod Moore went on to state:

'In Scotland and Ireland it is not insisted upon as a pass to the Templar, Royal Arch Masons being alone eligible; why it should have been in any way mixed up with the Order of the Temple is difficult to explain, as the Degree is only a combination of the Royal Arch commemorating the dangers encountered by the Jews in building the second Temple, and being of Jewish and Persian origin, has no connection with the Christian Order of Knight Templar.' [29]

Twenty-Ninth Triennial Conclave
Knights Templar
San Francisco, Cal., September MDCCCCIV

An advertisement from 1903 announcing the 29th Triennial Conclave to be held in San Francisco, California in 1904. Triennial celebrations were marked with lavish parades featuring marching American templars in full regalia, a peculiarity which caught the eye of many Canadian Templars.
Author's collection

Although MacLeod Moore permitted Canadian encampments to confer the degree, so as to allow Canadian Fratres to be admitted south of the border, his distaste for the Order of the Red Cross did not dissipate over the years. More than two decades later, in 1888 MacLeod Moore, then Supreme Grand Master of the independent Sovereign Great Priory of Canada, had more to say on the Order. In a circular sent to Provincial Priors, the Canadian Grand Master said:

'They [the American Templars] also add the degree called Knights of the Red Cross, peculiar to the American Masonic system, not practised outside the jurisdiction of their Grand Encampment, fabricated from the degrees known in Great Britain and Ireland as the Babylonish Pass, Knights of the Sword and East, etc., etc. It has no connection whatever with the Templar Order, and is neither a chivalric, nor, strictly speaking, a Masonic degree, the history of Masonry being always looked upon as having reference to the building of the Solomonic Temple.' [30]

MacLeod Moore was not alone in his opinion on the Order of the Red Cross. In October of 1888 General Roome, a Past Grand Master of the Knights Templar in the United States wrote to MacLeod Moore, stating:

'I agree with you that the Order of the Red Cross should never have been introduced into our system, and cannot see any connection between it and the Order of the Temple. It in no way refers to the Christian religion, and should never, therefore, have been part of a system whose foundation is Christianity. Templars in this country, however, believe differently.' [31]

However, not all American Templars were supportive of the degree as Roome concluded. Alfred Creigh in the introduction to his *History of the Knights Templar of the State of Pennsylvania* had unfavourable comments on the degree's placement within the American Templar system:

'We look forward with hope to that day when the present Ritual will give place to the one used by our Fathers, pre-eminently teaching the Christianity of the New Testament and discard the Red Cross degree, as not only an interpolation, but having been surreptitiously taken from the Ineffable degrees of the Scottish Rite. In the name of Christianity we protest against the Red Cross being acknowledged as the first degree of the Order of Christian Knighthood.' [32]

A New Country and a New Grand Body

ALTHOUGH we have jumped ahead several decades in our previous digression, let us return to the early years of Templary under MacLeod Moore. Over the next decade Canadian encampments grew in number and by 1867, the year of Canadian Confederation, there were eight encampments. These were Hugh de Payens, William de la More (in Ottawa, which had moved from its former home of Quebec), Richard de Coeur de Lion (in London), Godfrey de Bouillon (in Hamilton), King Baldwin (in Belleville), Richard de Coeur de Lion (in Montreal), Plantagenet (in St Catherines) and Sussex (in Stanstead). [33] Absent from the roster was Geoffrey de St Aldemar, of Toronto. This encampment, having lost all of its property and equipment in a fire, had become a dormant encampment. It was later revived in 1870. One of the most interesting of the additions was Godfrey de

Bouillon, which had received its warrant from Ireland in 1855, but joined the Provincial Grand Conclave in 1859.

At the 1867 meeting, which was the 12th Annual Assembly of the Provincial Grand Conclave, two important recommendations were made:

'1/ The Provincial Grand Conclave apply to the Supreme Grand Conclave of England for the appointment of a Colonial Deputy Grand Master for the Dominion of Canada, with power to establish Provincial Grand Conclaves in the Provinces of the Dominion and…

2/ that correspondences be originated with the Supreme Grand body in England to express the desire to form a Supreme Grand Conclave for the Dominion of Canada, with Colonel W. J. B. MacLeod Moore as its first Grand Master.' [34]

In answer to the Colonials' request, MacLeod Moore was appointed the Grand Prior of the Dominion of Canada by William Stuart, then Supreme Grand Master in England. [35] The new Grand Priory of the Dominion of Canada held its first assembly on 12 August 1868 at Montreal, Quebec, where 12 Templars assembled to conduct the business of the order.

In his Grand Historian's report of 1984, Forest-Jones recounts an incident at the Annual Assembly where the members of the order expressed a desire to change the uniform of the order and adapt garments similar to that of their American Brethren in order to be able to take part in Masonic processions. Forest Jones quotes the words of MacLeod Moore as follows:

'For my part, I cannot agree with the necessity for this change. The Order of the Temple as now constituted,

Traditional Calvary cross as used in the Order of the Temple in Canada.
Stephen Dafoe

The founding members of King Baldwin Encampment in Belleville, Ontario, are shown here in this photo c.1862. The Templar apron was done away with in 1873 in Canada.
Author's collection

The American-style chapeau and dress gained some popularity in Canada during McLeod Moore's term and although the Grand Master permitted a drill-type uniform for outdoor use, it was prohibited inside Canadian preceptories.
This did not stop Canadian Templars from embracing the American way. This particular chapeau belonged to a Preceptor as denoted by the double-barred cross.
Stephen Dafoe

The red pillbox chapeau used in Canada is like that used in the United Kingdom.
Stephen Dafoe

public at large… If the opportunity of exhibiting themselves in public with an attractive costume can really be the principal inducement for persons wishing to join the Order, such accessions to our rank would do us but little credit.' [36]

Canada and the Convent General

As we saw in Chapter 8, there was a movement in the 1870s to unite Scotland and Ireland with England and Wales through the Convent General. Although the Grand Bodies in England and Ireland proceeded, Scotland had withdrawn from the negotiations, as Pennsylvania had in the similar union proposed several decades earlier in the United States. As we have looked at the changes in Templary brought forth by the Convent General in Chapter 8, we will not reiterate them here. Suffice it to say that during the era of the Convent General Canadian Templars followed the changes adapted in England, to whose apron strings the Order was still clinging. One of these changes dealt with the ritual of Malta, heretofore permitted as an honorary degree with respect to Canadian Templary.

MacLeod Moore's instructions to the Canadian Fratres on this degree, which formed part of his annual address of 1873, offers further evidence of the errors contained in the 1824 warrant issue to the Kingston encampment:

was never intended for public gaze or street display, and the modern innovations of a military uniform and drill, so much thought of in the United States, do not convey to my mind the dignified position we ought to assume as successors although by adoption of our predecessors, the knights of old… I am strongly opposed to all public displays and deprecate them most strenuously … there is too great a desire to blazon forth all our doings, which can neither be understood or appreciated by the

'As we are now under the name of the United Orders of the Temple and Malta, it becomes necessary for each Preceptory to hold a Priory of Malta. The introduction of the Malta Order into that of Templary is comparatively very modern, irrespective of the legendary amalgamation, and many errors have been disseminated with respect to it by visionary and enthusiastic Masonic writers asserting as facts wild theories of their own relating to this supposed common origin in Freemasonry, and the old military orders of Knighthood. It has been stated that our Maltese ritual was brought from the Island of Malta; this I can positively say is not the case, for in 1849, I was the first to introduce the Templar Order there, and we did not work any degree of Malta. I have had for a long time in my possession, Malta rituals said to have been used by Templar Encampments in the last century, but I could find no trace whatever in Malta that any such ritual had belonged to the old Knights, or that they knew about our Encampments. It is from the Scottish Masonic degree of Knights of Malta our present ritual has been principally compiled.' [37]

Towards a More Perfect Union

THE CHANGES by the Convent General led the Canadian Templars to take steps towards a more autonomous existence. A memorial was sent to the Convent General on 25 April 1873 – a few weeks after William Stuart resigned as head of England, that read in part:

'The Templars of the Dominion of Canada, therefore, under the warmest impulse of Knightly courtesy and unswerving loyalty, present this their memorial, with the fullest confidence that after careful consideration their erection into a Great Priory may be conceded as a step calculated to subserve the best interests of the Christian and Chivalric Orders of the Temple and Hospital in this vast Dominion, and to perpetuate the ties of allegiance of a body which must, in the cause of events, become one of the most powerful and influential under the Convent General.' [38]

However, a year and a half later little had been done to accommodate Canada's desire for autonomy. During that time, Templary lost two of its important early leaders, William Stuart of England and the Duke of Leinster of Ireland, both of whom died in 1874. [39] But there was another death that would shine fortune on Canada's desire for independence. On 14 December 1873, Alexander Keith, Provincial Grand Prior of Nova Scotia died. Keith was a prominent Canadian, one-time Mayor of Halifax, Director of the Bank of Nova Scotia and President of the Upper House of the Nova Scotia legislature. [40] (Sadly, Keith is best known in Canada today for the beer that carries his name.) Until his death Keith had been in charge of Templars in Nova Scotia and New Brunswick. With his death, the Convent General gave MacLeod Moore dominion over the whole of British North America and two new preceptories entered the rolls: Nova Scotia of Halifax and Union de Molay of St John, New Brunswick. [41]

With the control he had desired for Canadian Templarism in his hands, there were still preceptories outside his governance. (These were the Scottish warranted preceptories at St Stephen and St John, New Brunswick as well as an Irish warranted preceptory in Hawkesbury, Ontario.) [42]

While MacLeod Moore was in effect the head of Canadian Templarism, autonomy was slow in coming. On 1 July 1876, the Convent General passed a resolution that allowed the formation of a National Great Priory for the Dominion of Canada. [43] On 10 August 1876, MacLeod Moore ascended the throne and became, by a patent issued by the pen of H.R.H. Albert Edward, the first Great Prior of the National Great Priory of the Dominion of Canada.

For reasons truly known to only those involved, there was some dissension among the ranks and in the autumn of 1875 a good number of Templars in Ontario tried to establish an independent Grand Commandery in alliance with the Grand Encampment of the United States. Fortunately for Canadian Templarism this movement died out and today all Canadian Masonic Preceptories are under the banner of the Sovereign Great Priory of Canada. [44] However, at the time, it seems to have eluded even the watchful eyes of MacLeod Moore, who in his address of that year said:

'I regret that my first official act, as Great Prior, should have been the necessity of issuing a circular to repudiate the advocacy of secession and the formation of another independent Templar Body in Canada. Had not the truth of such a movement been authenticated to me by an official of this Great Priory, I should not have thought it worthy of notice. There is, however, no difficulty, when desirable, in forming Provincial Priories for any of the Provinces, which would place them exactly in the same position to this Great Priory, as it formerly stood to that of England, and as the Grand Commanderies of the United States do to their Great National Council, "The Grand Encampment".' [45]

However, the protestations of the Ontario Templars were not the only complaints present at the time. MacLeod Moore was outraged that the Great Priory of England was making changes to the statutes of the Convent General, without the consent of the other

'The fact is, that the Great Priory of England has so long been the autocrat of the Templar Order, that it is difficult to persuade some of its members that it is now merely one of a Federated Union, and they seem to be indisposed to recognise either Ireland or Canada as an independent and co-equal member of the Federation; while it is equally plain that neither Ireland nor Canada will consent to assert and maintain other than her fullest rights under the same.' [46]

It is interesting that England appears to have been engaging in the very thing that Scotland had feared it would – thus preventing them from joining the Convent General at its outset.

Dissatisfaction with Canada's position within the Convent General grew among Canadian Templars over the next few years and at the Annual Assembly of 1883, the Canadian statutes were amended, effectively declaring itself a Sovereign Independent body of the Order. A letter to this effect was sent to the Arch Chancellor of the Convent General on 14 September 1883. [47] On 21 December 1883, MacLeod Moore followed up with a formal letter to Albert Edward requesting that Canada be absolved from all allegiances to the Supreme Grand Master. [48] Although the reply was not made until 17 April, 1884, it gave the Canadian Templars what they desired. [49]

Almost immediately upon receipt of the Arch Chancellor's letter, MacLeod Moore issued one of his own to the preceptories of Canada:

'MANIFESTO

'To all whom it may concern:

GREETINGS: –Whereas H.R.H., the Prince of Wales, Most Eminent and Supreme Grand Master of the United Orders of the Temple and Malta in England, Ireland and Canada, has been pleased to command the Arch-Chancellor of Convent General to acquaint the Great Prior of Canada, that H.R.H. having taken into consideration the prayer of the petition laid before him in behalf of the National Great Priory of Canada, to sever their connection with England, and to be absolved from their obligation to himself as Supreme Head, readily and willingly grants their request and absolves them from their allegiance to himself as members of the Convent General, and trusts that in their new position they may have a prosperous future. I, therefore, Lieutenant-

nationalities, one of which was MacLeod Moore's Dominion of Canada. To this end he sent a letter of protest to the Convent General, but was much harsher on the matter in his annual address:

Colonel W. J. B. MacLeod Moore, G.C.T., Most Eminent Great Prior ad vitam of the Great Priory of Canada, proclaim the Dominion of Canada occupied territory, and that all Commanderies and Preceptories of the Temple and all Knights Templars and Knights of Malta are subject to my authority, and owe me and the National Great Priory of Canada allegiance.

'Given under my hand and seal of the National Great Priory at St John, P.Q., Canada this 5th day of May, A.D. 1884.

'Fr. W. J. B. MACLEOD MOORE
'Gr. Prior Dom. Of Can.' [50]

In 1884, at what would be the final assembly of the National Great Priory of Canada, necessary resolutions were passed to change the name of the governing body to that of The Sovereign Great Priory of Canada. MacLeod Moore was elected as Supreme Grand Master *ad vitam*. The other officers of the new Sovereign Great Priory were elected to their positions and invested by Sir Knight Theodore S. Parvin who was then Grand Secretary of the Grand Encampment of the United States.

MacLeod Moore continued as Grand Master of Canadian Templars until his death on 1 September 1890. His funeral was held in Prescott, Ontario, and he was buried in Mount Royal Cemetery in Montreal, Quebec. As an interesting side note, each year Templars from across the country gather at the resting-place of our first Grand Master: a public procession that W. J. B. MacLeod Moore probably would not have approved of, given his distaste for the Americans' penchant for military procession.

It would seem to be a fitting

tribute to the memory of MacLeod Moore to close this chapter on Templary in Canada with the last words he is known to have written on the subject, for they beautifully exemplify, encapsulate and reflect upon the man's many years as a Freemason, but more especially a Knight Templar:

'Having passed through the ordeal of "seeking for hidden treasure," I had long been groping in the dark, expecting to find some occult science, the explanation of some philosophical problem, and to bring to light some wonderful secrets; in all of which I have been disappointed, until the true meaning of Masonry and Templary was placed before me in all its simplicity, purity, and sublime beauty; then all my anxiety vanished. I had been looking in the wrong direction, and for that which was not to be found. For this reason, I revere the degree of the Temple as taught in the British Dominion, not because it represents the once famous religious and military confraternity of that name in the Middle Ages, but because it holds up to the view of its members the Crucifixion, Death, Resurrection, and Ascension of Jesus, Lord and King of Glory, and Prince of Peace, teaching the Divinity of Christ and Trinity of the Godhead. Need I add, the object, the end, the result of the great speculation of antiquity was the ultimate annihilation of evil, and the restoration of man to his first state, by a Redeemer, a Messiah, a Christos — the Incarnate word?

This apron belongs to the English Knight Templar regalia of the 1850s. Canadian Templars wore this apron until its use was abolished on 14 August 1873 during the annual meeting of Sovereign Great Priory held at Kingston. *Stephen Dafoe*

Opposite: **This Masonic Templar apron of unknown date and origin is unique in that it permitted the owner to flip and turn the apron for use in the various orders of Masonic Templary. Image 1 shows the apron in its Red Cross form, Image 2 shows the reverse of the apron as used in the Order of Malta, and Image 3 depicts the reversible flap with skull and crossed bones to denote the Order of the Temple.** *Author's collection*

Left: **This badge from the 1908 meeting of the Sovereign Great Priory of Canada at Toronto shows the American-style chapeau and Templar cross, albeit with distinctly Canadian markings. Within a few years of Moore's death, American ideas had become firmly entwined around Canadian Templary.** *Stephen Dafoe*

'My views on this subject no doubt will be looked upon as expressing extreme opinions and be considered Utopian by the "wise" of this advanced age, being contrary to all preconceived ideas of Masonry. It may be so; but I have the consciousness of their abiding truth, and do not flinch or swerve from any criticisms that may be offered, or give the precious doctrines I hold and I am convinced that I have laid down the ancient and only true ground upon which the Order of the Temple should exist in Canada and elsewhere. Without a firm belief in the doctrine of the Trinity, there never would have been any Order of Knights Templar in the world. It was the very basis of the ancient Order, and continues to be so up to the present time. When this doctrine of the Holy Trinity is expunged from the Templar code, all my interest ceases, and I will have nothing to do with such a system of so-called Templary.' [51]

The seven-pointed star is an integral part of the Templar uniform in Canada and is worn on the breast of the Templar's jacket. As with the jewels, the gold colour denotes a centenary preceptory. The cross in the centre varies depending on the member's rank: a single-barred cross for a sir knight, a double-barred cross for a Preceptor and a triple-barred cross for the Grand Master.
Stephen Dafoe

References for Chapter 10

1. Stillson, Henry L. *History of the Ancient and Honourable Fraternity of Free and Accepted Masons and Concordant Orders*. London: The Fraternity Company, 1902. pp. 737, 738.

2. Quoted in Robertson, John R. *The History of the Knights Templars of Canada*. Toronto: Hunter, Rose & Co., 1890. p.20.

3. The St John's Lodge website claims that it was organised by dispensation under the 3rd Duke of Atholl in 1780. This would be impossible as the 3rd Duke died in 1774. However, there may be some confusion as both the 3rd and 4th Dukes of Atholl were named John Murray. The 4th Duke of Atholl was Grand Master of the Antients from 1775-1781; his predecessor and father served from 1771-1774.

4. Robertson. Op. cit.

5. Ibid. pp.30-31.

6. Ibid. p.30.

7. Ibid. pp.31-32.

8. 'Frequently Asked Questions.' The Grand Encampment of the United States of America. 28 January 2008
www.knightstemplar.org/faq1.html#order

9. Ibid.

10. 'Petition Back.' The Grand Encampment of the United States of America. 28 January 2008.
www.knightstemplar.org/newsrelease/Back.pdf

11. Between 2000-2002, I served the Sovereign Great Priory of Canada in the capacity of Grand Historian and the wording of the petition came up several times during this period. Although the petitions were to be changed, it seems that many preceptories are still using older versions of the document.

12. MacLeod Moore, William James Bury. 'British Templary: A History of the Modern or Masonic Templar Systems with a Concise Account of the Origin of Speculative Freemasonry and its Evolution since the Revival A.D. 1717.' *History of the Ancient and Honourable Fraternity of Free and Accepted Masons and Concordant Orders*. London, The Fraternity Company, 1902, p.743.

13. Robertson. Op. cit. p.32.

14. Ibid. p.32.

15. Ibid. p.39.

16. Ibid. pp.37-46.

17. Ibid. pp.38-39.

18. Ibid. p.48.

19. Ibid. p.48.

20. Ibid. p.49.

21. Ibid. p.49.

22. Dafoe, Stephen. 'A History of Canadian Masonic Templarism.' *The Templar Papers*. Franklin Lakes: New PageBooks, 2006, p.212. Robertson. Op. cit. p.49.

23. Robertson. Op. cit. p.71.

24. Ezra 5:1-17.

25. Maier, Paul L., trans. *Josephus: The Essential Writings*. Grand Rapids: Kregel Publications, 1988. pp.187-188. Also see I Esdras Chapters 3 and 4.

26. Smyth, Frederick. *Brethren in Chivalry*. London, Lewis Masonic, 1991, p.71.

27. Historical Sketch, found in the ritual of the Illustrious Order of the Red Cross as authorised by the Sovereign Great Priory of Canada. 1996, p.64.

28. Quoted in Robertson. Op. cit. p.75.

29. Ibid. p.75.

30. Ibid. p.350.

31. Creigh, Alfred. *History of the Knights Templar of the State of Pennsylvania*. Philadelphia: J. B. Lippincott & Co., 1868. p.373-374.

32. Ibid. pp.17-18.

33. Dafoe. Op. cit. p.213.

34. Dafoe. Op. cit. p.214.

35. Robertson. Op. cit. p.86.

36. Quoted in Dafoe. Op. cit. p.215.

37. Quoted in Robertson. Op. cit. p.115.

38. Quoted in ibid. p.117.

39. Ibid. p.122.

40. Dafoe. Op. cit. p.218.

41. Robertson. Op. cit. p.123.

42. Dafoe. Op. cit. p.219.

43. Robertson. Op. cit. p.146.

44. Dafoe. Op. cit. p.219.

45. Robertson. Op. cit. p.168.

46. Quoted in ibid. p.173.

47. Ibid. p.263.

48. Ibid. pp.264-265.

49. Ibid. p.266.

50. Ibid. p.266.

51. MacLeod Moore. Op. cit. p.794

Epilogue

The Knights Templar Today

It's a romantic tale, this story of the Knights Templar.

IN THE second decade of the twelfth century, a small group of knights gathered to start an Order of knighthood whose very name would put fear in the heart of every infidel and yet pride in the heart of every Christian. From this small band of knights arose an Order of Christian chivalry that accomplished what none had done before. And yet, less than two centuries after it was formed, it was struck down by the avaricious machinations of a greedy king and his subservient papal monkey. Despite the constant crack of the torturer's whip, these men remained steadfast in their hour of danger, upholding the great and proud name of the poor fellow soldiers of Christ and the Temple of Solomon. And how poetic it is, that while some of their number were undergoing the most horrendous of tortures, a small band of their brethren (not at all dissimilar in number to that of their forefathers who had created the Order) quietly slipped away by night disguised as humble stone masons. And how poetic it is, that these fugitive Templars would go on to create a new Order called the Freemasons, whose very name would strike fear into the hearts of every dictator and, yet, pride in the heart of every man who holds freedom dear. From eight humble knights arose the Templars and from eight humble Templars arose the Freemasons. And through it all, our Masonic Templar Order can claim an uninterrupted line of continuation that has spanned nearly nine full centuries, and stands a good chance of marking the millennial milestone if we can just hold out for another century.

It's a story of trials and tribulations, adventure and perseverance and, sadly, myth and reality. The opening paragraphs of this epilogue are the myth; the preceding chapters of this book are the reality. In the introduction to this book, I spoke of how I once believed that the superheroes I watched on television were real people and the events that were unfolding before my eyes were happening in real time. It is a myth that I accepted unconditionally and although I'd long since abandoned it by the time I'd joined the Masonic fraternity, I'd not yet given up the tendency to subscribe to myths. Indeed, for some time I was of the belief that there must be

TEN (K)NIGHTS IN A BARROOM

a connection between the Templars of old and their Masonic counterparts. But, as I said in the Introduction, I was certainly not alone in that belief. Indeed, even MacLeod Moore held to the idea during a significant portion of his Templar career. However, it is my hope that just as the idea of a Templar Freemason connection can be created through the pages of the copious books that make the claim, so too can the myth be dissolved through the same medium. If I have succeeded in my mission, then those of you who previously held to the notion that the dissolution of one great Order led to the creation of another, have a greater understanding of how the Templar Orders in Freemasonry were created. All one really needs to do is examine the chronology that forms the rear endpapers of this book and one can see that the evolution of Masonic Templary reads like a roadmap.

Having spent several chapters on the evolution of the Templars of old, the evolution of the myths that they continued after the dissolution and the evolution of the Templar degrees themselves, it is perhaps necessary to write a few words on the future of the order.

Quite some time ago I was sitting in my preceptory in Edmonton, Alberta listening to a discussion among the Fratres regarding the paying of a bill or some other mundane aspect of the regular business of the preceptory. I don't know what came over me, but as I looked around the room, I saw not my Masonic Brethren and fellow Knights Templar, but rather a sea of ageing, pot-bellied men in poorly fitting suits, dressed up in the most ridiculous garb I'd ever seen. And I wondered to myself, 'What would the original Knights Templar think of this lot?' I was immediately embarrassed by my internal thought process, but subconsciously there must have been some reason for the negative direction in which my mind wandered. Certainly I had no axe to grind with my fellow Templars. Since moving to Alberta in 2002, I have been welcomed into every body of Freemasonry with the same level of fellowship I had enjoyed in my native Province of Ontario.

No, there must have been something else at play for my mind to turn from fraternal admiration to an immediate sense of contempt. It is, I suppose, possible that, having recently entered my middle years, the sense of revulsion I felt was from looking at my own future. As my own Templar mentor Clare Faulkner was so fond of saying, 'I have more steps behind me than I have left ahead of me.' And yet, my age has never bothered me. In fact, I looked forward to turning 40 with the same enthusiasm that I looked forward to reaching my age of majority.

Throughout the course of writing this book, as I've reflected on the history of the original Templars and the history of the Masonic Orders that bear their proud name, I've often thought back to that brief moment of disgust, wondering why I felt the way I did.

It is only now, as I write these closing words, that I feel I can finally wrap my head around what troubled me so. My preceptory, like many preceptories in Canada and the United Kingdom, as well as in the commanderies of the United States, seems to be going through the motions of Templary. We meet once or twice a month to pass bills and vote on how much to give to this cause or that and occasionally to discuss who will deliver what lecture on the rare opportunity that we get to confer the Orders. To this end, we are engaging in the same activities we engage in at our lodge and chapter meetings; the only thing different is the regalia we wear on any given night of the week.

Perhaps having studied the history of the original Templars for some 15 years now, my love of Templary has dwindled over the years, or perhaps it has grown for exactly the same reason. Perhaps it is the latter that caused me to briefly recoil in disgust at the slouching posture of those seated around me.

With respect to the Templars of old, we see an Order that arose from a common desire to defend the interests of Christianity, an Order comprised of men who lived and died for the cause which united them into life-long bonds of brotherhood. We see an Order that remained steadfast in that faith although they suffered the crack of the torturer's whip and the stinging agony of being stretched on the rack. And while many confessed to the most horrendous of crimes to alleviate their afflictions, they none the less remained devout in their faith well after the dying embers of their last Grand Master's ashes were no more. It is from this chivalrous Order of Christian knights that Freemasons who subscribe to the doctrine of the Holy and Undivided Trinity take their name.

And yet, those who patterned themselves after the Templars of old were not without their share of trials and tribulations. As we have seen through the course of the preceding pages, the Masonic Templar story has been a tale of uphill battles, all of which were successfully overcome by the Fratres who went before us. Whether it was surviving the Unlawful Societies Act of 1799 in England, rebounding from the persecutions brought on by the Morgan Affair in the United States or struggling for autonomy, as was the case of the Templars in Canada, the work of the Masonic Templars who have gone before us has preserved the Order for in excess of two centuries.

Given that the original Templars survived for but 194 years, it is ridiculous for us to hold on to the myth that we are a direct continuation of the Order to which we pay homage.

The fact of the matter remains that the Templar Orders in Freemasonry originated not in a group of fleeing Templars who disguised themselves as operative Masons, but in an address written by the son of a humble Scottish baker: a man who, despite his modest beginnings, embraced the liberal arts and sciences as every Freemason ought. This lecture, rightly or wrongly, put ideas into the minds of other Freemasons who built chivalric rites upon the Craft degrees and in so doing paved the road for the system, as it exists today.

It is no little irony that chivalric Masonry began with stories of Templars dressed as Masons, which resulted in a large number of Masons returning the favour by dressing up as Templars. But since we are dressed up as Templars, whether in the mantle and chapeau of the United Kingdom and Canada or the civil war uniforms of our American Fratres, let us pay honour and respect to the men who once took great pride in wearing them.

The author front row, (third from left) with officers of the Grand Encampment of Indiana in 2005. Indiana code allows Commanderies to choose which style of regalia it will use. The Sir Knight in mantle and chapeau in the back row is an American Templar.
Stephen Dafoe

APPENDIX I

Augustin Barruel's Templar History

The text, which follows, is an extract from The Abbé Augustin Barruel's *Memoirs Illustrating the History of Jacobinism*, and comes from an English edition published in 1799 by Hudson & Goodwin. The text presented in this appendix is a complete reprinting of Chapter 12 of Barruel's book and presents Barruel's belief that Freemasonry originated from the dissolved Order of the Knights Templar. It is presented to give the reader a contrast to the works of Laurie, whose history of Freemasonry was written partly to respond to Barruel's accusations. A chapter from Laurie's work is contained in Appendix II. It is hoped that both texts will provide the reader with an insight into the thoughts and opinions of eighteenth and nineteenth century writers regarding the history of the Knights Templar and Masonic Templarism.

Antimonarchical Conspiracy

By Augustin Barruel

CHAP. XII

Proofs of the Origin of Free-masons drawn from their own systems.

Let us begin by rejecting the opinions of all those demi-adepts, who in their research of Masonry, led away by the similarity of name, really believe themselves descended from the Masons who built the Tower of Babel, or who raised the pyramids of Egypt, or more particularly from those who erected Solomon's Temple, or who worked at the Tower of Strasbourg; in fine, or those who laid the foundations of so many Churches in Scotland in the tenth century. Those men of mortar had never been admitted to the mysteries. If it be true that they ever constituted a part of the Brotherhood, they were soon excluded; their minds were too blunt and not sufficiently Philosophic.

They were no longer wanted, when once the trowel, the compasses, the cubic stone, the truncated or entire columns, became nothing more than systematic emblems; and the learned adepts blush at an origin which they consider as too ignoble.

We will subdivide into two classes the divers opinions set forth in order to ennoble their origin. In the first class, we comprehend all those who ascend back to the mysteries of the Egyptian priests, to those of Eleusis or the Greeks, or those who pretend to filiate from the Druids, or even who call themselves descendents of the Jews. In the second class, we consider those who only trace themselves from the Knights Templars, or the Age of the Crusades.

If we examine never so carefully the reasons on which the learned Masons ground their filiation from the ancient Philosophers, they will be found to contain merely this assertion:

'That in those ancient times when men first began to desert the primitive truths, to follow a religion and morality founded on superstition, some sages were to be met with who segregated themselves from the general mass of ignorance and corruption. These sages, perceiving that the grossness or the stupidity of the people rendered them incapable of profiting by their lessons, formed separate schools and disciples, to whom they transmitted the whole science of the ancient truths and of the discoveries they had made by their profound meditations on the nature, the religion, the polity, and the rights of man. In these lessons some insisted on the unity of God or true Deism, others on the unity of the Great Being, or Pantheism. The morality deduced from these principles was pure; it was grounded on the duties of charity, on the rights of Liberty, and on the means of living peaceably and happily. Lest these doctrines should lessen in value, should be falsified or be entirely lost, these sages commanded their disciples to keep them secret. They also gave them signs and a particular language by which they were to recognise each other. All those who were admitted to this school and to these mysteries were the children of Light and Liberty, while all the rest of mankind were with respect to them but slaves and prophane beings; and hence their contempt for the vulgar. This was also the reason why the disciples of Pythagoras observed such a profound silence, the origin of that particular and secret science of the divers schools. Hence the mysteries of Egyptians and afterwards of the Greeks and of the Druids, even the very mysteries of the Jews themselves, or of Moses initiated in all the secrets of the Egyptians.

'These divers schools and the secrets of these mysteries have not been lost; the Philosophers of Greece transmitted them to those of Rome, and the Philosophers of all nations followed the same line of conduct after the establishment of Christianity. The secret was always preserved, because it was necessary to avoid the persecutions of an intolerant Church and of its Priests. The sages of divers nations by means of the signs, which had been originally established, recognised each other, as the Free-masons do every where at this present day. The name only has been changed; and the secret has been handed down under the denomination of Free-masonry, as it was formerly under the sanction of the Magi, of the Priests of Memphis or of Eleusis, and of the Platonic or Eclectic Philosophers. Such is the origin of Masonry, such are the causes which perpetuate it, and which render it the same in all parts of the world.'

This is the faithful result of what the most learned Masons have published on their origin.—It is not our object to examine how false are such ideas on the pretended doctrine of the Persian, Egyptian, Grecian, Roman or Druid sages, nor how contrary to all history. In the first place, can any thing be more absurd than to suppose, that there existed a unity of religious opinions, of morality, and of secrets among Philosophers, who have left behind them systems as variegated, and as opposite to each other, and as absurd as those of our modern sophisticated Philosophis? Nor do I undertake to examine the erroneous assertion, that the mysteries of Eleusis has no other secret but the unity of God, and the purest morality.— How is it possible to suppose that those mysteries were not universally known to the people, when it is certain that all the citizens of Athens were initiated into both the lesser and greater mysteries, according to their age? Nor do I ask how it came to pass, that these same Athenians under the ground were all taught their catechism on the unity of God, and how when above ground they adored such a multitude of Gods; or, again, how it happened that they condemned Socrates to death on the accusation that he did not adore all the Gods; or else, why all the priests of the different idols only acquired by their initiation new zeal for the defence of that multitude of Gods and their altars. In fine, I will not ask how it is possible to persuade oneself that those Priests, so ardent and so zealous in their temples for the worship of Jupiter, of Mars, of Venus, and of so many other Deities, should be the very persons who assembled the people during the solemnity of the grand mysteries, to tell them that all their worship of the Gods was nothing but imposture, and that they themselves were the authors, ministers, or priests of imposture!

I know that such reflections are more than sufficient to stamp with falsehood the origin in which the learned Masons glory. But let us for a moment suppose, that these mysteries were what they had represented them to be; the very pretension of a society springing from such ancestry and glorifying in perpetuating their spirit and their Dogmas, this pretension alone, I say, must class this Brotherhood among the most ancient conspirators. It would entitle us to say to the Craft, 'Such then is the origin of your mysteries; such the object of your Occult Lodges! You then descend from those pretended sages, and those Philosophers, who, reduced to the lights of reason, had no farther knowledge of the true God than what their reason inspired. You are the children of Deism or Pantheism, and, replete with the spirit of your forefathers, you wish to perpetuate it! Like them you look upon every thing, which the rest of mankind have learned from the lights of Revelation, as superstition and prejudice. Every Religion, which adds to the worship of the Theist or detests the Pantheist, in a word Christianity and its mysteries, are with you objects of hatred and contempt! You abhor whatever the Sophists of Paganism, or the Sophists initiated in the mysteries of the idolatrous Priests abhorred;–but those Sophists detested Christianity, and showed themselves its most inveterate enemies. From your own avowals, then, in what light can we view your mysteries, if not as a perpetuation of that hatred and of that wish of annihilating every other Religion but the pretended Deism of the Ancients?

'You also say that you are what those Jews were, and still are, who, for all their religious tenets, only acknowledge the unity of God (provided there have existed Jews who did not believe in the Prophets and in *Emmanuel* the Saviour.)—You have then the same sentiments toward the Christian which the Jews have. Like them, you insist on *Jehovah*, but to curse Christ and his mysteries.'

The more the Masonic works above-mentioned are read, the more conspicuous will be the justice of the reproaches we make. With some, matter is eternal; with others, the Trinity of the Christians is only an alteration of Plato's system. Others again adopt the follies of the Martinists, or of the ancient Dualism. Nothing then can be more evident. All these learned Masons who pretend to descend from the Egyptian Priests, from those of Greece, or from the Druids, only seek to establish what may appear to be the religion of nature. Nor do they say less as to its

tenets than did the ancient and modern Sophisters. They all agree in destroying faith in the minds of their adepts, by systems in direct opposition to Christianity. If they do not run in wild declamation like Voltaire, Diderot, or Raynal, it is because they wished themselves to deduce their consequences. To have expressed them too openly would have been divulging their mysteries; but one must be more than ignorant not to comprehend their meaning— How can we be blind to their intentions, when we peruse the writing of those who declare themselves to have originated in the Templars, or in those sectaries who infected all Europe under the name of Albigeois [Cathars]? These two sources have more analogy between them than may be supposed.—Let us examine them separately, and then judge what we have to expect from men who glory in such an origin.

As to the Templars, let us suppose that this famous order was really innocent of all the crimes which occasioned its dissolution; what object either religious or political can the Free-masons have in perpetuating the mysteries under the name and emblems of that order? Had the Templars brought into Europe a religion, or a code of morality, that was not known? Is that their inheritance?—In that case neither your religion nor your morality can be that of Christ. Is it their fraternity, their charity, which is the object of your secrets? Did the Templars really add any thing to those Evangelical virtues? Or is it the religion of *Jehovah*, or the Unity of God, coinciding with the mysteries of Christianity?— If so, why do you reject all *Christians* who are not *Masons*, as prophane?

It is too late to reply, that the alarms of religion are vain and ungrounded; that religion never was the object of the Lodges. What then is that name, that worship of *Jehovah*, which the learned Masons declare to have been handed down from the Knights Templars. Whether these Knights were the authors of it, or whether they received it by tradition, or borrowed it from the ancient mysteries of Paganism and of its sages, this name I say, this worship cannot he foreign to Christianity; and is not every Christian entitled to say, 'You would not be so secret nor so ardent to revenge it, if it were similar to the worship established throughout the Christian world?'

Should governments partake of the same alarms, to what subterfuge will the adepts have recourse who have sworn to avenge Liberty, Equality, and every right of their association, which has been so desperately outraged in the destruction of the Templars? It will be in vain to assert the innocence real or fictitious of those too

famous Knights. That vow of vengeance which has been perpetuated for nearly five centuries can hardly fall on *Philip le Bel* or *Clement V*. or on the other Kings and Pontiffs who in the beginning of the fourteenth century contributed to the dissolution of that order? Nor will it be renewed in these days on account of the ties of blood, or through any pity for the particular individuals of the order? This vow, this oath of vengeance must be instigated by other causes— It has been perpetuated as the very object, the very doctrine of the school, as the principles and mysteries which the Masons have received from the Templars. What then can those principles be, which can only be avenged by the death of Kings and Pontiffs? And what are those lodges wherein for four hundred and four-score years this vow, this oath of vengeance has been perpetuated?

It is evident: Nor is it necessary in this place to examine whether Molay and his order were innocent or criminal, whether they were the real progenitors of the Free-masons or not; what is incontestable is sufficient; it is enough that the Masons recognise them for their ancestors; then the oath of avenging them and every allegory recalling that oath decidedly points out an association, continually threatening and conspiring against Religion and its Pontiffs, against Empires and their Governors.

But it may be asked, what lights can history throw on such an intimate connection between the mysteries of Masonry and the order of Templars? Such a question requires much research, nor will I withhold from my reader the result of the inquiries which I have made on that subject.

The order of Knights Templars established by Hugo de Paganis, and confirmed by Pope Eugenius III. was originally founded with all that charity which Christian zeal could inspire, for the service of those Christians who, according to the devotion of the times, went to visit the Holy Land. At first mere Hospitallers, these Knights, following the manners of the age, soon acquired great celebrity by their exploits against the Saracens. Their first repute originated in the services which were naturally to be expected from their great valour and eminent virtues: and such is the general testimony which history bears in their favour, making a wide distinction between the former and latter part of their existence. The order soon spread through Europe, and acquired immense riches. They then began to forget their religious state, courted only the celebrity of the field, and were no longer led to it by the same spirit. It is worthy of remark, that many years before their dissolution, history already reproached them not only with being lax in their former virtue, but with those very crimes which caused their destruction. In the very zenith of their glory, and at a time when it required much courage to upbraid them with their vices, we see *Matthew Paris* accusing them of converting into darkness the lights of their *predecessors*, of having abandoned their first vocation for plans of ambition, pleasure, and debauchery, and of unjust and tyrannical usurpation. They were already accused of holding correspondence with the Infidels, which rendered abortive all the plans of the Christian Princes; they were accused particularly of having treasonably communicated the whole of Frederic II's plan to the Soudan of Babylon, who, detesting such perfidy, informed the Emperor of the treachery of the Templars. This testimony, to which the Historian may add many others, will serve to render less surprising the catastrophe, which befell this famous order.

In the reign of *Philip le Bel*, two men who had been imprisoned for their crimes declared that they had some important discoveries to make concerning the Knights Templars. Such a declaration under circumstances so peculiar could not be thought entitled to much credit; it sufficed nevertheless to make the King determine on the dissolution of the order, and he caused all the Templars in his kingdom to be arrested on the same day. This step may be thought too precipitate: But interrogatories and a thorough examination followed; and it is on those proofs alone, and the authentic minutes of that examination, that the Historian is to found his judgement. If their avowals are perfectly free, numerous, and coincident with each other, not only in different tribunals, but in different countries, enormous as their crimes may have been, still we are forced to believe them, or reject all history, and the juridical acts of the tribunals. These juridical minutes have survived the ravages of time, and their importance has caused the Historian to refer to the collection made by Mr. Dupuy, the King's librarian; I know no other way of forming one's judgement, and of dissipating prejudices.

It has been said, that *Philip le Bel* and *Clement V.* had concerted between them the dissolution of the Templars. The falsity of such an assertion is evident on the inspection of their letters. Clement V. at first will give no credit to the accusations against the Templars; and even when he receives incontestable proofs from *Philip le Bel*, he had still so little concerted the plan with that Prince, that every step taken by the one or the other occasions disputes on the rights of the Church or of the Throne.

It was also said, that the King wished to seize on the great riches of these Knights; but at the very commencement of his proceedings against the order, he solemnly renounced all share in their riches; and perhaps no Prince in Christendom was truer to his engagement. Not a single estate was annexed to his domain, and all history bears testimony to the fact.

We next hear of a spirit of revenge which actuated this Prince; and during the whole course of this long trial, we do not hear of a single personal offence that he had to revenge on the Templars. In their defence not the most distant hint either at the revengeful spirit or at any personal offence against the King is given; so far from it, until the period of this great catastrophe the Grand Master of the order had been a particular friend of the King's, who had made him godfather to one of his children.

In fine, the rack and torture is supposed to have forced confessions from them which otherwise they never would have made; and in the minutes we find the avowal of at least two hundred Knights all made with the greatest freedom and without any coercion. Compulsion is mentioned but in the case of one person, and he makes exactly the same avowal as twelve other Knights, his companions, freely made. Many of these avowals were made in *Councils* where the Bishops begin by declaring that all who had confessed through fear of the torture should be looked upon as innocent, and that no Knight Templar should be subjected to it. The Pope, *Clement V.* was so far from favouring the King's persecutions, that he began by declaring them all to be void and null. He suspended the Archbishops, Bishops, and Prelates, who had acted as inquisitors in France. The King accuses the Pope in vain of favouring the Templars; and *Clement* is only convinced after having been present at the interrogatories of seventy-two Knights at Poictiers in presence of many bishops, Cardinals, and Legates. He interrogated them not like a Judge who fought for criminals, but like one who wished to find innocent men, and thus exculpate himself from the charge of having favoured them. He hears them repeat the same avowals, and they are freely confirmed. He desired that these avowals should be read to them after an interval of some days, to see if they would still freely preserve in their depositions. He hears them all confirmed. *Qui perseverantes in illis, eas expresse et sponte prout recitate suerant approbarrunt.* He wished still further to interrogate the Grand Master and the principal superiors, *praeceptores majores*, of the divers provinces of France, Normandy and Poitou, and of the Transmarine countries. He sent the most venerable persons to interrogate those of the superiors whose age or infirmities hindered them from appearing before him. He ordered the depositions of their brethren to be read to them, to know if they acknowledged the truth to them. He required no other oath from them than to answer freely and without compulsion; and both the Grand Master and the superiors of these divers provinces depose and confess the same things, confirm them some days after, and approve of the minutes of their depositions taken down by public notaries.

Nothing less than such precautions could convince him of his error: it was then only that he revoked his menaces and his suspension of the French bishops, and that he allows the King to proceed in the trials of the Templars.

Let such pretexts be forgotten, and let us dwell on the avowals which truth alone forced from these criminal knights.

Their depositions declare, that the Knights Templars on their reception denied Christ, trampled on the cross, and spit upon it; that Good Friday was a day which was particularly consecrated to such outrages; that they promised to prostitute themselves to each other for the most unnatural crimes; that every child begotten by a Templar was cast into the fire; that they bound themselves by oath to obey without exception every order coming from the Grand Master; to spare neither the sacred nor prophane; to look upon every thing as lawful when the good of the order was in question; and above all, never to violate the horrible secrets of their nocturnal mysteries under pain of the most terrible chastisement.

In making their depositions many of them declared they had only been forced into these horrors by imprisonment and the most cruel usage; that they wished, after the example of many of their brethren, to pass into other orders, but that they did not dare, fearing the power and vengeance of their order. That they had secretly conferred their crimes and had craved absolution. In this public declaration they testified by their tears the most ardent desire of being reconciled to the church.

Clement V. convinced at length, conceives whence the treachery proceeded, of which the Christian Princes so often complained they had been the victims in their wars against the Saracens. He permits the trials of the Templars to be continued, and a hundred and forty are heard in Paris.

All repeat the same deposition, except three, who declare they have no knowledge of the crimes imputed to their order. The Pope, not content with this information taken by Religions and by French Noblemen, requires that a new trial should take place in Poitou before Cardinals and others whom he himself nominates: Again, with the same freedom and for the third time, the Grand Master and other Chiefs in presence of Clement V. repeat their depositions. Molay even requested that one of the Lay Brothers who was about his person should be heard, and this Brother confirms the declaration. During many years these informations were continued and renewed at Paris, in Champagne, in Normandy, in Quercy, in Languedoc, in Provence. In France alone above two hundred avowals of the same nature are to be found; nor did they vary in England, where the synod of London, held in 1311, seventy-eight English Knights were heard, and two whole months were spent in taking informations and in verifying their declarations. Fifty-four Irish were also heard, and many Scotch, in their respective countries. It was in consequence of these declarations, that the order of the Templars was abolished in those kingdoms, and that the Parliament disposed of their goods. The same declarations were taken and proved in Italy, at Ravenna, at Bologna, at Pisa, and at Florence, though in all these councils the Prelates were very ready to absolve all those Knights who could succeed in their justifications.

When I hear the crimes of this order called in question, it appears to me that a sufficient attention has not been paid to the multiplicity of the avowals of these Knights, and of the diversity of nations which judged them. It would be one of the most extraordinary facts in history to see two hundred of these Knights accusing themselves of the greatest abominations. It would be a still greater atrocity to see so many Bishops, Noblemen, Magistrates, and Sovereigns, of different nations, sitting in judgement on the Templars, and publishing to the world, as free and uncontrolled, declarations which had only been extorted from them by the fear of torture. Such a conduct would be still more horrible than that of the Templars themselves; and would it not be equally extraordinary to see so many different nations agreeing to use the rack to extort such depositions from them? But for the honour of humanity such means were not employed in the trials of the Templars, by the Bishops and Grand Bailiffs, the King's Commissaries, the Cardinals, and Commissaries of Clement V. nor by himself in France. Such methods were not resorted to by the councils nor by the tribunals of other nations. Never was a cause of greater importance pleaded; and, from the numerous and authentic documents which are still extant, it is evident, that Judges never were more fearful of confounding the innocent with the guilty.

Let not the dissolution of another celebrated order, though in a very different way, be objected. The Jesuits were abolished, but they were not brought to trial; not a single member of the order has been heard in its defence, nor have any members deposed against it. I should be the first to condemn them, could proofs similar to those against the Templars, be adduced against them.

Let us for a moment suppose the Templars entirely innocent of the crimes imputed to them, what could have been the virtue and courage of an order, which could demean itself so much, as to make such declarations against itself? How can the Free-masons glory in such an ancestry, who, if their crimes were not monstrous, must themselves have been monsters of the basest cowardice.

The vulgar may be led away by the tardy protestations of Guy and Molay; but do the vulgar ever distinguish between the obstinacy of despair and that serene firmness and constancy which are the attendants on virtue? They are not aware that false honour, like truth, may have its martyrs. During three years Molay persevered in his avowal, and he repeated it at least three times; when he pretends at length to deny it, his expressions are those of rage, and he throws down the gauntlet to whoever shall pretend to assert that he *had made any deposition* against his order; at the place of execution he declares *that all he had said* against his order was false, and that if he deserved death it was *for having accused his order falsely* both before the Pope and the King. Amidst these contradictions, can the Historian receive such protestations of innocence? Much less is he to attend to the popular fable of Molay having cited Philip le Bel and Clement V. to the tribunal of God within a year and a day, and that both the Pope and King died within the year; for history not only varies as to the day, but even as to the year of Molay's execution.

As a last resource in defence of the order, the very nature and infamy of the crimes of which the Templars were accused have been alleged as a proof of their innocence. But most certainly the more infamous those crimes, the more debased must have been the members of the order to accuse each other of them. But all these crimes, however infamous and incredible, only serve to discover the abominable sect which introduced them among their adepts, and from whom the Templars evidently learned their frightful mysteries. That hatred of Christ, that execrable immorality, even to the atrocious infanticide, all are to be found in the tenets, they are even in the principles of that incoherent medley of Begards, Cathares, and of that shoal of sectaries which flocked from the East to the

Western States about the beginning of the eleventh century.

I would willingly assert that it was the smaller part of the Templars who suffered themselves to be carried away by such abominations. Some even at Paris were declared innocent. In Italy a still greater number were absolved; of all those who were judged at the Councils of Mayence and Salamanca none were condemned; and hence we may conclude, that of the nine thousand houses belonging to the order many had not been tainted, and that whole provinces were to be excepted from the general stain of infamy. But the condemnations, the juridical depositions, the method of initiating the knights, almost became general; the secrecy of their receptions, where neither Prince nor King, nor any person whatever, could be present during the last half century, are so many testimonies which corroborate the divers accusations contained in the articles sent to the Judges; that is to say, that at least two thirds of the order knew of the abominations practised, without taking any steps to extirpate them. *Quos omnes, vel quass due partes Ordinis scientes dictos errors corrigere neglecxerint.*

This certainly cannot mean that two thirds of the Knights had equally partaken of these abominations. It is evident on the contrary that many detested them as soon as they were acquainted with them; and the others not only submitted to them, though initiated, after the harshest treatment and most terrible threats. Nevertheless, this proves that the greatest part of these Knights were criminal, some through corruption, others through weakness, or connivance; and hence the dissolution of the order became necessary.

Another reflection which strikes me as being of weight, though I do not know that any one has made it, is, that between thirty and forty thousand Knights not only survived the condemnation of the order, but also survived Philip le Bel and Clement V. The greater part of these had only been condemned to canonical penance, to so many days fasting or prayer, or to a short imprisonment. They lived in different parts of the world, where they had nothing to fear from their *persecutors and tyrants*. Conscience, honour, and many other motives, should have induced these survivors to make their recantations after having made juridical depositions of such an abominable nature against the order; most certainly if they had made them through fear or seduction, it was a duty incumbent on them. Nevertheless, of those thousands of Knights heard in so many different states there is not a single one that makes his retraction, not one who leaves such a declaration to be published after his death. What men then are these Knights? If there depositions be true, how monstrous must that order have been by its crimes; if they be false, what monsters of calumny was it composed of? That fear may have made them swerve from truth during the reign of Philip le Bel, I will admit; but that King being dead, what becomes of such a plea.

Such nevertheless are the men whom the Masons glory in their decent from. Yes, and their descent is real. Their pretensions are no longer chimerical. Were they to deny it we should force them to recognise as their progenitors not the whole of the order, but that part whose ancient corruption and obstinate hatred against the altar and the throne, when added to their thirst of revenge, must render them still more formidable to both Kings and Pontiffs.

Were we to trace the decent of the Free-masons by the Templars, we should not have the assurance of those who suppose the Grand Master Molay, when in the Bastille, creating the four Lodges, that of Naples for the East, of Edinburgh for the West, of Stockholm for the North, and of Paris for the South. Yet, following nothing but the archives of the Free-masons themselves, and the apparent affinities which subsist between them and the Knights Templars, we are entitled to say to them—'Yes, the whole of your school and all your Lodges descend from the Templars. After the extinction of their order a certain number of criminal Knights, who had escaped the general proscription, formed a body to perpetuate their frightful mysteries. To their pre-existing code of Impiety they added the vow of vengeance against Kings and Pontiffs who had destroyed their order, and against all Religion, which proscribed their tenets. They formed adepts who were to perpetuate and transmit from generation to generation the same mysteries of iniquity, the same oaths, and the same hatred against the God of the Christians, Kings and Priests.—These mysteries have descended to you, and you perpetuate their impiety, their oaths, and hatred.—Such is your origin. Length of time, the manners of each age may have varied some of your signs and of your shocking systems; but the essence is the same, the wishes, oaths, hatred and plots are similar—You would not think it, but every thing betrayed your forefathers, and every thing betrays their progeny.'

Let us compare the tenets, language and signs. What a similarity, and how many are common to both! In the mysteries of the Templars the initiator begins by opposing the God who cannot die to the God who dies on the cross for the salvation of mankind. 'Swear,' he says to the candidate, 'that you believe in a God the Creator of all things, who neither did nor will die;' and then follow blasphemies against the God of Christianity. The new adept is taught to say, that Christ was but a false prophet, justly condemned in expiation of his own crimes and not of those of mankind. *Receptores dicebant illis quos recipiebant, Christum non esse verum Deum et ipsum fuisse falsum Prophetum; non Fuisse passum pro redemptione humanus generic, sed pro sceleribus suis.* Can anyone here mistake the Jehovah of the Masons, of the Iew [Jew] of Nazareth led by Raphael into Iudea [Judea] to suffer for his crimes?

The God of the Templars, which *never could die*, was represented by the *head* of a man, before which they prostrated themselves as before their real idol. This head is to be found in the Masonic Lodges in Hungary, where Free-masonry has preserved the greatest number of its original superstitions.

This head is to be found again in the *Magic Mirror* of the Cabalistic Masons. They call it the Being of Beings, and reverence it under the title of SUM (I am.) It represents their great Jehovah, source of all beings. And we may look upon it as one of the links which compose the general chain by which the Historian may connect the History of Masonry with that of the Templars.

These same Knights in hatred to Christ celebrated the mysteries of Jehovah more particularly on Good Friday, *precipue in die Veneris Sancta*; and it is the same hatred, which assembles the Rosicrucians on that day, according to their statutes, to dedicate it more particularly to their blasphemies against the God of Christianity.

Among the Templars, Liberty and Equality was masked under the name of Fraternity.

Qu'il est bos, qu'il est doux, de vivre en freres.
was the favourite canticle during their mysteries. It has since been adopted by the Masons, and is the mark that conceals their political errors.

The Templars were bound to secrecy by the most terrible oaths, subjected themselves to the vengeance of the Brethren and to death itself, if ever they revealed the mysteries of the order. *Injungebant eis per sacramentum, ne predicta revelarent sub paean mortis.* The same oath subsists among Masons, and the same threats for any one who shall violate secrecy.

The precautions lest any profane being should be present at their mysteries are similar. The Templars always began by sending out of their houses whoever was not initiated. Armed brethren were placed at the doors to keep off all curious people, and sentries were placed on the roofs of their houses, which they always called Temples. Hence originates the Brother Terrible, or the Tyler, who stands at the doors with a drawn sword, to defend the entrance of the Lodge against the prophane multitude. Hence that common expression among the Masons the *Temple is covered*, to say the sentries are placed; no prophane Being can gain admittance, not even by the roof, we may now act with full liberty. Hence also the expression *it rains*, signifying the Temple is not covered, the Lodge is not guarded, and we may be seen and over-heard.

Thus every thing to the very symbols, their language, the very names of Grand Master, of Knight, of Temple, even to the columns *Jachin and Boaz*, which decorated the Temple of Jerusalem, and which are supposed to have been given to the care of the Templars, all in a word betray our Free-masons to be the descendants of those proscribed Knights. But what 'a damning proof' do we not find in those trials, where the candidate is taught to strike with his poniard the pretended assassin of their Grand Master; in common with the Templars it is on Philip le Bel that they wreak their vengeance; and in every other King the sect behold this pretended assassin. Thus with all the blasphemous mysteries against Christ we see them perpetuating those mysteries of vengeance, hatred, and combination against Kings. The Masons then are correct when they claim the proscribed Knights for their forefathers. The same perhaps, the same means, the same horrors could not be more faithfully transmitted from father to son.

We shall conclude this chapter by a few observations which will not leave any subterfuge to those who may still entertain doubts concerning the crimes that brought dissolution on this proscribed order. Let us suppose the whole of this order to have been perfectly innocent of all the accusations of impiety, or of the principles dangerous to governments. It is not in this state of innocence that they are recognised by the Masons as their forefathers. The profound adepts only acknowledge the Templars as their progenitors, because they are convinced that those Knights were guilty of the same impiety and of the same plots as themselves. It is in these crimes alone, and in these conspiracies, that they recognise their masters; and as infidels and conspirators it is that they invoke them.

Under what tile do the Condorcets and Syeyes, under what tile does Fauchet or Mirabeau, Guillotin or Lalande, Bonneville or Volney, and so many others who are known to be at once the profoundest adepts of Masonry and the heroes of Impiety and Revolutionary Rebellion—under what title can such men challenge the Knights Templars as their progenitors, if not because they believe that they have inherited those principles of Liberty and Equality which are no other than hatred to Christ and hatred to Kings? When Condorcet, summing up the studious research of thirty years, falsifying all the facts of history, and combining all the cunning of Sophistry to extort our gratitude for those *secret associations destined to perpetuate privately and without danger among a few adepts*, what he calls *a small number of plain truths, as certain preservatives against the predominant prejudices*; when he extols the French Revolution as the triumph so long preparing and expected by these *secret societies*; when he promises to solve the question hereafter, whether the Knights Templars, whose dissolution was the summit of *barbarity and meanness, are not to be numbered among these associations*. When he holds such language, under what point of view can the Knights Templars have inspired him with such deep concern? With him, these secret associations, so deserving of our gratitude, are those of the pretended sages, 'indignant at feeling oppressed, even in sanctuary and conscience, by Kings the superstitious or political slaves of the priesthood.' They are the associations of those *generous* men 'who dare examine the foundations of all power or authority, and who revealed to the people the great truths, that their Liberty is inalienable; that no prescription can exist in behalf of tyranny; that no convention can irrevocably subject a nation to any particular family: That Magistrates, whatever may be their titles, functions, or powers, are only the officers, and not the masters of the people: That the people always preserve the right of revoking those powers emanating from them alone, whether they judge it has been abused, or consider it to be useless to continue them. In short that the people have the right of punishing the abuse as well as of revoking the power.'

Thus we see Condorcet tracing back the germ at least of all principles of the French Revolution to these secret associations, which he represents as the benefactors of nations, and as preparing the triumph of the multitude against the altar and the throne. All therefore he does or promises to do in the future, when he proposes the question, whether the Knights Templars are not to be numbered among those secret associations, can only originate in the hope of tracing to them principles, oaths, and means which in time would operate similar revolutions. All this zeal of Condorcet for the secret association of the

Templars, is no other than the hopes of finding them guilty of that same hatred against Royalty and the Priesthood with which his own heart is inflamed.

The secret which he has half disclosed more daring adepts have betrayed; it has escaped them amidst their declamations. In the delirium of fury, and in the cavern as it were of their regicide trials, they publicly invoke the *reeking dagger*, they exclaim to their brethren, 'Let the interval of ages disappear and carry nations back to the persecutions of Philip le Bel—*You who are or are not Templars*—help a free people to build in three days and for ever, a Temple of honour of Truth—*May tyrants perish*, and may the earth be delivered from them!'

Such then is the explanation which the profound adepts give the mysterious names of Philip le Bel and of the Templars. The first recalls to their mind, that in all Revolutions Kings are to be immolated, and the second, that there existed a set of men leagued in the oath of delivering the earth from its Kings. That is what they call restoring Liberty to the people, and building the Temple of Truth!—I had long feared to exaggerate the depravity and the plots of the proscribed Knights; but what crimes can history impute to them which are not comprehended in this terrible invocation of the adepts at the dawn of the Revolution? It is when they grow more daring, and stimulate each other to those crimes which overthrow the altar and the throne; it is at that period that the most furious adepts, at once Masons and Jacobins, recall the name and honour of the Templars to be avenged, and their oaths and plots to be accomplished. The Templars were then, what the Jacobin Masons are at this day; their mysteries were those of Jacobins.—It is not to that objections are to be made on this accusation. Let the profound adepts of Masonry and Jacobinism defend their own assertions; let the offspring be persuaded that they have wronged their forefathers: and even could that be demonstrated, still it would be evident that the mysteries of the Occult Lodges consist in that hatred of the altar and the throne, and in those oaths of rebellion and impiety, which the adepts extol as their inheritance from the Templars. Still it would be evident that the oath (the essence of Jacobinism) of overturning the altar and the throne is the last mystery of the Occult Masons, and that they only recognise the Templars as their progenitors, because they believed the mysteries of those famous though proscribed Knights contained all the principles, oaths, and wishes which operated the French Revolution.

APPENDIX II

William Alexander Laurie's Templar History

The following appendix is a verbatim transcript of Chapter II of William Alexander Laurie's *History of Free Masonry and the Grand Lodge of Scotland with Chapters on The Knights Templar, Knights of St John, Mark Masonry and R. A. Degree to which is added an Appendix of Valuable Papers.* The extract contains Laurie's original footnotes so that the reader may fully understand where the author derived his erroneous ideas and notions. In addition to painting a fictitious story of a Freemasonry embraced by the Knights Templar, Laurie does a reasonable job of refuting the claims of Barruel's anti-Masonic claims found in his 1797 book *Memoirs Illustrating the History of Jacobinism.*

CHAPTER II (pages 26-44)

PARTIAL EXTINCTION OF SECRET ASSOCIATIONS DURING THE DARK AGES – TRAVELLING ARCHITECTS – FREE MASONRY EXTINGUISGED THROUGHOUT EUROPE WITH THE EXCEPTION OF BRITAIN – ORIGIN OF THE KNIGHT TEMPLARS – THEIR PERSECUTION – THEIR INNOCENCE MAINTAINED –CONNECTION BETWEEN CHIVALRY AND FREE MASONRY – INITIATION OF THE TEMPLAR INTO THE SYRIAN FRATERNITY

Having in the preceding Chapter finished what may be properly be denominated the Ancient History of Free Masonry, we are now to trace its progress from the abolition of the heathen rites, in the reign of Theodocius, to the present day; and though the friends and enemies of the Order seem to coincide in opinion upon this part of its history, the materials are as scanty as before, and the incidents equally unconnected. In those ages of ignorance and disorder which succeeded the destruction of the Roman Empire, the minds of men were too debased by superstition and contracted by bigotry to enter into associations for promoting mental improvement and mutual benevolence. The spirit which then raged was not one of inquiry. The motives which then influenced the conduct of men were not those benevolent and correct principles of action which once distinguished their ancestors, and which still distinguish their posterity. Sequestered habits and unsocial dispositions characterised the inhabitants of Europe in this season of mental degeneracy, while Free Masons, actuated by very different principles, inculcate on their Brethren the duties of social intercourse, and communicate to all within the pale of their Order the knowledge which they possess and the happiness which they feel. But if science had existed in these ages, and if a desire of social intercourse had animated the minds of men, the latter must have languished for want of gratification as long as the former was imprisoned within the walls of a convent by the tyranny of superstition or the jealousy of power. Science was in these days synonymous with heresy; and had any bold and enlightened man ventured on philosophical investigations, and published his discoveries to the world, he would have been regarded as a magician by the vulgar, and punished as a heretic by the Church of Rome. These remarks may be exemplified and confirmed by an appropriate instance of the interfering spirit of the Romish Church even in the sixteenth century, when learning had made considerable advancement in Europe. The celebrated Baptists Porta having, like the sage of Samos, travelled into distant countries for scientific information, returned to his native home and established a society which he denominated the Academy of Secrets. He communicated the information which he had collected to the members of this association, who in their turn imparted to their companions the knowledge which they had individually obtained. But this little Fraternity, advancing in respectability and science, soon trembled under the rod of ecclesiastical oppression, and experienced in its dissolution that the Romish hierarchy was determined to check the ardour of investigation, and retain the human mind in its former fetters of ignorance and superstition. How then could Free Masonry flourish when the minds of men had such an unfortunate propensity to monkish retirement, and when every scientific and secret association was so thoroughly overawed and persecuted?

But though the political and intellectual condition of society was unfavourable to the progress of Free Masonry, and though the secret associations of the ancients were dissolved in the fifth century by the command of the Roman Emperor, yet there are many reasons for believing that the ancient mysteries were observed in private, long after their public abolition, by those enemies of Christianity who were still attached to the religion of their fathers. Some authors [1] even inform us that this was actually the case, and that the Grecian rites existed in the eighth century, and were never completely abolished. [2] These considerations enable us to connect the heathen mysteries with that trading association of architects which appeared during the dark ages under the special authority of the See of Rome.

The insatiable desire for external finery and gaudy ceremonies which was displayed by the catholic priests in the exercise of their religion, introduced a corresponding desire for splendid monasteries and magnificent cathedrals. But as the demands for these buildings were urgent, and continually increasing, it was with great difficulty that artificers could be procured even for the erection of such pious works. In order to encourage the profession of architecture, the bishops of Rome and the other potentates of Europe conferred on the Fraternity the most important privileges, and allowed them to be governed by laws, customs, and ceremonies peculiar to themselves. This association was composed of men of all Nations, of Italian, Greek, French, German, and Flemish artists, who were denominated Free Masons, and who, ranging from one country to another, erected those elegant churches and cathedrals which, though they once gratified the pride and sheltered the rites of a corrupted priesthood, now excite the notice of antiquarians and administer to the grandeur of kingdoms. The government of this association was remarkably regular.

Its members lived in a camp of huts reared beside the building on which they were employed. A surveyor or master presided over and directed the whole. Every tenth man was called a warden, and overlooked those who were under his charge; and such artificers as were not members of this Fraternity were prohibited from engaging in those buildings which they alone had a title to rear. [3] It may seem strange, and perhaps inconsistent with what we have already said, that the Fraternity of Free Masons should have been sanctioned, and even protected by the bishops of Rome, secret associations being always a terror to temporal and spiritual tyranny. But these heads of the Church, instead of approving of Free Masonry by the encouragement and patronage which they gave to architects, only employed them as instruments for gratifying their vanity and satiating their ambition; for, in after ages, when Masons were more numerous, and when the demand for religious structures was less urgent than before, the Roman Pontiffs deprived the Fraternity of those very privileges which had been conferred upon them without solicitation, and persecuted with unrelenting rage the very men whom they had voluntarily taken into favour, and who had contributed to the grandeur of their ecclesiastical establishment.

Wherever the catholic religion was taught, the meetings of Free Masons were sanctioned and patronised. The principles of the Order were even imported into Scotland, [4] where they continued for many ages in their primitive simplicity, long after they had been extinguished in the continental kingdoms. In this manner Scotland became the centre from which these principles again issued, to illuminate not only the Nations on the continent but every part of the civilised portion of the habitable world. What those causes were which continued the Societies of Free Masons longer in Britain than in other countries it may not perhaps be easy to determine; but as the fact itself is unquestionably true, it must have arisen either from some favourable circumstance in the political state of Britain which did not exist in the other governments of Europe, or from the superior policy by which the British Masons eluded the suspicion of their enemies, and the greater prudence with which they maintained the simplicity and respectability of their Order. The former of these causes had, without doubt, a considerable share in producing the effect under consideration; and we know for certain that in our own days the latter has preserved Free Masonry in a flourishing condition throughout these United Kingdoms, while in other countries the impudence and foolish innovations of its members have exposed it to the severest and justest censures, and, in many cases, to the most violent persecutions. It is a fact requiring no confirmation, and resulting from the obvious causes, that Free Masonry never flourishes in seasons of public commotion; and during these, even in Great Britain, though the seat of war is commonly in foreign countries, it has universally declined. But in those lands which are the theatre of hostilities it will be neglected in a still greater degree; and if these hostilities are long continued or of frequent recurrence, the very name and principles of the Order must soon be extinguished. Amid the continual wars, therefore, which during the middle ages distracted and desolated the continent of Europe, the association of architects would be easily dissolved, while on the western coast of Scotland, in the humble village of Kilwinning, they found a safe retreat from the violent convulsions of continental wars.

Before we detail the progress of Free Masonry after its importation into Britain, it will be necessary to give some account of The Knight Templars, a fraternity of Free Masons whose affluence and virtues aroused the envy of contemporaries and whose unmerited and unhappy end must have frequently excited the compassion of posterity. To prove that the Order of the Knight Templars was a branch of Free Masonry would be a useless labour, as the fact has been invariably acknowledged by Free Masons themselves, and none have been more zealous to establish it than the enemies of the Order; [5] the former have admitted the fact, not because it was creditable to them but because it was true; and the latter have supported it, because, by the aid of a little sophistry, it might be employed to disgrace their opponents.

The Order of Knight Templars was instituted during the Crusades, in the year 1119, by Hugo de Payens and Godfrey de St Omer, and received the appellation because its members originally resided near the church in Jerusalem which was dedicated to our Saviour. Though their professed object was to protect those Christian pilgrims whose mistaken piety had led them to the Holy City, yet it's almost beyond a doubt that their chief and primary intention was to practise and preserve the rites and mysteries of Free Masonry. We know at least that they not only possessed the mysteries, but performed the ceremonies and inculcated the duties of Free Masons; and it is equally certain that the practising of these rites could contribute nothing to the protection and comfort of the catholic pilgrims. Had they publicly avowed the real object of the institution, instead of that favour which they so long enjoyed, they would have experienced the animosity of the Church in Rome. But as they were animated with a sincere regard for the Catholic faith, and with a decided abhorrence for the infidel possessors of Judea, it was never once suspected that they transacted any other business at their sacred meetings but that which concerned the regulation of their Order, the advancement of religion and the extirpation of its enemies. The prodigies of valour which they performed towards the distressed pilgrims; and the virtues which adorned their private character, procured for them from the rulers of Europe that respect and authority to which they were so justly entitled, and which they so long maintained. But these were not the only rewards which they purchased by their virtues and military prowess.

From the munificence of the Popes, the generosity of the pious princes and nobles of Europe, and from the gratitude of those wealthy pilgrims who had experience in the moments of distress their kind assistance, they had acquired such immense possessions in every kingdom of Europe, but particularly in France, that the revenues often exceeded those of the secular princes. Thus independent in their circumstances, and being fatigued with those unsuccessful struggles against the infidels which

they had maintained with such heroic courage, they returned to their native land to enjoy peace and quiet the recompense of their toils. But like all men who are suddenly transported from danger and fatigue to luxury and ease, many of them deviated from that virtuous course which they had hitherto pursued, and indulged too freely in those amusements to which they had hitherto pursued, and indulged too freely in those same amusements to which they were invited by opulence and impelled to by inactivity. Thus, from the indiscretions of a few, the Order lost a considerable share of those honours and that celebrity which they had long enjoyed. But this relaxation of discipline and attachment to luxurious indolence were the principle faults chargeable against them; and to men of their spirit the forfeiture of popularity which was the consequence of their apostasy, would be a sufficient punishment. This, however, was not the sentiment of Philip the Fair. That rapacious monarch, instigated by private resentment, and encouraged by the prospect of sharing in their ample revenues, [6] imprisoned in one day all the Templars in France, merely at the instance of two worthless members of the Order who had been disgraced and punished by their superiors for their vices. [7]

It was pretended by these base accusers that the Templars abjured the Saviour,–that they spit upon his cross, –that they burned their children, –and committed other atrocities from which the mind recoils with horror, and which could have been perpetrated only by men as completely abandoned as the informers themselves. Under the pretence of discovering what degree of credit might be attached to the accusations the Knights were extended on the rack till they confessed the crimes with which they were charged. Several of them, when stretched on this instrument of agony, made every acknowledgement with which their persecutors desired. But others–retaining that fortitude and contempt of death which they had exhibited on the field–persisted in denying the accusations, and proclaimed with their last breath the innocence of their Order; and many of those who had tamely submitted to their persecutors retracted the ignominious confessions which the rack had extorted, and maintained the integrity in the midst of those flames which the barbarous Philip kindled for their destruction. Fifty-nine of these unhappy men were burnt alive at Paris by a slow fire; and the same vindictive spirit was exhibited in the other provinces of France and in the other nations of Europe. The fortitude which in every country was displayed by these unfortunate sufferers could have been inspired by innocence

alone, and is strong proof that their minds were neither so enervated by indolence, nor their bodies so enfeebled by luxury, as has been generally believed. The only murmurs which escaped from their lips were those which expressed their anguish and remorse that they had betrayed in the hour of pain the interests of the Order, and had confessed themselves guilty of crimes unworthy of men and of Templars.

But the scene which was to complete their ruin and satiate the vengeance of their enemies was yet to be enacted. Their Grand Master, Jacques de Molay, [8] and other dignitaries of the Order, still survived; and though they had made the most submissive acknowledgements which could have been desired, yet the influence which they had over the minds of the vulgar, and their connection with the many princes of Europe, rendered them formidable and dangerous to their oppressors. By the exertion of that influence they might restore union to their dismembered party, and inspire them with courage to revenge the murder of their companions; or, by adopting a more cautious method, they might repel by incontrovertible proofs the charges for which they suffered, and by interesting all men in their behalf, they might expose Philip to attacks of his own subjects and to the hatred and contempt of Europe. Aware of the danger to which his character and person would be exposed by pardoning the survivors, the French Monarch commanded the Grand Master and his brethren to be led out to a scaffold erected for the purpose, and there to confess before the public the enormities of they had been guilty, and the justice of the punishment which had been inflicted on their brethren. If they adhered to their former confessions a full pardon was promised to them, but if they should persist in maintaining their innocence, they were threatened with destruction on a pile of wood which the executioners had erected in their view to awe them into compliance.

While the multitude were standing around in awful expectation, ready from the words of the prisoners to justify or condemn their king, the venerable Molay, with a cheerful and undaunted countenance, advanced in chains to the edge of the scaffold, and with a firm and impressive tone thus addressed the spectators: –'It is but just that in this terrible day, and in the last moments of my life, I lay open the iniquity of falsehood, and make truth to triumph. I declare then, in the face of heaven and earth, and I confess to my eternal shame and confusion, that I have committed the greatest of crimes; but it has been only in acknowledging those that have been charged with so much virulence upon an Order which truth obliges me to pronounce innocent. I made the first declaration they required of me only to suspend the excessive tortures of the rack, and mollify those that made me endure them. I am sensible what torments they prepare for those that have the courage to revoke such a confession; but the horrible sight which they present to my eyes is not capable of making me confirm one lie by another. On a condition so infamous as that I freely renounce like, which is already but too odious to me, for what would it avail me to prolong a few miserable days when I must owe them only to the blackest of calumnies.' [9] In consequence of this manly revocation, the Grand Master and his companions were hurried into the flames, where they retained that contempt of death which they had exhibited on former occasions in the field. This mournful scene extorted tears from the most abandoned of the people. Four valiant knights, whose charity and valour had procured them the gratitude and applause of mankind, suffering without fear the most cruel and ignominious death, was indeed a spectacle well calculated to excite emotions of pity in the hardest hearts; and whatever opinion we may entertain concerning the character of that unhappy Order, every mind of sensibility will compassionate their fate, and denounce the inhuman policy of Philip the Fair.

From this short and imperfect account of the origin, progress, and dissolution of the Knight Templars, the reader will be enabled to understand the merits of the question respecting their innocence, which it is necessary here to consider. The opinions of contemporary writers were too much influenced by party spirit and religious zeal to merit any regard in this investigation. All those writers, [10] however, who are generally deemed impartial, and who were in no respect interested either in their condemnation or acquittal, have without hesitation pronounced them innocent of the charges to them, and ascribed their destruction to the avarice and private resentment of Philip. In the decision of these historians the public had in general acquiesced till the sentiments were unsettled by the bold pretentious and the sophistical reasoning of Barruel. This writer has charged upon them all those crimes with which their enemies had formerly loaded them. He has attempted to justify the severity of the French king, and has reproached, with the bitterest invective, the Society of Free Masons, because they were once connected with a Fraternity, which, in his opinion, was so wicked and profane. While we endeavour, therefore, to defend the

Templars against these recent calumnies, we shall at the same time be maintaining the respectability of our own Order by vindicating its members from that imputed depravity which, according to Barruel, they have inherited from their fathers.

In order to form an impartial judgment respecting any sentence which has been passed without proper evidence, either against individuals or associations, it is necessary to be acquainted with the motives and character of the accusers, and with the benefits which might accrue to them and the judges by the punishment or liberation of the accused. In the case before us the latter had been disgraced and imprisoned by the former. Sordid and private motives actuated their chief prosecutor and judge, and many rival Orders, who had been languishing in obscurity and indigence, propagated with assiduity slanderous accusations, in the hope of sharing in those ample possessions and that public favour which had been acquired by the superior abilities of the Templars. To all ranks of men, indeed, the veneration which their name inspired was an object of envy. Their revenues were calculated to create uneasiness in a covetous mind, and the remarkable regularity of their conduct was no small incitement to detraction. Such were the motives and prospects of their judges and accusers. Let us attend now to the accusations which were brought against them, and we shall find that these could scarcely come under the cognizance of law, as their pretended crimes were committed against themselves and not against society. Did they perpetrate murder upon any of their fellow-citizens? This was never laid to their charge. Did they purloin any man's treasures? Of theft they were never accused. Did they instigate to rebellion the subjects of any Government, or plot destruction against the person of any king?

Under such a character they were never known till Barruel called them traitors and regicides; because forsooth, it was his opinion that their successors, the Free Masons of France, were accessory to the murder of their Sovereign. What then were these crimes? It was said that they burned their own children! And yet an instance was never adduced in which the child of a Templar had disappeared, and in which the tenderness of a mother, as certainly would have happened, remonstrated against the murder of her infant. They were said to have committed upon one another the most unnatural of all crimes! And yet no individual produced a specific instance which could corroborate by indubitable proof. They were accused of insulting the Cross

of Christ; and yet they had shed their blood in the defence of His religion. Of deeds like these one may conceive a depraved individual to have been guilty, but to believe that a respectable Fraternity, consisting of thousands of members, could be capable of such enormities, requires a degree of faith to which the most credulous will scarcely attain.

Their innocence, and the injustice of Philip, will be still more apparent by considering the conduct of the latter, as related even by Barruel. This writer observes, 'That two men who had been imprisoned for their crimes declared that they had some important discoveries to make concerning the Knight Templars, and that this declaration, though entitled to little credit, made the king determine on the dissolution of the Order and the arrest in one day all the Templars in his kingdom.' [11] Here then, at the very outset, was the most flagrant injustice. Without summoning a single witness, without examining a single Knight, without consulting a single friend, without even knowing what the important discoveries were which the criminals had to make, the French king determined on the destruction of an Order whose Grand Master had been his particular friend, and even the godfather of one of his children. [12] This latter circumstance, indeed, is brought forward by Barruel to justify the conduct of Philip, because he sacrificed the duties of friendship to the principles of justice; but, taken in connection with the other parts of his conduct, it says little for either the head or the heart of that unscrupulous monarch.

Such being the premature and precipitate determination of Philip, we may consider the Order as at that time dissolved, and regard all those examinations, inquiries, confessions, trials, and councils which succeeded, as mere phantoms of justice, conjured up by that crafty prince to dazzle the eyes of his subjects, and sanctify the depravity of his own conduct. By keeping this circumstance in view, the intelligent reader will be enabled to understand the minute though sometimes contradictory details of historians respecting the trial and confessions of the Templars; and, notwithstanding the veil of justice with which the judges attempted to cover their proceedings, he will be aided in developing those detestable principles upon which their trial was conducted, and the despicable motives which induced Clement the fifth to partake in the guilt of Philip the Fair.

The most formidable, and indeed the only plausible argument by which Barruel supports his opinions, is drawn from the confessions of the Templars. He maintains that these were free from compulsion, and that no set of men could be so base as to accuse their Brethren of crimes of which they believed them to be entirely innocent. But the fallacy of his reasoning will manifest itself upon the slightest reflection. It is a curious, though unquestionable fact, that when an avowal must be made, men are more ready to accuse themselves of actions of which they have never been guilty than to confess those which they have actually committed. Such as have attended to the operation of their own minds, particularly in the earlier part of life, will acquiesce in this extraordinary truth; and those who have not had the occasion to observe it, will find, upon consideration, that it is consonant to the constitution of the human mind.

When a man confesses himself guilty of a crime which he has really perpetrated, he is exposed not only to the reproaches of his own conscience but to those of the world, and should he at any time retract his confessions he must be aware that every subsequent inquiry would only confirm the truth of his first deposition. But when a man, from a principle of fear, acknowledges the truth of accusations with which he is unjustly charged, a sense of his integrity and innocence supports him under the opprobrium of the world; he is conscious that his character will be vindicated by every investigation, and that the confessions which he has made may at any time be proved to have been the offspring of necessity. Such undoubtedly were the feelings by which the Templars were actuated.

Convinced that the crimes which they were required to acknowledge were of such an unnatural kind that they could never be imputed to them by any reasonable man, they yielded to the solicitations of their persecutors, in the well-grounded assurance that future inquiry would remove the stain which the irresistible desire of self-preservation had prompted them to throw upon their character. From this very consideration indeed, namely, from the nature of the crimes charged upon them, many eminent historians have maintained their innocence. But were we even to allow, with Barruel, in opposition to all history, that their avowals were entirely voluntary, we would from that circumstance, by an application of the principles already laid down, prove not the guilt but the innocence of the Order.

It is not, however, upon speculative principles alone that we can account for their confessions and subsequent recantations. There are fortunately some historical facts which furnish a rational explanation of their conduct, but which Barruel, either from ignorance of design, has totally overlooked. About the commencement of the persecution, Molay, the Grand Master, had been examined at Paris. From the causes which we have already explained, but particularly from a dread of those torments to which an obstinate avowal of his innocence would expose him, he made every confession which his persecutors demanded; and at the same time he transmitted circular letters to an immense number of his Brethren, requesting them to make the same confessions with himself, [13] for it was only by submissive conduct that they could hope to disarm the fury of their enemies and avert the blow with which the Order was threatened.

Agreeably to the request of Molay, many of the Templars made the same acknowledgements; while others, whose morality was more inflexible, and whose courage was more undaunted, disdained in the avowal of their own innocence and that of their companions. Molay, however, and those who had followed his example, soon perceived that though their admissions had protected them from injury as individuals, they had nevertheless rather inflamed the rage of Philip against the Order generally; and being convinced that their acknowledgements had produced an effect opposite to what they expected, boldly retracted their former avowals, and adopted that intrepid line of conduct of which we have already given a brief outline. There is another circumstance connected with this part of our subject which, though not taken notice of by historians, is well deserving of the reader's attention.

It is asserted by all contemporary writers, whether the friends or adversaries of the Templars, that all those who maintained their innocence were condemned either to death or to a punishment equally severe; while all who confessed, and adhered to their confessions, were either completely acquitted, or sentenced to a few days' fasting and prayer, or a short imprisonment. [14] It is allowed also by these historians, and even by Barruel, that a very considerable number were altogether ignorant of the crimes perpetrated by the others, and that some who were privy to them were not partakers in their guilt. In which class, then, are we to rank these innocent men? Among those who suffered, or among those who were saved? If among the former, their enemies were guilty of the most flagrant injustice and cruelty in consuming the innocent on the same pile with the guilty. If among the latter, they must have been compelled to confess themselves guilty of crimes of which they were entirely innocent.

In order to show that the confessions were voluntary and not extorted, Barruel is obliged to deny facts which are admitted by every historian. But lest his readers should not be so sceptical on that point as himself, he takes care to inform them that the bishops declared that all those whose confessions were extorted by the rack should be regarded as innocent, and that no Templar should be subject to it: That Clement the Fifth rather favoured them, and that he sent the most venerable persons to interrogate those whose *age and infirmities* prevented them from appearing before him. But who, pray, were those aged and infirm Templars to whom Clement is so compassionate? Were they men who were smarting under diseases inflicted by the hand of Providence? Were they men whose aged limbs were unfit for the fatigues of a journey, of whose grey hairs had excited the pity of the Roman Pontiff? No! They were a few undaunted Knights, whom the blood-extorting screws of their tormentors had tortured and disabled, whose flesh had been lacerated on the rack, and whose bones had been disjointed or broken on the wheel. These are the men who, in the language of the above writer, were prevented by their *age and infirmities* from travelling to the Poictiers, or who, in the mere simple style of the Pope himself, were unable to *ride on horseback, or to bear any other method of conveyance whatsoever*. Such was the mildness of Clement which Barruel applauds! And such too, we may add, is the integrity of Barruel.

Having thus endeavoured to vindicate the character of our ancestors from the accusations of their enemies, it is necessary to make a few remarks respecting the ceremonial observances which are attributed to them and their posterity by the author of the Memoirs of Jacobinism. But this, our opponents well know, is ground on which Free Masons are prohibited to enter by the rules of their Order. It is here, consequently, that the most numerous, and apparently the most successful attacks have been made, for we can be provided with no means of defence without laying open the mysteries of the Fraternity. Conscious of the disadvantages under which we labour, our adversaries have invented the most frightful and foolish ceremonies, and imposed them upon the world as those of Free Masonry; among these may be reckoned those rites and oaths which Barruel ascribes to the Templars and their posterity, but which, we solemnly aver, have no connection with either the one or the other; and were we permitted to divulge the whole of our ritual system, many who have duped the public by deceitful information would stand abashed at their conduct, while others who have confided therein would be astonished at the extent of their credulity. Then might Free

Masons defy, as they have done on every other point, the fabrications of the malicious and the conjectures of the ignorant; then, too, might they mock at the ingenuity of the wise. But as they are bound to preserve from public view the rites of their Order, it is highly disingenuous to assail them in the quarter where resistance is impossible, and where every unprincipled man may triumph with impunity. Is not this to assassinate an enemy with his hands tied behind his back? Is not this to reproach a foe who is deprived of the power to reply?

But there is another important consideration which, while it points out in a more striking manner the disingenuity of such conduct, should at the same time incite the candid inquirer to reject every calumny against secret associations, arising from reports concerning their rites and ceremonies. If ever the secrets of Free Masonry were betrayed they must be betrayed by men who were completely destitute of religious principle, who paid no respect to those ties which unite the members of civil as well as secret associations; who, in short, neither feared God nor regarded man. Suppose then that a person pretending to be a Free Mason offered to communicate either to an individual or to the public the rites and ceremonies of the Order. What degree of credit should men of probity attach to the information which they might in this way receive? A person addresses them under the character of a perjurer, offering to violate the most solemn engagements, and to divulge mysteries which have been concealed for ages. He may give them accurate information, or he may not. If the secrets which he offers to betray have been hitherto unknown, there is no possible method of ascertaining the truth of his deposition, and it is rather to be suspected that he will dupe his hearers by a fictitious narrative than trample upon an engagement guarded by the most awful sanctions. He might indeed confirm by an oath the truth of his asseveration, but as he must have violated an oath equally solemn, no man of any sense will give him the slightest credit. But granting that he really divulges the rites and ceremonies of Free Masonry, it is either clear that he has not understood their true import, or at least that they have made no impression upon his mind; and it is almost certain, therefore, that from ignorance or misapprehension of their meaning, he will exhibit under an aspect calculated to excite ridicule, that which, if properly explained, would command respect. If then, it be so difficult for the uninitiated to discover those secrets, and still more so to ascertain their signification if they should discover them, what must we think of

those who open their ears to every slanderous tale against Free Masons, which unprincipled individuals may impose upon their credulity? What must we think of those who reproach and vilify us upon the doubtful statements of cunning and interested men? We appeal to the impartial reader if they are not equally base with the informers themselves.

Such are some of the considerations by which we would attempt to repel those charges and distorted facts with which Barruel has calumniated the character and disfigured the history of the Templars. They will be sufficient, we hope, to remove those erroneous impressions which the perusal of the Memoirs of Jacobinism may have left upon the reader's mind; but although we have adopted the opinion of those who maintain their innocence, we cannot coincide with them in believing that, as individuals, they were totally exempt from blame. They were possessed of the same corrupted nature, and influenced by the same passions as their fellow men, and were unquestionably exposed to stronger and more numerous temptations. Some of them, therefore, may have been guilty of crimes, and these, too, of an aggravated kind, which by a strange though not uncommon mistake, may have been transferred to their Order. But it was never proved that they were traitors, child-murderers, regicides, and infidels. A certain class of historians, indeed, have imputed to them such iniquities, and were unable to establish their assertions have fixed upon them the more probable charges of drunkenness and debauchery. But amidst all these accusations we hear nothing of that valour which first raised them to pre-eminence; nothing of that charity and beneficence which procured them the respect of contemporaries; nothing of that fortitude and patience which most of them exhibited on the rack and in the flames. In their case it has been too true that:

The evil which men do lives after them;
The good is oft interred with their bones.

But allowing them to be as guilty as their enemies have represented, upon what principles of sound reasoning or common sense does Barruel transfer their guilt to the Fraternity of Free Masons? Is it absolutely necessary that the son should inherit the bodily diseases and the mental debility of his forefathers? or is it fair that one Order, proposing to itself the same object, and instituted upon the same principles as another, should be charged also with the same crimes? Certainly not. If virtue and vice were

hereditary qualities we might arrogate to ourselves much honour for our connection with the Templars; but as we have not been applauded for their virtues, we should not be reproached for their crimes. But the reasoning of Barruel is as repugnant to the dictates of experience as it is to those of common sense. Were not the inhabitants of England at one period fanatics, rebels, and regicides? But where now is the Nation that is more liberal in its religion and more steady in its loyalty! Did not the French at one time torture, burn and massacre their fellow-citizens, from the fury of their religious zeal and the strength of their attachment to the Catholic communion? But what Nation is at the present less influenced by religious principles, and less attached to the Church of Rome! Did not the rulers of France at one time torment and assassinate hundreds of the Templars because they deemed them infidels, traitors, and regicides? And have we not seen, in these latter days, the rulers of France themselves infidels, traitors and regicides! If, however, the impartial reader should upon farther inquiry give credit to the guilt of the Templars, in order to remove the imputed stain which has been transferred to Free Masons it may be sufficient to address him in the words of the poet:

Tempora mutantur, et nos mutamor in illis.
[The times are changing, and we are changing with them.]

About the time of the Knights Templar, Chivalry had attained its highest perfection. It had its existence indeed prior to this period; but as it continued to influence the minds of men long after the destruction of that Order, we have deferred its consideration till the present stage of our history. When it made its appearance the moral and political condition of Europe was in every respect deplorable. The religion of Jesus existed only in name. A degrading superstition had usurped its place, threatening ruin to the reason and the dignity of man. The political rights of the lower orders were sacrificed to the interests of the higher. War was carried on with a degree of savage cruelty, equalled only by the sanguinary contentions of the beasts of prey, –no clemency was shown to the vanquished, –no humanity to the captive. The female sex were sunk below the natural level, were doomed to the most laborious occupations, and were deserted and despised by that very sex on whose protection and sympathy they have so natural a claim.

To remedy these disorders, a few intelligent and pious men formed an association whose members obligated themselves to defend the

Christian religion, to practise its morals, to protect widows and orphans, and to decide judicially, and not by arms, the disputes which might arise about their goods or effects. It was from this body undoubtedly that chivalry arose, [15] and not, as some think, from the public investiture with arms, which was customary among the ancient Germans. But whatever was its origin, it produced a considerable change in the opinions and customs of society. It could not indeed eradicate that ignorance and depravity which engendered those evils that we have already enumerated. It has softened however the ferocity of war. It restored woman to that honourable rank which she now possesses, and which at all times she was entitled to hold. It has inspired those sentiments of generosity, sympathy, and friendship, which have already contributed very much to the civilisation of the world, and introduced that principle of honour which, though far from being a laudable motive to action, often checks the licentious when moral and religious considerations would make no impression upon their minds. Such was its origin, and such the blessings which it imparted.

That it was a branch of Free Masonry may be inferred from a variety of considerations, from the consent of those who have made the deepest researches into the one, and who were intimately acquainted with the spirit, rites, and ceremonies of the other. They were both ceremonial institutions, and important precepts were communicated to the members of each for the regulation of their conduct as men and as brethren. Its ceremonies, like those of Free Masonry, though unintelligible to the vulgar, were always symbolic of some important truths. The object of both institutions was the same, and the members bound themselves by an oath to promote it with ardour and zeal. In chivalry there were also different degrees of honour, through which the youths were obliged to pass before they were invested with the dignity of knighthood; and the Knights, like Free Masons, were formed into Fraternities or Orders, distinguished by different appellations. [16]

From these circumstances of resemblance, we do not mean to infer that Chivalry was Free Masonry under another name; we mean only to show that the two were intimately connected; that the former took its origin from the latter, and borrowed from it not only some of its ceremonial observances but the leading features and the general outline of its constitution. These points of similarity, indeed, are in some cases so striking that several learned men have affirmed that Free Masonry was a secondary Order of Chivalry, and derived its origin from the usages of that

institution; [17] but by what process of reasoning these authors arrive at this conclusion is impossible to conjecture. The only argument which they adduce is the similarity of the institutions; but they do not consider that this proves with equal force that Free Masonry is the parent of Chivalry. We have already shown that there were many secret societies among the ancients, particularly the Dionysian architects, which resembled Free Masonry in everything but the name; and it requires no proof that this brotherhood arose many hundred years before the existence of chivalry. If then there are points of resemblance between the institution we have been comparing, we must consider Free Masonry as the fountain and Chivalry as the stream.

The one was adapted to the habits of intelligent artists, and could flourish only in times of civilisation and peace; the other was accommodated to the dispositions of a martial age, and could exist only in seasons of ignorance and war. With these observations, indeed, the history of both fraternities entirely corresponds. In the enlightened ages of Greece and Rome, when Chivalry was unknown, Free Masonry flourished under the sanction of government, and the patronage of intelligent men. But during the reign of Gothic ignorance and barbarity which followed the destruction of Imperial Rome, Free Masonry languished in obscurity, while Chivalry succeeded in its place, and proposed to accomplish the same object by different means, which, though more rough and violent, were better suited to the manners of the age. And when science and literature revived in Europe and scattered those clouds of ignorance and barbarism with which she had been overshadowed, Chivalry decayed along with the manners that gave it birth, while Free Masonry arose with increasing splendour, and advanced with the same pace as civilisation and refinement. The connection between them is excellently exemplified in the Knights Templars. It is well known that this was an order of Chivalry, and that the members thereof performed its ceremonies and were influenced by its precepts, and we know that they were also initiated into the mysteries, regulated by the maxims, and practised the rites, of Free Masonry. [18]

But though they then existed in a double capacity, it must be evident to all who study their history that their Masonic character chiefly predominated; and that they deduced the name of their institution, and their external observances, from the usages of chivalry, in order to conceal from the Roman Pontiff their primary object, and to hold their secret meetings free from suspicion and alarm. About this time,

indeed the Church of Rome sanctioned the Fraternity of Operative Masons, and allowed them to perform their ceremonies without molestation or fear. But this clemency, as we have already observed, was a matter of necessity; [19] and the same interested motive which prompted his Holiness to patronise that trading association, could never influence him to countenance the duplicity of the Templars, or permit them to exist in their Masonic capacity. It was the discovery, indeed, of their being Free Masons, of their assembling secretly, and performing ceremonies to which no stranger was admitted, that occasioned those calamities which befell them. It will no doubt appear surprising to some readers that such zealous defenders of the Catholic religion should practise the observances of a body which the Church of Rome has always persecuted with the bitterest hostility. But their surprise will cease, when they are informed that about the middle of the eighteenth century, when Free Masonry was prohibited in the Ecclesiastical States by a papal bull, the members of the Romish church adopted the same plan, and, being firmly attached to the principles and practice of the Fraternity, established what they called a new association, into which they professed to admit none but zealous abettors of the papal hierarchy. In this manner, by flattering the pride of the church they eluded its vigilance, and preserved the spirit of Free Masonry by merely changing its name, and professing to make it subservient to the Pontificate.

Before leaving this subject, it may be interesting to some readers, and necessary for the satisfaction of others, to show in what manner the Knight Templars became the depositaries of the Masonic mysteries. We have already seen that almost all the secret associations of the ancients either flourished or originated in Syria and the adjacent countries. It was here that the Dionysian artists, the Essenes, and the Kasideans arose. From this country also came several members of the trading community of Masons which appeared in Europe during the dark ages; [20] and we are assured that notwithstanding the unfavourable condition of that province, there exists at this day on Mount Libanus. [21] As the order of the Knight Templars therefore was originally formed in Syria and existed there for a considerable time, it is no improbable supposition that they received their Masonic knowledge from the Lodges in that quarter. But we are fortunately, in this case, not left to conjecture, for we are expressly informed by a foreign author [22] who was well acquainted with the history and customs of Syria, that they were actually members of the Syriac Fraternities.

References for Appendix II

1. Gibbon, vol. v. chap. Xxviii, p.110.

2. Psellus, Vide also Anthologia Hibernica for January 1794, and pp.11-12, *supra*.

3. Wren's Parantalis, or a History of the Family of Wren, pp. 306-307. Henry's History of Great Britain, vol. viii, p.273, book iv, chap. V, sec. 1. Robinson's Proofs of a Conspiracy, p.21.

4. A.D. 1140. Vide Statistical Account of Scotland, parish of Kilwinning, Edinburgh Magazine for April 1802.

5. Vide Barruel's Memoirs of Jacobinism, vol. Ii, p. 379-383, where this is attempted at some length. As Barruel, was unacquainted with either the observances of the Templars or those of Free Masons, he has attributed to both many absurd rites which never existed but in his own mind. For the same reason he has omitted many points of resemblance, which would have established the common opinion upon an immovable foundation.

6. His darling object was to set the power of the monarchy above that of the church. In his celebrated controversy with Pope Boniface, the Templars had been on the side of the Holy See. Philip, whose animosity pursued Boniface even beyond the grave, wished to be revenged on all who had taken his side; moreover, the immense wealth of the Templars, which he reckoned on making his own if he could destroy them, strongly attracted the king, who had already tasted of the sweets of the spoliation of the Lombards and Jews; and he probably also feared the obstacle to the perfect establishment of despotism which might be offered by a numerous, noble and wealthy society such as the Templars formed.— Burnes's Sketch of the History of the Knights Templars, pp.26-27—E.

7. Squin de Flexian, who had been a Prior of the Templars, and had been expelled [from] the Order for heresy and various vices, and Noffo Dei, 'a man,' says Villani, 'full of all iniquity.'—Burnes's Sketch p.28—F.

8. Jacques de Molay was elected Grand Master in the year 1297, and was the second elevated to that dignity after the expulsion of the Christians from the Holy Land. He was of an ancient family in Besançon, Franche Compté, and entered the Order in the year 1265—Burnes's Sketch, p.27, *note*.—E.

9. Historie de Chevaliers Hospitaliers de Saint Jean de Jerusalem, par Abbé Vertot, tom. II, pp.101-102.

10. Among those were Hume, –History of England, vol. II, p.373; Henry, –History of Britain, vol. VIII; and Vertot, *ut supera*.

11. Memoirs of Jacobinism, vol. II, p.364.

12. Ibid, vol. II, p.366.

13. Historie de Chevaliers Hospitaliers de Saint Jean de Jerusalem, par Abbé Vertot, tom. II, p.86.

14. Some of them even received pensions for their confessions. Vertot, tom. II, p.91.

15. Bontainvilliers on the Ancient Parliaments of France, Letter 5; quoted in Brydson's Summary View of Heraldry, pp.24-26.

16. Brydson's Summary View of Heraldry, *passim*.

17. Chevalier Ramsay. Robinson's Proofs of a Conspiracy, p. 39. Leyden's Preliminary Dissertation to the Complaynt of Scotland, pp.67,71; and the Preface to the sixth edition of Guillim's display of Heraldry.

18. Vide pp.29, 30, *supra*.

19. Vide pp.27, 28, *supra*.

20. Mr. Clinch, who appears to have been acquainted with this fact, supposes that Free Masonry was introduced into Europe by means of the Gypsies. Anthologia Hibernica for April 1794. There was such an intimate connection between Asia and Europe in the time of the Crusades, that the customs and manners of the one must in some measure have been transferred to the other.

21. Anthologia Hibernica for April 1794.

22. Alder de Drusis Montis Libani.—Rome 1786.

APPENDIX III

Observations on the Orders of Knights Templar and Knights of Malta

The following is an extract from Webb's monitor 1859 – compare against 1818 version.

According to the Abbe de Vertot, the Order of Knights of Malta, who were originally called Hospitallers of St. John of Jerusalem, took its rise about the year 1099; from which time to the year 1118, their whole employment was works of charity, and taking care of the sick.

Some time after the establishment of this Order, nine gentlemen (of whose names two only remain on record, viz.: Hugho de Paganis and Godfrey Adelman) formed a society to guard and protect Christian pilgrims who travelled from abroad to visit the Holy Sepulchre.

These men were encouraged by the Abbot of Jerusalem who assigned them and their companions a place of retreat in the Christian church, called the Church of the Holy Temple, from which they were called Templars, and not from the temple of Jerusalem, that having been destroyed by Titus Vespasian, 982 years before the society of Templars was instituted.

The society increased rapidly, and was much respected; but had neither habit, order, or mark of distinction, for the space of nine years, when Pope Honorius II, at the request of Stephen, Patriarch of Jerusalem, laid down a rule and manner of life for them; and ordained that they should be clothed in white; to which garment Pope Eugenius III. added a red cross, to be worn on the breast, which they promised by a solemn oath to observe forever. Incited by the example of the Knights Templar, about the year 1118, the Hospitallers also took up the profession of arms, in addition to their original charitable profession; occupying themselves at one time in attending upon the sick, and at others in acts of hostility against the Turks and Saracens. At this time they took the name of knights hospitallers.

Both Orders flourished and increased daily; but that of the Templars, though the younger of the two, having from its original establishment been wholly employed in the profession of arms, was by many esteemed to be the most honourable; and therefore many noblemen, princes and persons of the highest distinction, who thought the service of tending the sick too servile an employment, entered themselves among the knights templars, in preference to the other Order.

Both Orders, for years, generally took the field together, and, as well by themselves as in conjunction with the troops of the crusades, won many battles, and performed prodigies of valour. The emulation, however, which subsisted between them often occasioned warm disputes, which rose to such a height as produced frequent skirmishes between detached parties of the two Orders. This occasioned the Pope and the respective Grand Masters to interfere; who in a great measure suppressed these quarrels; but the Knights of the different Orders ever afterward continued to view each other with jealous eyes.

Some time after these difficulties were thus partially suppressed, the Turks assembled a great force and drove the whole of the Christians out of Palestine. The last fortress they had possession of was that of St. John d'Acre. This was long and bravely defended by the Knights Templar against their besiegers. The Turks, however, at last forced three hundred Knights, being all that remained of the garrison, to take refuge in a strong tower, to which also the women fled for safety. The Turks hereupon set about undermining it, which they in short time so effectually accomplished, that the Knights saw, in case they held out any longer, they must inevitably perish. They therefore capitulated, stipulating, among other things, that the honour of their women should not be violated. Upon this, the tower being opened, the Turks marched in; but, in total breach of the terms of capitulation, they immediately began to offer violence to the women. The enraged Knights instantly drew their swords, hewed in pieces all the Turks who had entered, shut the gates against those who remained without, and resigned themselves to inevitable death, which they soon met with, by the tower being undermined and thrown down upon their heads.

After this defeat, the two Orders found an asylum in the island of Cyprus; from whence, after some time, the Knights Templar, finding their number so diminished as to leave no hopes of effecting anything toward the recovery of the holy land, without new Crusades (which the Christian princes did not seem inclined to set on foot), returned to their different commanders in the various parts of Christendom.

From this time the Orders separated; the Knights Hospitallers remained a while at Cyprus, from whence they afterward went to Rhodes, and thence to Malta; which name they then assumed. The Knights Templar dispersed themselves throughout all Europe, but still enjoyed the princely revenues, and were extremely wealthy.

Vertot says, that Boniface VIII, having engaged in a warm dispute with Philip, king of France, the two Orders, as had too frequently happened before, took opposite sides. The Knights of Malta declared in favour of King Philip, while the Knights Templar espoused the cause of the Pope. This conduct, Philip, partly from a revengeful disposition, and partly from the hope of getting possession of the vast wealth of the Knights, never could forgive; but formed, thenceforward, the design of suppressing the Order, whenever a proper opportunity should offer. This, however, did not occur, until after the decease of Pope Boniface.

Immediately on the death of that pontiff, the cardinals assembled to elect his successor; but party disputes ran so high in the conclave, that there seemed no probability of again filling the papal chair very speedily. At length, through the intrigues and machinations of the friends of Philip, the Cardinals were all brought to consent to the election of any priest that he should recommend to them.

This was the darling object the monarch had in view: this being accomplished, he immediately sent for the Archbishop of Bordeaux, whose ambition he knew had no bounds, and who would hesitate at nothing to gratify it; and communicated to him the power he had received of nominating a person to the papal chair, and promising he should be the person, on his engaging to perform six conditions. The Archbishop greedily snatched at the bait, and immediately took an oath on the sacrament to the faithful performance of the conditions. Philip then laid upon him five of the conditions, but reserved the sixth until after the Archbishop's coronation as Pope; which soon took place in consequence of the recommendation of the king to the conclave; and the new Pope took upon himself the name of Clement V.

Vertot goes on to say, that a Templar and a citizen of Beziers, having been apprehended for some crime, and committed together to a dungeon, for want of a priest confessed to each other; that the citizen, having heard the Templar's confession, in order to save his own life, accused the Order to King Philip; charging them, on the authority of what his fellow prisoner had told him, with idolatry, sodomy, robbery and murder; adding that the Knights Templar being secretly Mohammedans [Muslims], each Knight, on his admission in the Order, was obliged to renounce Jesus Christ, and to spit on the cross in token of his abhorrence of it. Philip, on hearing these accusations, pardoned the citizen, and disclosed to the Pope his sixth condition, which was the suppression of the Order of Knights Templar.

Not only every Knight Templar must know to a certainty the absolute falsehood of these charges, but every unprejudiced reader of Vertot's history must also perceive that the whole of the accusation was the product of Philip's own brain, in order to accomplish his long-wished-for object of suppressing the Order, and getting possession of their vast riches in his dominions. It is therefore, evident that the story of the Templar's confession was all a forgery, and that the citizen was no other than a tool of Philip, who, to insure his own pardon, was prevailed on to make oath of such a confession having been made to him by a Templar.

The historian proceeds to say, that in consequence of this accusation, the Knights Templar in France, and other parts of the Pope's dominions, were imprisoned by his order, and put to the most exquisite tortures, to make them confess themselves guilty. They, however, bore these tortures with the most heroic fortitude, persisting to the last in asserting their own innocence, and that of the Order.

In addition to these proceedings, Pope Clement, in the year 1312, issued his bull for the annihilation of the order of knights templars, which he caused to be published throughout every country in Christendom. He at the same time gave their possessions to the Knights of Malta, which appropriation of the Templar's estates was assented to by most of the sovereigns of Europe; and there is now extant among the English statutes, an act of parliament, whereby, after setting forth the Order of Templars has been suppressed, their possessions in England are confirmed to the knights of St. John.

Vertot, however, further says, that in Germany, the historians of that nation relate, that Pope Clement having sent his bull for abolishing the Order to the Archbishop of Metey, for him to enforce, that prelate summoned all his clergy together, that the publication might be made with greater solemnity; and that they were suddenly surprised by the entry of Wallgruffor Count Sauvage, one of the principals of the Order, attended by twenty other Templars, armed, and in their regular habits.

The Count declared he was not come to do violence to any body, but having heard of the bull against his Order, came to insist that the appeal which they made from that decree to the next council, and the successor of Clement, should be received read and published. This he pressed so warmly, that the Archbishop, not thinking it proper to refuse men whom he saw armed, complied. He sent the appeal afterward to the Pope, who ordered him to have it examined in a council of the province. Accordingly, a synod was called, and after a lengthy trial, and various formalities which were then observed, the Templars of that province were declared innocent of the crimes charged upon them.

Although the Templars were thus declared innocent, it does not appear that either their possessions or their government, as a distinct order was restored; but that their estates in the German Empire were divided between the Knights of Malta and the Teutonic Knights; to the first of which Orders, many Knights Templar afterward joined themselves. This appears altogether probable from the following circumstances, viz.: It is unquestionable, that the habit of the Knights Templar was originally white; but we now observe they distinguish themselves by the same colour as the Knights of Malta, viz: black; which change cannot be accounted for in any other way than by a union with the Knights of that Order.

APPENDIX IV

Templar Text Book

The following history of the Knights Templar is an extract from the Templar's Text Book or Ritual of a council of the Red Cross and or an encampment of Knights Templar and Knights of Malta. – 1859

Order of Knights Templar

This Order, which fills so large a space in the history of the world during the twelfth and thirteenth centuries, took its rise in Jerusalem about the year eleven hundred and eighteen. Nine gentleman, among whom were Hugh de Payens and Godfrey Adelman, associated themselves together and formed a society for the purpose of guarding and protecting pilgrims to the Holy Sepulchre from the insults and attacks of the infidels. Hence the order partakes of both the religious and military character. Baldwin I., at that time king of Jerusalem, approved of the organisation and objects of the Order, and appointed for their residence a part of the royal palace near the site of the Temple of Solomon, in consequence of which they were called Templars, or soldiers of the Temple. By other historians it is said a place of retreat was assigned them in a Christian church, called the church of the Holy Temple, (perhaps from the fact of its being supposed to stand on the spot originally occupied by Solomon's Temple) and hence their name.

This Order had no connexion with ancient Freemasonry, save that the rites and mysteries of Masonry were practised and preserved by them; and from an early date, none could be admitted to the honours of the Order until they had first received the several degrees of Masonry up to the Royal Arch.

The history of this Order is an interesting study. For a long time it flourished in Europe and the Holy Land; men of the first distinction united themselves to it, and the attainment of honourable place in its ranks was considered an object worthy of their highest ambition. In connexion with the Knights Hospitallers, who took their rise about the same time, they took the field against the infidels, won many battles during the crusades, and performed prodigies of valour. The emulation which existed between these two Orders, at last produced hostilities between them, and it proceeded to such an extent that they finally turned their arms against each other. At length the Grand Masters of the respective Orders, assisted by the Pope, interfered, and to a great extent suppressed the quarrel, but there still remained a lingering jealousy between them.

Some time after this, the Turks succeeded in driving the Christians out of Palestine, and at the capture of the last fortress held by the Knights, put a large number of Templars to the sword. After this, the remnants of the two Orders found an asylum in the Island of Cyprus; but from their diminished numbers, and the disinclination of the Christian princes to renew the crusades, they saw no prospect of recovering the Holy Land, and the Templars returned to their different Commanderies in various parts of the world. The Knights Hospitallers afterwards went to Rhodes and thence to Malta, where they remained and assumed its name; since which time they have been known as the Knights of Malta.

The early history of the Templars, as well as those of Malta, is a history of magnanimous warfare in the defence of the Christian religion, and in the protection of Christian pilgrims on their journeys going to, and returning from, the Holy City. That feature in their character, however, has long since ceased to be practical; a love for the Christian religion and the practice of Christian virtues have taken its place.

But to resume the history of the Order. From the time of Hugh de Payens to that of James de Molay, the Templars continued to be governed by a succession of the noblest and bravest knights of which the chivalry of Christendom could boast. They continued to increase in power, in fame and in wealth; and thus independent in their circumstances, and fatigued with those unsuccessful struggles against the infidels which they had maintained with such manly courage, they returned to their native land to enjoy in peace and quiet, the recompense of their toils. But, like all men who are suddenly transported from danger and fatigue to opulence and ease, many of the Templars deviated from the virtuous course which they had hitherto pursued, and indulged too freely in those luxuries and fashionable amusements to which they were invited by opulence, and impelled by inactivity. Thus, from the indiscretions of a few, did the Knights Templars lose a considerable share of those honours and that celebrity which they had long enjoyed. But this relaxation of discipline and attachment to luxurious indolence, were the only crimes of which the Templars were guilty; and to men of honour and spirit like them, the forfeiture of popularity, which was the consequence of their apostasy, would be a sufficient punishment.

This, however, was not the sentiment of Philip the Fair, then King of France, and he soon found a pretence for the exhibition of his ambitious and avaricious spirit by the most unjust and revengeful proceedings against the Order. In his celebrated controversy with Pope Boniface VIII, in the beginning of the fourteenth century, as Vertot observes, the Templars had, as was usual with them, sided with the Pontiff and opposed the king. This conduct, Philip, partly from a revengeful disposition and partly from the hope of gaining possession of the vast wealth of the Knights, never could forgive, but formed thenceforward the design of suppressing the Order whenever a proper opportunity should offer. This, however, did not occur till after the decease of Pope Boniface.

Immediately after the death of the pontiff the cardinals assembled to select his successor; but party spirit ran so high in the conclave that there seemed no probability of filling the papal chair very speedily. At length, through the intrigues and machinations of the friends of Philip, the cardinals were induced to assent to the election of any priest whom he should recommend. This was the darling object which the monarch had in view, which being accomplished, he immediately sent for the archbishop of Bordeaux, whose ambition he well knew had no bounds, and communicated to him the power which he had received of nominating a person to the papal chair, and promised that he should be the person, provided he would engage to perform six conditions. The archbishop greedily accepted the proposal, and forthwith took an oath on the sacrament to the faithful performance of the conditions. Philip at once disclosed to him the five of these conditions, but reserved the sixth until the archbishop should be crowned pope. His coronation soon took place and he assumed the name of Clement V.

Vertot proceeds to say that a Templar and a citizen of Beziers having been apprehended for some crime and committed together to a dungeon, for want of a priest confessed to each other; that the citizen having heard the Templar's confession, in order to save his own life, accused the Order to King Philip, charging them, on the authority of what his fellow prisoner had told him, with idolatry, sodomy, robbery and murder; adding that the Knights Templar being secretly Mahometans [Muslims], each Knight, at his admission into the Order, was obliged to renounce the Saviour, and to spit on the cross in token of his abhorrence of it. Philip, on hearing these accusations, pardoned the citizen, and disclosed to the Pope his sixth condition – the suppression of the Order of Knights Templar.

Clement, by Philip's direction wrote in June, 1306 to De Molay, the Grand Master, who was then at Cyprus, inviting him to come and consult with him on some matters of great importance to the Order. De Molay obeyed the summons and arrived in the beginning of 1307, at Paris, with sixty Knights and a large amount of treasure. He was immediately imprisoned, and on the 13th of October following, under the pretence of discovering what degree of credit might be attached to the accusations which had been made against the Order, every Knight in France was, by the secret orders of the king, arrested and put to the most excruciating tortures. Several of the Knights, when extended on the rack, made every acknowledgement which their persecutors desired. But others retaining on this instrument of agony that fortitude and contempt of death which they had exhibited on the field, persisted in denying the crimes with which they were charged, and maintained with their last breath the innocence of their Order. Many of those, even, who had tamely submitted to their persecutors, retracted those ignominious confessions which the rack had extorted, and maintained their integrity in the midst of those flames which the barbarous Philip had kindled for their destruction.

On the 12 May 1310, fifty-four of the Knights after a mock trial were publicly burnt at Paris. The same vindictive and inhuman spirit was exhibited in other provinces of France and the other nations of Europe. They bore their sufferings with unparalleled fortitude. The only murmurs which parted their lips, were those which expressed their anguish and remorse that they had in the hour of pain betrayed the interest of their Order, and confessed themselves guilty of crimes unworthy of a Templar and a man.

But the atrocious scene was yet to come which was to complete the ruin of the Templars and satiate the vengeance of their enemies. Their Grand Master, Molay, and other dignitaries of the Order still survived: and though they had made the most submissive acknowledgements of their unrelenting persecutors, yet the influence which they had over the minds of the vulgar, and their connexions with many of the princes of Europe, rendered them formidable and dangerous to their oppressors. In order, therefore, that these might not restore union to their dismembered party, and inspire them with courage to revenge the murder of their companions, and that they might not live to prove the innocence of their Order and the vile motives of Philip in persecuting them, the French monarch commanded the Grand Master and four of his brethren to be led out to a scaffold, erected for the purpose, and there to confess before the public the enormities of which their Order had been guilty, and the justice of their punishment.

If they adhered to their former confessions, a full pardon was promised to them; but if they persisted in maintaining their innocence, they were threatened with destruction on a pile of wood which the executioners had erected in their view to awe them into compliance. While the multitude were standing around in awful expectation, ready from the words of the prisoners to justify of condemn their king, the venerable Molay, with a cheerful and undaunted countenance, advanced in chains to the edge of the scaffold, and in a firm and impressive tone thus addressed the spectators: 'It is but just, that in this terrible day, and in the last moments of my life, I lay open the iniquity and falsehood and make truth to triumph. I declare then, in the face of heaven and earth, and I confess, though to my eternal shame and confusion, that I have committed the greatest crimes; but it has been only in acknowledging those that have been charged with so much virulence upon an Order, which truth obliges me to pronounce innocent. I made the first declaration they required of me, only to suspend the excessive tortures of the rack, and mollify that made me endure them. I am sensible what torments they prepare for those that have courage to revoke such a confession. But the horrible sight which they present to my eyes, is not capable of making me confirm one lie by another. On a condition so infamous as that, I freely renounce life with is already too odious to me. For what would it avail me to prolong a few miserable days, when I must owe them only to the blackest of calumnies,' [the writer takes this quotation from *Historie des Chevaliers de Saint Jean de Jerusalem*, by Abbé Vertot tome ii pp. 101, 102] In consequence of this manly revocation, the Grand Master and his companions were hurried into the flames, where they retained that contempt of death which they had exhibited on former occasions.

But notwithstanding the efforts of King Philip and the Pope, the Order of Templars was not annihilated. De Molay, in anticipation of his fate, appointed John Mark Larmenius as his successor in office, and from that time to the present, there has been a regular and uninterrupted succession of Grand Masters.

The following is a list of the names of these Grand Masters and the date of their elections. [*the author credits his list to Mackey's Lexicon of Freemasonry.*]

No.	Name	Date	No.	Name	Date
1.	Hugh de Payens	1118	27.	Thomas Theobald Alexandrius	1324
2.	Robert of Burgundy	1139	28.	Arnold de Braque	1340
3.	Everard de Barri	1147	29.	John de Claremont	1349
4.	Bernard de Trenellape	1151	30.	Bertrand de Guesclin	1357
5.	Bertrand de Blanchefort	1154	31.	John Arminiacus	1381
6.	Andrew de Montbar	1165	32.	Bernard Arminiacus	1392
7.	Philip of Naplus	1169	33.	John Armanacius	1419
8.	Odo de St. Amand	1171	34.	John de Croy	1451
9.	Arnold de Troye	1180	35.	Bernard Imbault	1472
10.	John Terricus	1185	36.	Robert Senoncourt	1478
11.	Gerard de Ridefort	1187	37.	Galeatius de Salazar	1497
12.	Robert Sablaeus	1191	38.	Philip Chabot	1516
13.	Gilbert Gralius	1196	39.	Gaspard de Jaltiaco Travanensis	1544
14.	Philip de Plessis	1201	40.	Henry de Montmorency	1574
15.	William de Carnota	1217	41.	Charles de Valois	1615
16.	Peter de Montagu	1218	42.	James Ruxellius de Granceio	1651
17.	Armand de Petragrossa	1229	43.	Duc de Duras	1681
18.	Herman de Petragorious	1237	44.	Philip, duke of Orleans	1705
19.	William de Pupefort	1244	45.	Duc de Maine	1724
20.	William de Sonnac	1247	46.	Louis Henry Bourbon	1737
21.	Reginald Vichierius	1250	47.	Louis Francis Bourbon	1741
22.	Thomas Beraud	1257	48.	Duc de Cosse Brisac	1776
23.	William de Beaujeau	1274	49.	Claude M. R. de Chevillon	1792
24.	Theobald Gaudinius	1291	50.	Bernard R. F. Palaprat	1804
25.	James de Molay	1298	51.	Sir Sidney Smith	1838
26.	John Mark Larmenius	1314			

APPENDIX VI

Ramsay's Oration of 1737

The noble ardour which you, gentlemen, evince to enter into the most noble and very illustrious Order of Freemasons, is a certain proof that you already possess all the qualities necessary to become members, that is, humanity, pure morals, inviolable secrecy and a taste for the fine arts.

Lycurgus, Solon, Numa and all the political legislators have failed to make their institutions lasting. However wise their laws may have been, they have not been able to spread through all countries and ages. As they only kept in view victories and conquests, military violence and the elevation of one people at the expense of another, they have not had the power to become universal, nor to make themselves acceptable to the taste, spirit and interests of all nations. Philanthropy was not their basis. Patriotism badly understood and pushed to excess, often destroyed in these warrior republics love and humanity in general. Mankind is not essentially distinguished by the tongues spoken, the clothes worn, the lands occupied or the dignities with which it is invested. The world is nothing but a huge republic, of which every nation is a family, every individual a child. Our Society was at the outset established to revive and spread these essential maxims borrowed from the nature of man. We desire to reunite all men of enlightened minds, gentle manners and agreeable wit, not only by a love of the fine arts but, much more, by the grand principles of virtue, science and religion, where the interests of the Fraternity shall become those of the whole human race, whence all nations shall be enabled to draw knowledge and where subjects of all kingdoms shall learn to cherish one another without renouncing their own country. Our ancestors, the Crusaders, gathered together from all parts of Christendom in the Holy Land, desired thus to reunite into one sole Fraternity the individuals of all nations. What obligations do we not owe to these superior men who, without gross selfish interests, without even listening to the inborn tendency to dominate, imagined such an institution, the sole aim of which is to unite minds and hearts in order to make them better, to form in the course of ages a spiritual empire where, without derogating from the various duties which different states exact, a new people shall be created, which, composed of many nations, shall in some sort cement them all into one by the tie of virtue and science.

The second requisite of our Society is sound morals. The religious orders were established to make perfect Christians, military orders to inspire a love of true glory and the Order of Freemasons to make lovable men, good citizens, good subjects, inviolable in their promises, faithful adorers of the God of Love, lovers rather of virtue than of reward.

> Polliciti servare fidem, sanctumque vereri
> Numen amicitiae, mores, non munera amare.
> To faithfully keep a promise, to honour the holiness of friendship
> To love virtue, not its reward.

Nevertheless, we do not confine ourselves to purely civic virtues. We have amongst us three kinds of brothers: Novices or Apprentices, Fellows or Professed Brothers, Masters or Perfected brothers. To the first are explained the moral virtues, to the second the heroic virtues; to the last the Christian virtues; so that our Institution embraces the whole philosophy of sentiment and the complete theology of the heart. This is why one of our brothers has said:

> Freemason, illustrious Grand Master
> Receive my first transports,
> In my heart the Order has given them birth,
> Happy I, if noble efforts
> Cause me to merit your esteem
> By elevating me to the sublime,
> The primeval Truth,
> To the Essence pure and divine,
> The celestial Origin of the soul
> The Source of life and love.

Because a sad, savage and misanthropic philosophy disgusts virtuous men, our ancestors, the Crusaders, wished to render it lovable by the attractions of innocent pleasures, agreeable music, pure joy and moderate gaiety. Our festivals are not what the profane world and the ignorant vulgar imagine. All the vices of heart and soul are banished there and irreligion, libertinage, incredulity and debauch are proscribed. Our banquets resemble those virtuous symposia of Horace, where the conversation only touched what could enlighten the soul, discipline the heart and inspire a taste for the true, the good and the beautiful.

> O noctes coenaeque Deum ...
> Sermo oritur, non de regnis domibusque alienis
> ...sed quod magis ad nos
> Pertinet, et nescire malum est, agitamus;
> utrumne

> Divitis homines, an sint virtute beati;
> Quidve ad amicitias usus rectumve trahat nos,
> Et quae sit natura boni, summumque quid ejus.

> O nights, o divine repasts!
> Without troubling ourselves with things that do not matter
> But to dwell on those which concern us
> ...and it would be bad to ignore:
> If wealth or virtue give happiness to Man
> What use do friendship or virtue bring us
> What is the nature of good, and what is the highest good.
> Horace, Satire VI Book II

Thus the obligations imposed upon you by the Order, are to protect your brothers by your authority, to enlighten them by your knowledge, to edify them by your virtues, to succour them in their necessities, to sacrifice all personal resentment, to strive after all that may contribute to the peace and unity of society.

We have secrets; they are figurative signs and sacred words, composing a language sometimes mute, sometimes very eloquent, in order to communicate with one another at the greatest distance, to recognise our Brothers of whatsoever tongue. These were words of war which the Crusaders gave each other in order to guarantee them from the surprises of the Saracens, who often crept in amongst them to kill them. These signs and words recall the remembrance either of some part of our science, of some moral virtue or some mystery of the faith. That has happened to us which never befell any former Society. Our Lodges have been established, are spread in all civilised nations and, nevertheless, amongst this numerous multitude of men never has a Brother betrayed our secrets. Those natures most trivial, most indiscreet, least schooled to silence, learn this great art on entering our Society. Such is the power over all natures of the idea of a fraternal bond! This inviolable secret contributes powerfully to unite the subjects of all nations, to render the communication of benefits easy and mutual between us. We have many examples in the annals of our Order. Our Brothers, travelling in diverse lands, have only needed to make themselves known in our Lodges in order to be there immediately overwhelmed by all kinds of succour, even in the time of the most bloody wars, while illustrious prisoners have found brothers where they only expected to meet enemies.

Should any fail in the solemn promises which

bind us, you know, gentlemen, that the penalties which we impose upon him are remorse of conscience, shame at his perfidy and exclusion from our Society, according to those beautiful lines of Horace:

Est et fideli tuta silentio
Merces; vetabo qui Cereris sacrum
Vulgarit Arcanae, sub isdem
Sit tragibus, fragilemque mecum
Solvat Phaselum...

Loyal silence is surely rewarded
But he who reveals the sacred secret of Ceres
Him I will not allow to dwell under my roof
Or to share my shallow skiff
Horace, Odes, Book III

Yes, sirs, the famous festivals of Ceres at Eleusis, of Isis in Egypt, of Minerva at Athens, or Urania amongst the Phoenicians, of Diana in Scythia were connected with ours. In those places mysteries were celebrated which concealed many vestiges of the ancient religion of Noah and the Patriarchs. They concluded with no banquets and libations when neither that intemperance nor excess were known into which the heathen gradually fell. The source of these infamies was the admission to the nocturnal assemblies of persons of both sexes in contravention of the primitive usages. It is in order to prevent similar abuses that women are excluded from our Order. We are not so unjust as to regard the fair sex as incapable of keeping a secret. But their presence might insensibly corrupt the purity of our maxims and manners.

The fourth quality required in our Order is the taste for useful sciences and the liberal arts. Thus, our Order exacts of each of you to contribute, by his protection, liberality or labour, to a vast work for which no academy can suffice, because all these societies being composed of a very small number of men, their work cannot embrace an object so extended. All the Grand Masters in Germany, England, Italy and elsewhere, exhort all the learned men and all the artisans of the Fraternity to unite to furnish the materials for a Universal Dictionary of the liberal arts and useful sciences, excepting only theology and politics.

This work has already been commenced in London and, by means of the union of our Brothers, it may be carried to a conclusion in a few years. Not only are technical words and their etymology explained, but the history of each art and science, its principles and operations, are described. By this means the lights of all nations will be united in one single work, which will be a universal library of all that is beautiful, great, luminous, solid and useful in all the sciences and in all noble arts. This work will augment in each century, according to the increase of knowledge, it will spread everywhere emulation and the taste for things of beauty and utility.

The word Freemason must therefore not be taken in a literal, gross and material sense, as if our founders had been simple workers in stone, or merely curious geniuses who wished to perfect the arts. They were not only skilful architects, desirous of consecrating their talents and good to the construction of material temples; but also religious and warrior princes who designed to enlighten, edify and protect the living temples of the Most High. This I will demonstrate by developing the history or rather the renewal of our Order.

Every family, every republic, every Empire, of which the origin is lost in obscure history, has its fable and its truth, its legend and its history. Some ascribe our institution to Solomon, some to Moses, some to Abraham, some to Noah, some to Enoch, who built the first city, or even to Adam. Without any pretence of denying these origins, I pass on to matters less ancient. This, then, is a part of what I have gathered in the annals of Great Britain, in the Acts of Parliament, which speak often of our privileges and in the living traditions of the English people, which has been the centre of our Society since the eleventh century.

At the time of the Crusades in Palestine many princes, lords and citizens associated themselves and vowed to restore the temple of the Christians in the Holy Land, to employ themselves in bringing back their architecture to its first institution. They agreed upon several ancient signs and symbolic words drawn from the well of religion in order to recognise themselves amongst the heathen and the Saracens. These signs and words were only communicated to those who promised solemnly, even sometimes at the foot of the altar, never to reveal them. This sacred promise was therefore not an execrable oath, as it has been called, but a respectable bond to unite Christians of all nationalities in one confraternity. Some time after our Order formed an intimate union with the Knights of St John of Jerusalem. From that time our Lodges took the name of Lodges of St John. This union was made after the example set by the Israelites when they erected the second Temple who, whilst they handled the trowel and mortar with one hand, in the other held the sword and buckler.

Our Order, therefore, must not be considered a revival of the Bacchanals, but as an Order founded in remote antiquity, renewed in the Holy Land by our ancestors in order to recall the memory of the most sublime truths amidst the pleasures of society. The kings, princes and lords returned from Palestine to their own lands and there established divers Lodges. At the time of the last Crusades many Lodges were already erected in Germany, Italy, Spain, France and, from thence, in Scotland, because of the close alliance between the French and the Scotch. James, Lord Steward of Scotland, was master of a Lodge at Kilwinning, in the West of Scotland, MCCLXXXVI, shortly after the death of Alexander III, King of Scotland, and one year before John Balliol mounted the throne. This lord received Freemasons into his Lodge the Earls of Gloucester and Ulster, the one English, the other Irish.

By degrees our Lodges and our Rites were neglected in most places. This is why of so many historians only those of Great Britain speak of our Order. Nevertheless it preserved its splendour amongst those Scotsmen to whom the Kings of France confided during many centuries the safeguard of their royal persons.

After the deplorable mishaps in the Crusades, the perishing of the Christian armies and the triumph of Bendocdar, Sultan of Egypt, during the eighth and last Crusade, that great Prince Edward, son of Henry III, King of England, seeing there was no longer any safety for his Brethren in the Holy Land, whence the Christian troops were retiring, brought them all back and this colony of Brothers was established in England. As this prince was endowed with all the heroic qualities, he loved the fine arts, declared himself protector of our Order, conceded to it new privileges and then the members of this Fraternity took the name of Freemasons after the example set by their ancestors.

Since that time Great Britain became the seat of our Order, the conservator of our laws and the depository of our secrets. The fatal religious discords which embarrassed and tore Europe in the sixteenth century caused or Order to degenerate from the nobility of its origin. Many of our Rites and usages which were contrary to the prejudices of the times were changed, disguised and suppressed. Thus it was that many of our Brothers forgot, like the ancient Jews, the spirit of our laws and retained only the letter and shell. The beginnings of the remedy have already been made. It is necessary only to continue and, at last, to bring everything back to its original institution. This work cannot be difficult in a State where religion and Government can only be favourable to our laws.

From the British Isles the Royal Art is now repassing into France, under the reign of the most amiable of Kings, whose humanity animates all his virtues and under the ministry of a Mentor, who has realised all that could be imagined most fabulous. In this happy age when love of peace has become the virtue of heroes, this nation one of the most spiritual in Europe, will become the centre of the Order. She will clothe our work, our statutes, our customs with grace, delicacy and good taste, essential qualities of the Order, of which the basis is wisdom, strength and beauty of genius. It is in future in our Lodges, as it were in public schools, that Frenchmen shall learn, without travelling, the characters of all nations and that strangers shall experience that France is the home of all nations. Patria gentis humanae.

BIBLIOGRAPHY

Anderson, James. *Anderson's Constitutions of 1723*. Washington: Masonic Service Association of the United States, 1924.

Ashe, Jonathan. *The Masonic Manual or Lectures of Freemasonry*. London: Richard Spencer, 1853.

Barber, Malcolm. *The Trial of the Templars*. Cambridge: Cambridge UP, 1996.

Barruel, Augustin. *Memoirs Illustrating the History of Jacobinism Part II – Volume II: the Antimonarchical Conspiracy*. Hartford: Hudson & Goodwin, 1799.

Bennett, Burton E. 'The Rite of Strict Observance.' *The Builder* September-October 1926.

Bernheim, Alain, and Arturo De Hoyos. 'Introduction to the Rituals of the Rite of Strict Observance.' *Heredom: Transactions of the Scottish Rite Research Society Volume 14*. Washington: Scottish Rite Research Society, 2006. pp.47-104.

Bernheim, Alain. 'Ramsay and His Discours Revisited.' *Pietre-Stones Review of Freemasonry*. 28 January 2008.
www.freemasons-freemasonry.com/bernheim_ramsay03.html

Bogdan, Henrik. 'An Introduction to the Higher Degrees of Freemasonry.' *Heredom: Transactions of the Scottish Rite Research Society Volume 14*. Washington: Scottish Rite Research Society, 2006, pp.9-46.

Brown, William M. *Highlights of Templar History*. Greenfield: Wm. Mitchell Printing Co., 1944.

Burnes, James. *Sketch of the History of the Knights Templars*. Edinburgh: Wm. Blackwood & Sons, 1840.

Carlisle, Richard. *Manual of Freemasonry*. Kessinger, 1825.

Carson, J. L. 'Irish Masonry.' *The Builder* January 1916.

Cooper, Robert. *The Rosslyn Hoax*. London: Lewis Masonic, 2006.

Creigh, Alfred. *History of the Knights Templar of the State of Pennsylvania*. Philadelphia: J. B. Lippincott & Co., 1868.

Cross, Jeremy L. *The True Masonic Chart or Hieroglyphic Monitor*. New York: Jeremy L. Cross, 1851.

Dafoe, Stephen. 'A History of Canadian Masonic Templarism.' *The Templar Papers*. Franklin Lakes: New PageBooks, 2006. pp.207-222.

Dafoe, Stephen. *Nobly Born: An Illustrated History of the Knights Templar*. London: Lewis Masonic, 2007.

Dafoe, Stephen. 'Reading, Writing and Apathy: the Rise and Fall of Masonic Education.' *Heredom: Transactions of the Scottish Rite Research Society Volume 14*. Scottish Rite Research Society, 2006. pp.145-178.

Demurger, Alain. *The Last Templar*. London: Profile Books. p.173.

Franco, Barbara. 'Many Fraternal Groups Grew From Masonic Seed Part 1.' *The Northern Lights* September 1985: pp.4-8.

Franco, Barbara. 'Many Fraternal Groups Grew From Masonic Seed Part 2.' *Northern Lights* November 1985: pp.10-15.

'Frequently Asked Questions.' *The Grand Encampment of the United States of America*. 28 January 2008
www.knightstemplar.org/faq1.html#order

From Geyser to Canon with Mary: Pilgrimage of Mary Commandery No. 36 Knights Templar of Pennsylvania to the Twenty-Ninth Triennial Conclave of the Grand Encampment U.S. At San Francisco, Cal. Philadelphia: Thomson Printing Company, 1904.

Gould, Robert F. *A Concise History of Freemasonry*. London: Gale & Polden Ltd., 1903.

Hardie, James. *The New Freemason's Monitor or Masonic Guide for the Direction of Members of That Ancient and Honourable Fraternity*. New York: George Long, 1819.

Haywood, H. L. *A Story of the Life and Times of Jacques De Molay*. The Order of DeMolay, 1925.

Haywood, H. L. 'Thomas Smith Webb.' Grand Lodge of Iowa Bulletin 56 (1955).

Henry, Fowle. *The Autobiography of Henry Fowle of Boston (1766-1837)*. Comp. David H. Kilmer. New York: Heritage Books, 1991.

Hodapp, Christopher, and Alice Von Kannon. *The Templar Code for Dummies*. Hoboken: Wiley, 2007.

Hodapp, Christopher. 'On Making Knights.' *Templar History Magazine* December 2006, pp.2-7.

Hutchens, Rex R. *A Bridge to Light*. Washington: The Supreme Council of 33 Degree Ancient and Accepted Scottish Rite Southern Jurisdiction, 1992.

Hutchinson, William. *The Spirit of Masonry in Moral and Elucidatory Lectures*. Carlisle: F. Jollie, 1795.

'In eminenti.' Papal Encyclicals Online. 28 April 1738. 28 January 2008. www.papalencyclicals.net/Clem12/c15inemengl.htm

Kahler, Lisa. 'Andrew Michael Ramsay and His Masonic Oration.' Heredom: Transactions of the Scottish Rite Research Society Volume 1. Washington: Scottish Rite Research Society, 1992. pp.19-47.

Laurie, William A. *The History of Free Masonry and the Grand Lodge of Scotland with Chapters on the Knights Templars, Knights of St John, Mark Masonry and R. A. Degree to which is added an Appendix of Valuable Papers*. Edinburgh: Seton & Mackenzie, 1859.

Mackey, Albert G. *Encyclopaedia of Freemasonry and its Kindrid Sciences Volumes I & II*. Comp. William J. Hughan. Chicago: The Masonic History Company, 1927.

Mackey, Albert G. *Lexicon of Freemasonry*. Philadelphia: Barnes and Noble Books, 2004.

Mackey, Albert G. 'The Story of the Scottish Templars.' *The History of Freemasonry*. New York: Gramercy Books, 1996. pp.255-266.

MacLeod Moore, James B. 'British Templary: A History of the Modern or Masonic Templar Systems with a Concise Account of the Origin of Speculative Freemasonry and Its Evolution Since the Revival A.D. 1717.' *History of the Ancient and Honourable Fraternity of Free and Accepted Masons and Concordant Orders*. London: The Fraternity Company, 1902. pp.741-794.

Maier, Paul L., trans. *Josephus: The Essential Writings*. Grand Rapids: Kregel Publications, 1988.

McBride, Harriet W. 'Business and the Brethren: the Influences of Regalia Houses on Fraternalism.' *Heredom: Transactions of the Scottish Rite Research Society Volume 12*. Washington: Scottish Rite Research Society, 2004. pp.163-202.

McGregor, Martin I. *A Biographical Sketch of the Chevalier Andrew Michael Ramsay*. Research Lodge of Southland No. 415. 14 August 2007. 28 January 2008. www.freemasons-freemasonry.com/ramsay_biography_oration.html

Moore, Charles W. *The Freemasons' Monthly Magazine Volume XX*. Boston: Hugh H. Tuttle, 1861.

Moore, Cornelius, comp. *The Craftsman, and Templar's Text Book and, Also Melodies for the Craft*. Cincinnati: Jacob Ernst and Company, 1859.

Morris, S. B. *The Complete Idiots Guide to Freemasonry*. New York: Alpha, 2006.

Morris, S. B. 'The High Degrees in the United States.' The Blue Friars. Blue Friars Lecture. 1998.

Naudon, Paul. *The Secret History of Freemasonry: Its Origins and Connection to the Knights Templar*. Trans. Jon Graham. Rochester: Inner Traditions, 2005.

Oliver, George. *The Historical Landmarks of Freemasonry*. London: Richard Spencer, 1846.

Pearson, Norman. 'The Preceptory (Knights Templar).' *Light Beyond the Craft in Canada*. London, Ontario: Lux Quaro Chapter the Philalethes Society, 1997. pp.75-79.

'Petition Back.' *The Grand Encampment of the United States of America*. 28 January 2008.

www.knightstemplar.org/newsrelease/Back.pdf

Prescott, Andrew. 'The Unlawful Societies Act of 1799.' Centre for Research Into Freemasonry. Second International Conference of the Canonbury Masonic Research Centre. University of Sheffield, Sheffield. 4 November 2000. 28 January 2008.

www.freemasonry.dept.shef.ac.uk/?q=book/print/46&PHPSESSID=eed5bdedf9947288165c3d626d29cf2c

Preston, William. *Illustrations of Masonry by the Late William Preston, Esq*. London: Whittaker, Treacher & Co., 1829.

Ridley, Jasper. *The Freemasons*. London: Constable, 2003.

Ritual No. 1: The Order of the Temple and Drill. London: The Great Priory of the Religious, Military and Masonic Orders of the Temple and St John of Jerusalem, Palestine, Rhodes and Malta of England and Wales and Its Provinces Overseas, 2007.

Robertson, John R. *The History of the Knights Templars of Canada*. Toronto: Hunter, Rose & Co., 1890.

Robinson, John J. *Born in Blood: The Lost Secrets of Freemasonry*. New York: Evans, 1989.

Searing, Richard A. *History of Monroe Commandery No. 12 Knights Templars Stationed At Rochester New York 1826-1914*. Genesee, The Genesee Press, 1913.

Smyth, Frederick. *Brethren in Chivalry*. London: Lewis Masonic, 1991.

Speed, Frederic. 'The Knights Templar of the United States of America, and Government by a Grand Encampment, Grand Commanderies, and Commanderies. The Ritual and Ethics of American Templary.' *History of the Ancient and Honourable Fraternity of Free and Accepted Masons and Concordant Orders*. London: The Fraternity Company, 1902. pp.699-738.

Stevenson, David. 'James Anderson: Man & Mason.' *Heredom: Transactions of the Scottish Rite Research Society Volume 10*. Washington: Scottish Rite Research Society, 2002. pp.93-138.

Tabbert, Mark A. *American Freemasons: Three Centuries of Building Communities*. New York: New York UP, 2006.

Templar's Companion. Boston: Grand Commandery of Knights Templars, and Appendant Orders of Massachusetts and Rhode Island, 1876.

'The Historical Background of the Order.' *The Great Priory of Scotland*. 30 January 2008. 31 January 2008.

www.greatprioryofscotland.com/history.htm

Upton-Ward, Judith. *The Rule of the Templars*. Woodbridge: The Boydell Press, 2001.

Waite, Arthur E. *A New Encyclopaedia of Freemasonry*. New York: University Books, 1996.

Waite, Arthur E. *The Templar Orders in Freemasonry*. Morinville: Stephen A. Dafoe, 2006.

Webb, Thomas S. *The Freemason's Monitor or Illustrations of FreeMasonry*. Cincinnati: Moore, Wilstavh, Keys & Co., 1859.

Webb, Thomas S. *The Freemason's Monitor or Illustrations of FreeMasonry*. Salem: Cushing and Appleton, 1818.

INDEX

Pictorial references are in **bold**.